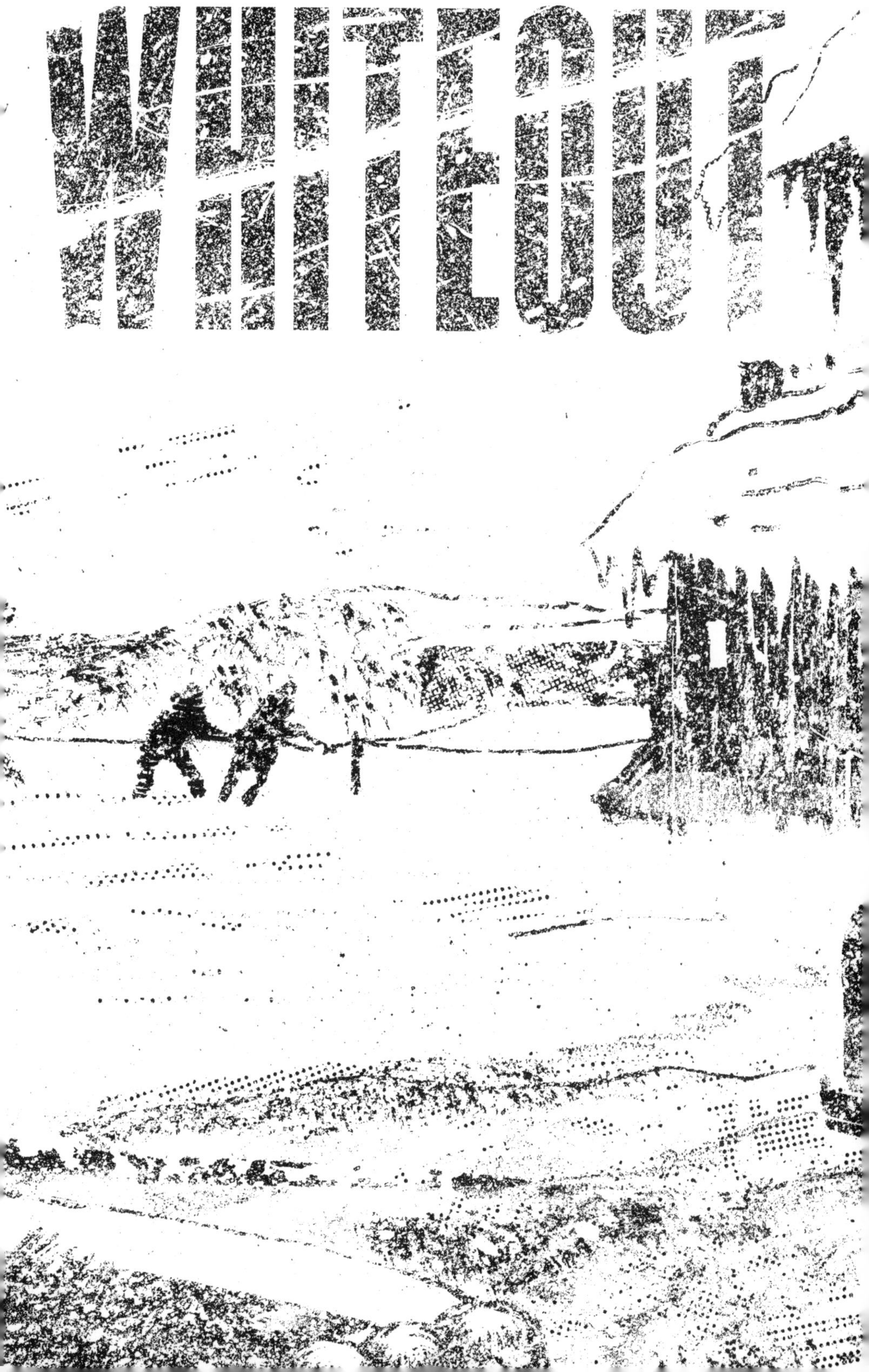
WHITEOUT

WRITTEN BY
GREG RUCKA

ILLUSTRATED & LETTERED BY
STEVE LIEBER

BOOK DESIGN BY
STEVEN BIRCH @ SERVO

ADDITIONAL PRODUCTION BY
RANDAL C. JARRELL

ORIGINALLY EDITED BY
BOB SCHRECK & JAMIE S. RICH

NEW EDITION EDITED BY
JAMES LUCAS JONES

PUBLISHED BY ONI PRESS, INC.

JOE NOZEMACK, PUBLISHER
JAMES LUCAS JONES, EDITOR IN CHIEF
RANDAL C. JARRELL, MANAGING EDITOR
DOUGLAS E. SHERWOOD, EDITORIAL ASSISTANT
JILL BEATON, EDITORIAL INTERN

THIS VOLUME COLLECTS ISSUES 1-4 OF THE
COMIC BOOK MINISERIES *WHITEOUT*.

ONI PRESS, INC.
1305 SE MARTIN LUTHER KING JR. BLVD.
SUITE A
PORTLAND, OR 97214
USA

WWW.ONIPRESS.COM
WWW.GREGRUCKA.COM
WWW.STEVELIEBER.COM

FIRST EDITION: JUNE 2007
ISBN 978-1-932664-70-6
ISBN-10 1-932664-70-X

1 3 5 7 9 10 8 6 4 2
PRINTED IN CANADA.

CHAPTER ONE

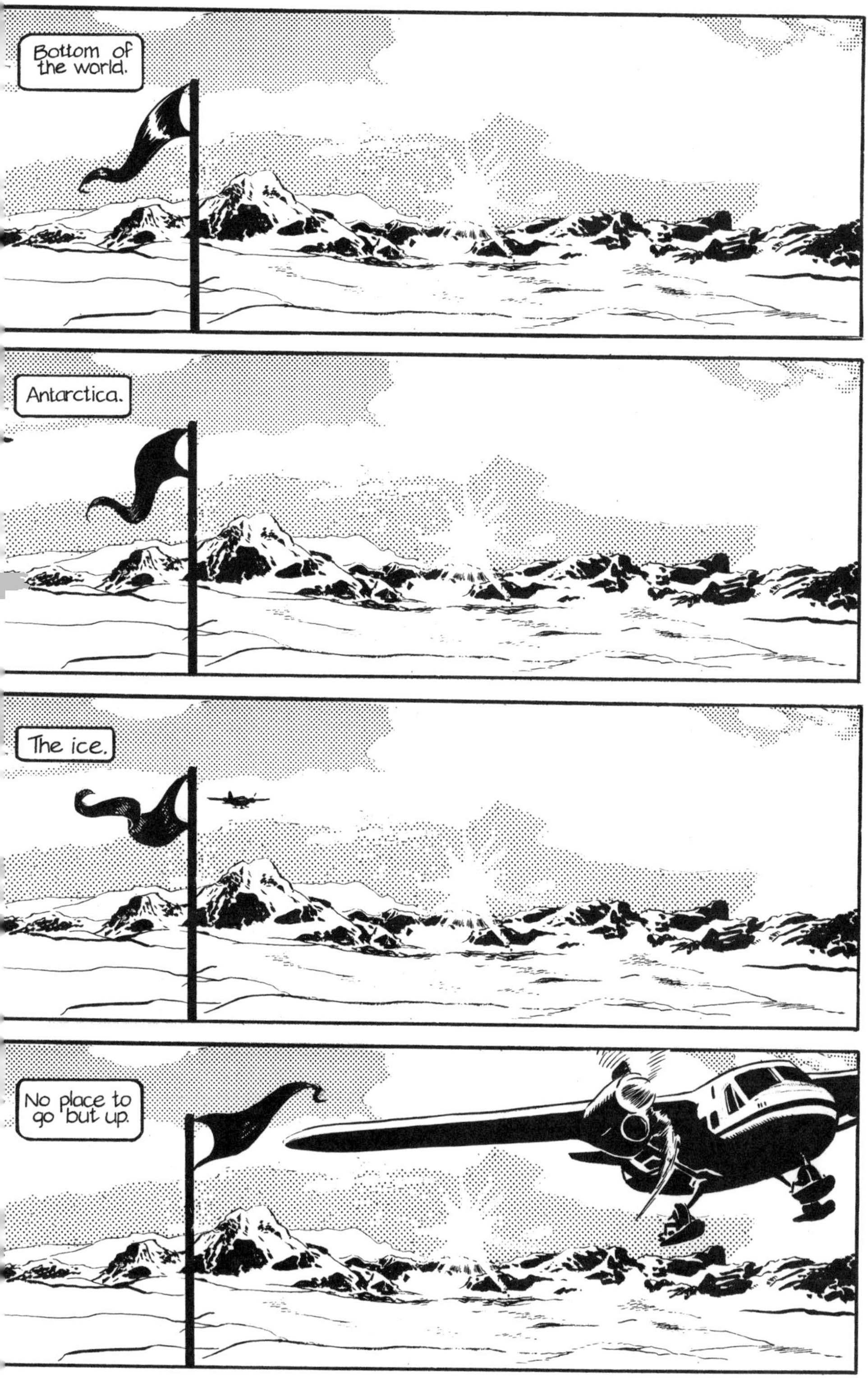
Bottom of the world.
Antarctica.
The ice.
No place to go but up.

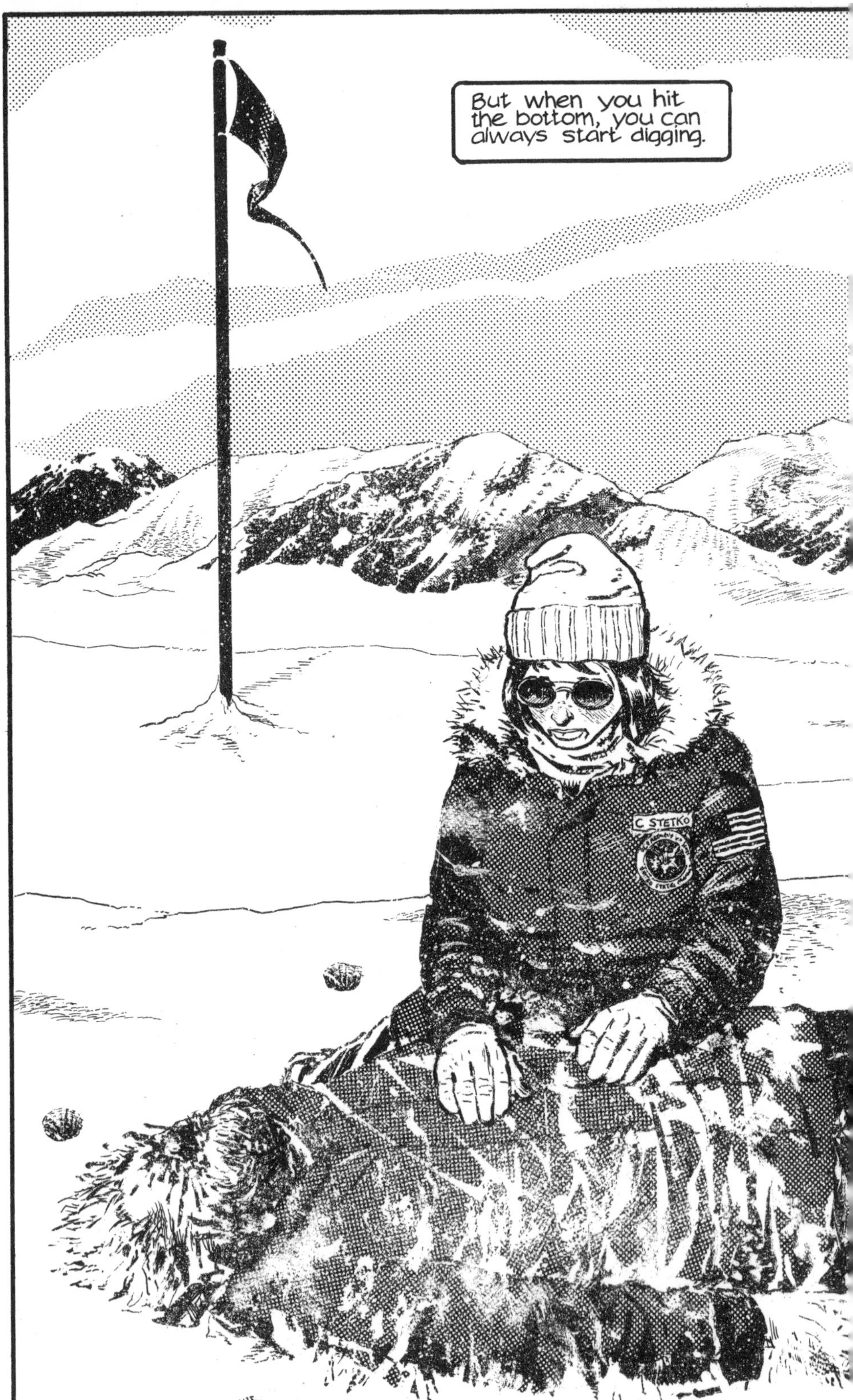
But when you hit the bottom, you can always start digging.
C STETKO

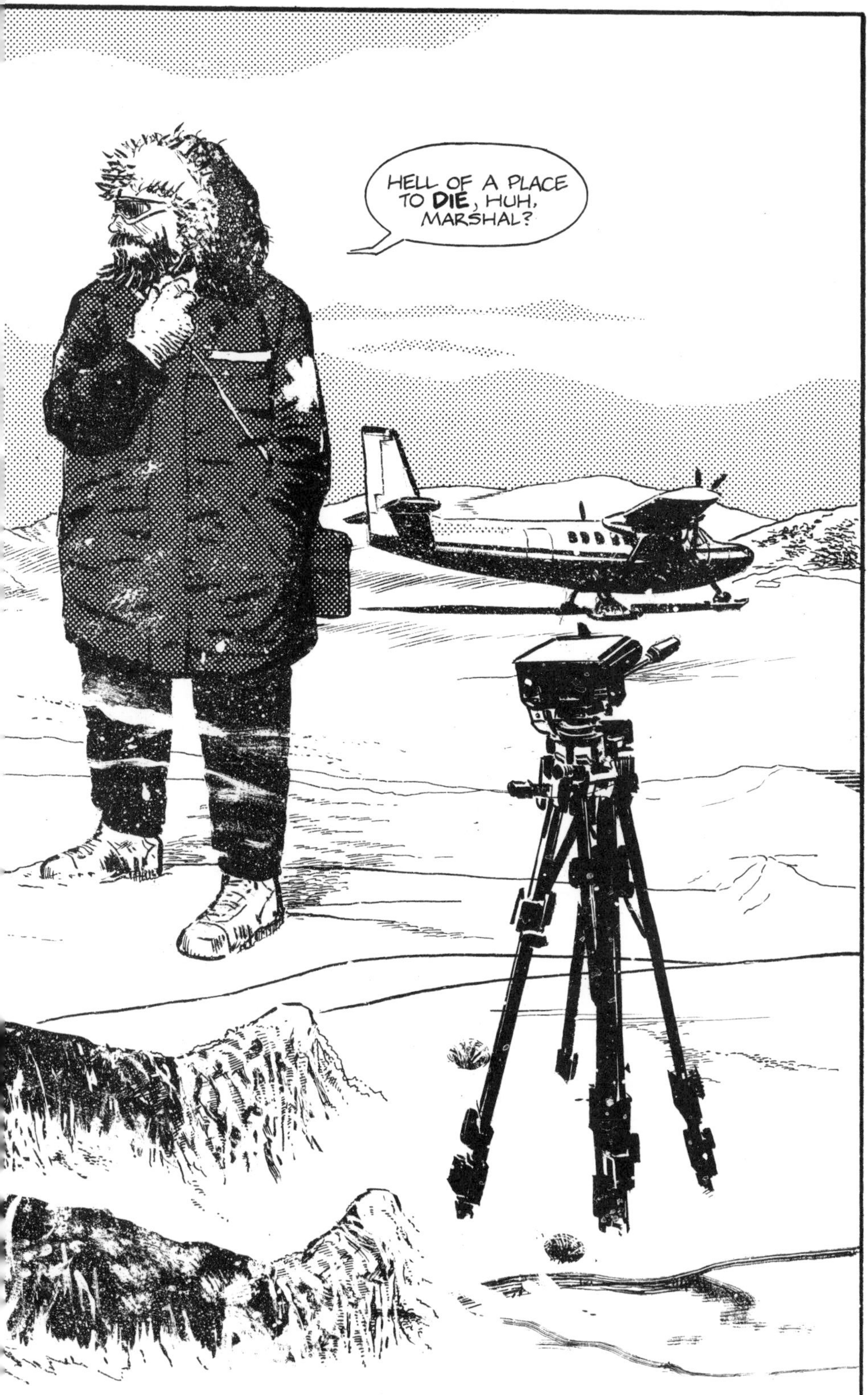
HELL OF A PLACE TO DIE, HUH, MARSHAL?

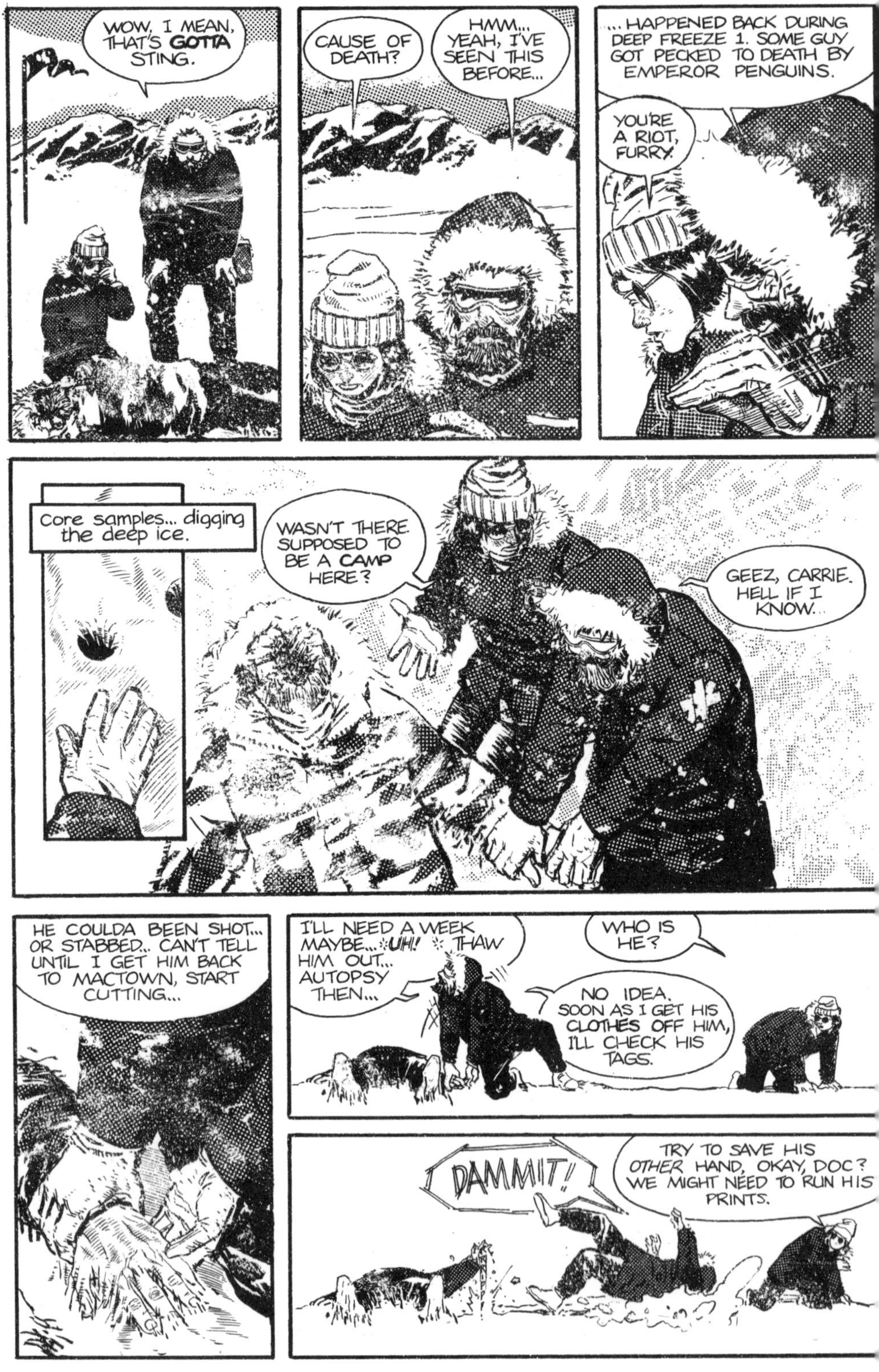
WOW, I MEAN, THAT'S **GOTTA** STING.
CAUSE OF DEATH?
HMM... YEAH, I'VE SEEN THIS BEFORE...
...HAPPENED BACK DURING DEEP FREEZE 1. SOME GUY GOT PECKED TO DEATH BY EMPEROR PENGUINS.
YOU'RE A RIOT, FURRY.
Core samples... digging the deep ice.
WASN'T THERE SUPPOSED TO BE A **CAMP** HERE?
GEEZ, CARRIE. HELL IF I KNOW...
HE COULDA BEEN SHOT... OR STABBED... CAN'T TELL UNTIL I GET HIM BACK TO MACTOWN, START CUTTING...
I'LL NEED A WEEK MAYBE... *UH!* THAW HIM OUT... AUTOPSY THEN...
WHO IS HE?
NO IDEA. SOON AS I GET HIS **CLOTHES OFF** HIM, I'LL CHECK HIS TAGS.
DAMMIT!
TRY TO SAVE HIS *OTHER* HAND, OKAY, DOC? WE MIGHT NEED TO RUN HIS PRINTS.

DEFINITELY MURDERED?

FURRY CAN'T DO AN AUTOPSY YET, BUT THAT'S HOW IT LOOKS.

ONE OF OURS?

WE DON'T KNOW.

U.S. Marshal Brett McEwan—safe and warm in Hawaii—knows dick about The Ice.

But The Ice and I, we're kindred spirits, now.

We don't care.

DID YOU CHECK HIS TAGS, **DEPUTY** STETKO?

HE WASN'T WEARING TAGS, **MARSHAL** McEWAN. BUT HE HAD THE FLAG ON HIS PARKA.

SOMEONE **TOOK** HIS TAGS?

I DON'T KNOW.

RESEARCH CAMPS JUST DON'T UP AND DISAPPEAR. WHERE ARE THE OTHERS?

I DON'T KNOW.

YOU'RE FUCKING USELESS.

THERE WERE **FIVE MEN** ON THAT TEAM, FOR GOD'S SAKE.

COULD BE ANYWHERE. COULD STILL BE OUT THERE.

ALL THE BASES ARE GOING TO WINTER STAFF IN THE NEXT TWO WEEKS. NINETY PERCENT OF ALL PERSONNEL ON THE ICE ARE SHIPPING BACK HOME. YOU'VE GOT UNTIL THEN, DEPUTY...

...OR ELSE I'LL HAVE YOUR BADGE.

I WANT YOUR JOHN DOE IDENTIFIED. I WANT THIS DAMN THING SOLVED. FIND THE MEN. FIND THE CAMP. MAKE AN ARREST.

UNDERSTOOD?

YES.

...KICKING THE ICE QUEEN'S ASS! THESE GUYS JUST **DISAPPEARED** OUT THERE, AND IF SHE DOESN'T PUT OUT, HE'S PULLING HER PLUG! AND THE MARSHAL JUST **TOOK** IT, DIDN'T KICK BACK OR ANYTHING.

SHE'S BEEN DOWN HERE TOO LONG, SHE'S GONE COLD.

FRIGID.

FROZEN.

YOU KNOW IT! TALK ABOUT N.S.F.A.—

NO SEX FOR A WHILE.

NO SEX FUC EVER...

NO SEX FUCK ...TIGH

DOESN'T OW WHA HE'S MIS

WHOOPS.

CRASH.

11

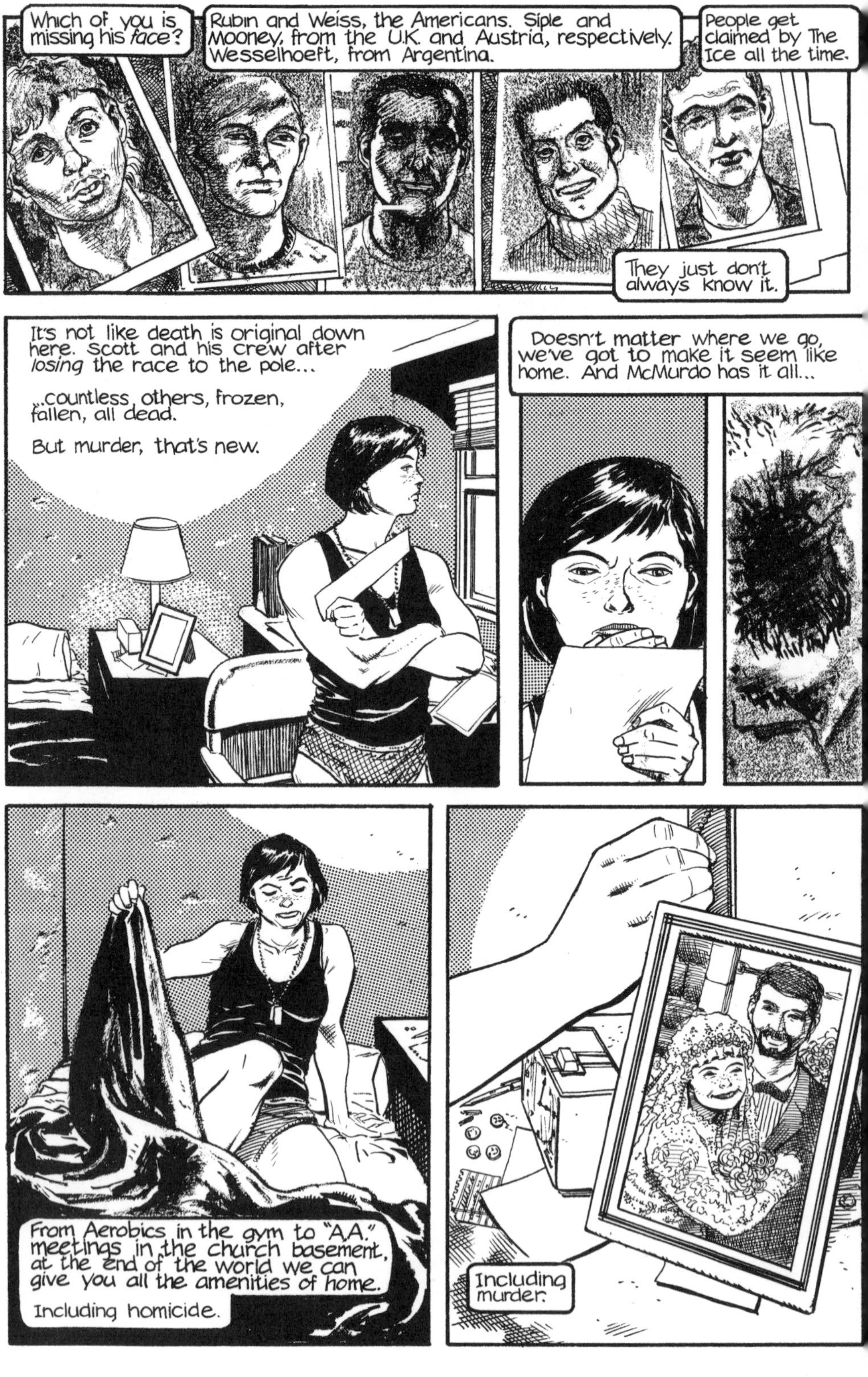

Which of you is missing his *face*?
Rubin and Weiss, the Americans. Siple and Mooney, from the U.K. and Austria, respectively. Wesselhoeft, from Argentina.
People get claimed by The Ice all the time.
They just don't always know it.
It's not like death is original down here. Scott and his crew after *losing* the race to the pole...
...countless others, frozen, fallen, all dead.
But murder, that's new.
Doesn't matter where we go, we've got to make it seem like home. And McMurdo has it all...
From Aerobics in the gym to "A.A." meetings in the church basement, at the end of the world we can give you all the amenities of home.
Including homicide.
Including murder.

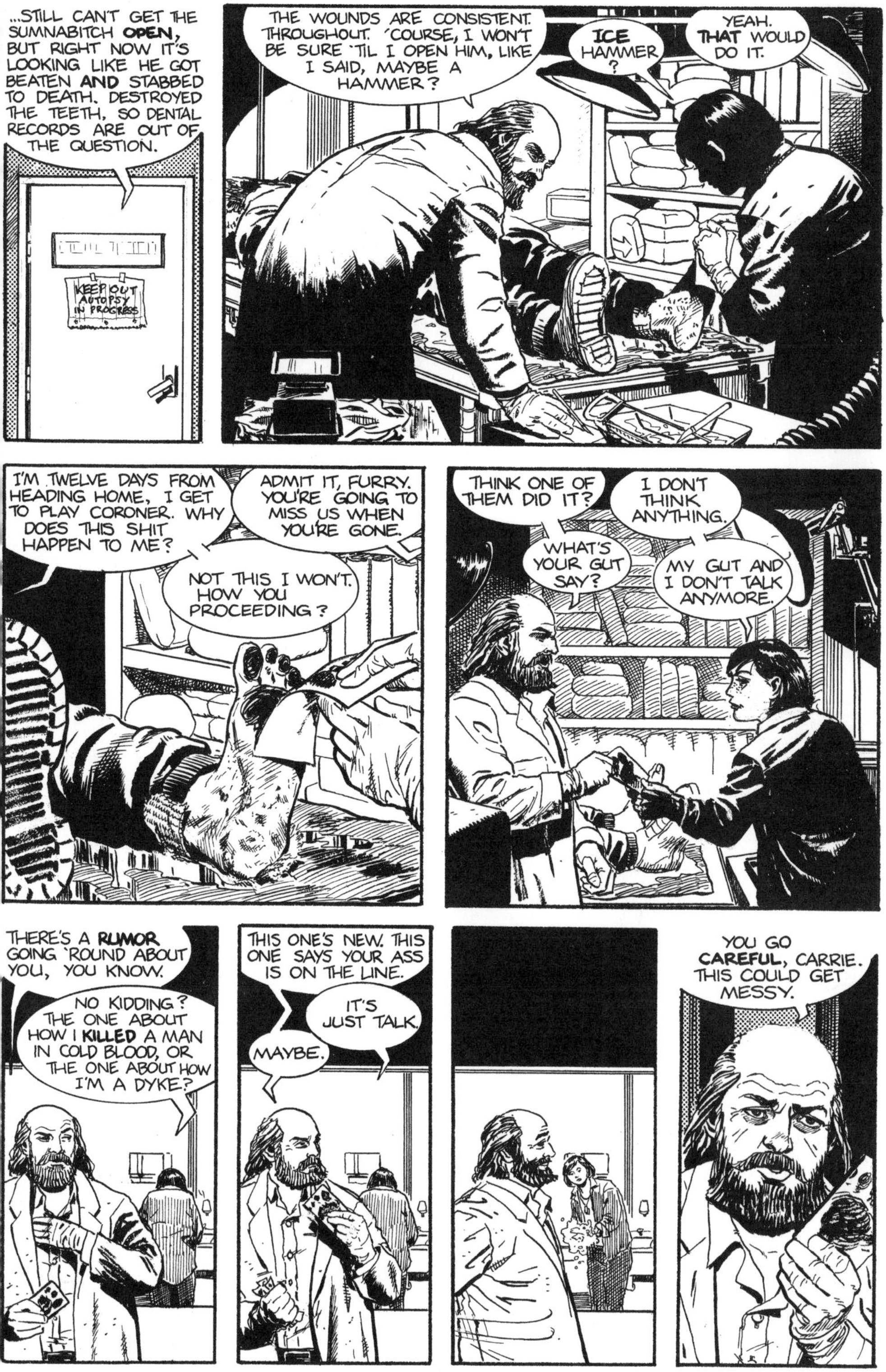

...STILL CAN'T GET THE SUMNABITCH **OPEN**, BUT RIGHT NOW IT'S LOOKING LIKE HE GOT BEATEN **AND** STABBED TO DEATH. DESTROYED THE TEETH, SO DENTAL RECORDS ARE OUT OF THE QUESTION.
KEEP OUT AUTOPSY IN PROGRESS
THE WOUNDS ARE CONSISTENT. THROUGHOUT. 'COURSE, I WON'T BE SURE 'TIL I OPEN HIM, LIKE I SAID, MAYBE A HAMMER?
ICE HAMMER?
YEAH. **THAT** WOULD DO IT.
I'M TWELVE DAYS FROM HEADING HOME, I GET TO PLAY CORONER. WHY DOES THIS SHIT HAPPEN TO ME?
ADMIT IT, FURRY. YOU'RE GOING TO MISS US WHEN YOU'RE GONE.
NOT THIS I WON'T. HOW YOU PROCEEDING?
THINK ONE OF THEM DID IT?
I DON'T THINK ANYTHING.
WHAT'S YOUR GUT SAY?
MY GUT AND I DON'T TALK ANYMORE.
THERE'S A **RUMOR** GOING 'ROUND ABOUT YOU, YOU KNOW.
NO KIDDING? THE ONE ABOUT HOW I **KILLED** A MAN IN COLD BLOOD, OR THE ONE ABOUT HOW I'M A DYKE?
THIS ONE'S NEW. THIS ONE SAYS YOUR ASS IS ON THE LINE.
IT'S JUST TALK.
MAYBE.
YOU GO **CAREFUL**, CARRIE. THIS COULD GET MESSY.

It'll take McEwan and his crew three hours to run the prints.

I kill the time hoping.

I don't want to know.

But of course...

...it's exactly what I **didn't** want.

ALEXANDER KELLER
age 28 UNIVERSITY of CHICAGO
Dept of Geology + Geophysical Sci.

United States Marshals Service

Office of the U. S. Marshal
District of Hawaii
US Courthouse
300 Moana Blvd. Room c-103
Honolulu, HI 96850

Stetko:

He's one of ours. Get to fucking work.

McEwan

P.S.- You DIDN'T...

ALEXANDER KELL
age 28 UNIVERSITY of CHI
Dept of Geology + Geophysi

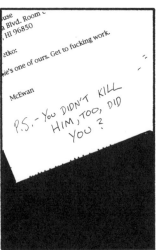

...use
Blvd. Room
HI 96850

...etko:

...e's one of ours. Get to fucking work.

McEwan

P.S.- YOU DIDN'T KILL HIM, TOO, DID YOU?

Bastard.

14

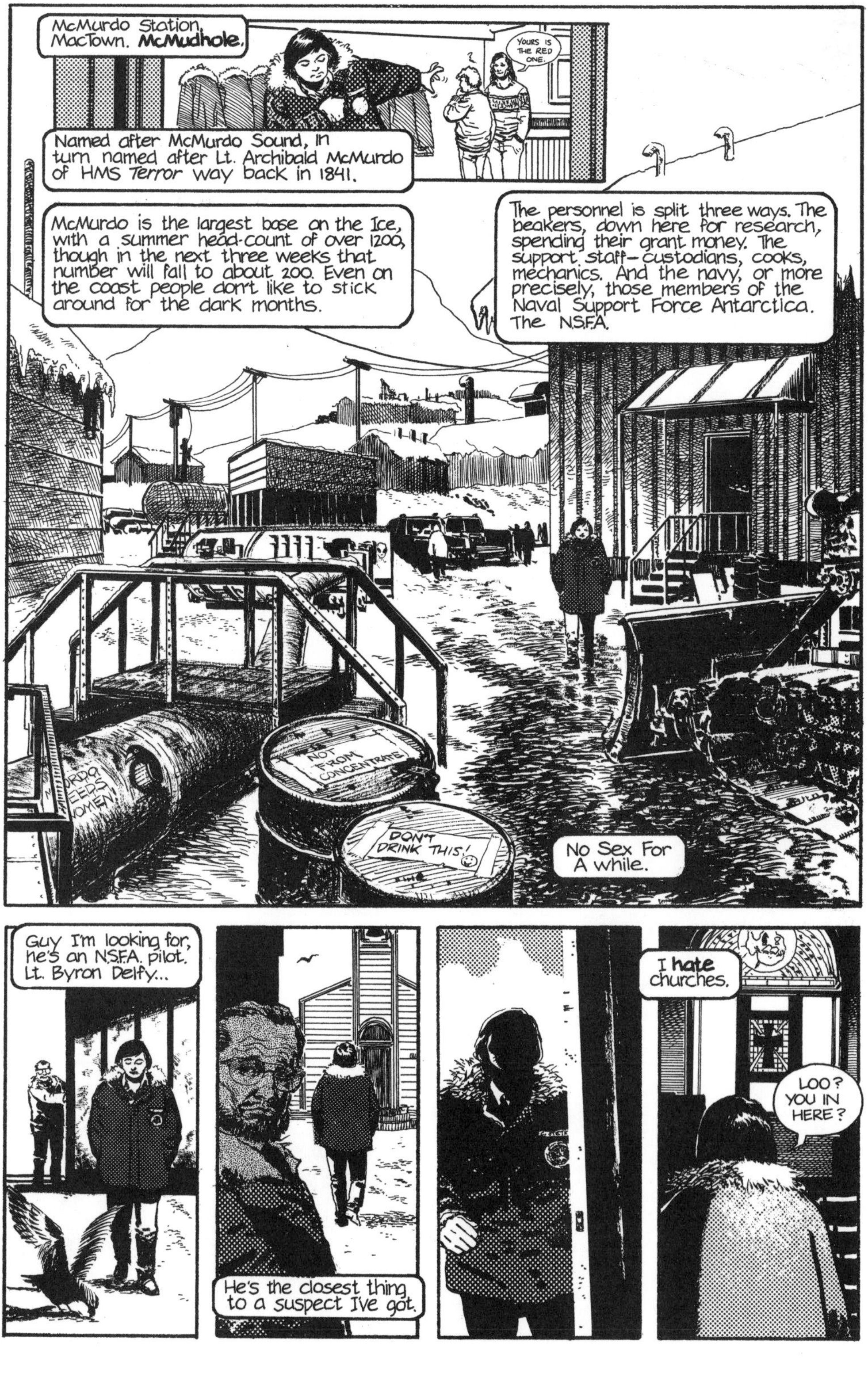
McMurdo Station. MacTown. **McMudhole.**
YOURS IS THE RED ONE.
Named after McMurdo Sound, In turn named after Lt. Archibald McMurdo of HMS *Terror* way back in 1841.
McMurdo is the largest base on the Ice, with a summer head-count of over 1200, though in the next three weeks that number will fall to about 200. Even on the coast people don't like to stick around for the dark months.
The personnel is split three ways. The beakers, down here for research, spending their grant money. The support staff—custodians, cooks, mechanics. And the navy, or more precisely, those members of the Naval Support Force Antarctica. The N.S.F.A.
NOT FROM CONCENTRATE
DON'T DRINK THIS!
No Sex For A while.
Guy I'm looking for, he's an N.S.F.A. pilot. Lt. Byron Delfy...
He's the closest thing to a suspect I've got.
I **hate** churches.
LOO? YOU IN HERE?

HOWDY, MARSHAL.

AM I LATE?

NAH, JUST GOT TO MAKE THE SLEIGH RIDE TOMORROW. PRAYING FOR GOOD WEATHER.

YOU'RE A **CHARACTER**, LOO. YOU KNOW THAT, DON'T YOU?

IF YOU HAD TO PILOT THIS FROZEN HELL FOR A LIVING, YOU'D PRAY, TOO.

I DON'T PRAY.

I KNOW.

YOU WERE FLYING SUPPORT FOR DELTA ONE-ONE?

YEAH, SINCE **WINFLY**, STANDARD STUFF. FOOD, MAIL, REPLACEMENT PARTS FOR THE DRILL INBOUND, WASTE AND OTHER CRAP OUTBOUND. NOTHING OUT OF THE ORDINARY.

AND YOUR LAST RUN?

THREE DAYS AGO. SUPPOSED. TO CLOSE THE CAMP, BRING THE AMERICANS BACK HERE. BUT WHEN I GOT THERE, THEY WERE GONE, EXCEPT FOR THE BODY.

YOU EVER TALK TO THIS GUY?

KELLER? SURE, I FLEW HIM AND BATES INTO TOWN, WHAT WAS IT, TWO WEEKS AGO. THEY HAD TO PICK UP REPLACEMENT GEAR. WE HAD A FEW DRINKS.

... ALEX KELLER IS A HOOT.

HE'S THE POPSICLE.

I LIKED HIM. GOOD KID.

SOMEBODY **DIDN'T.** MAYBE ONE OF HIS BUNK MATES.

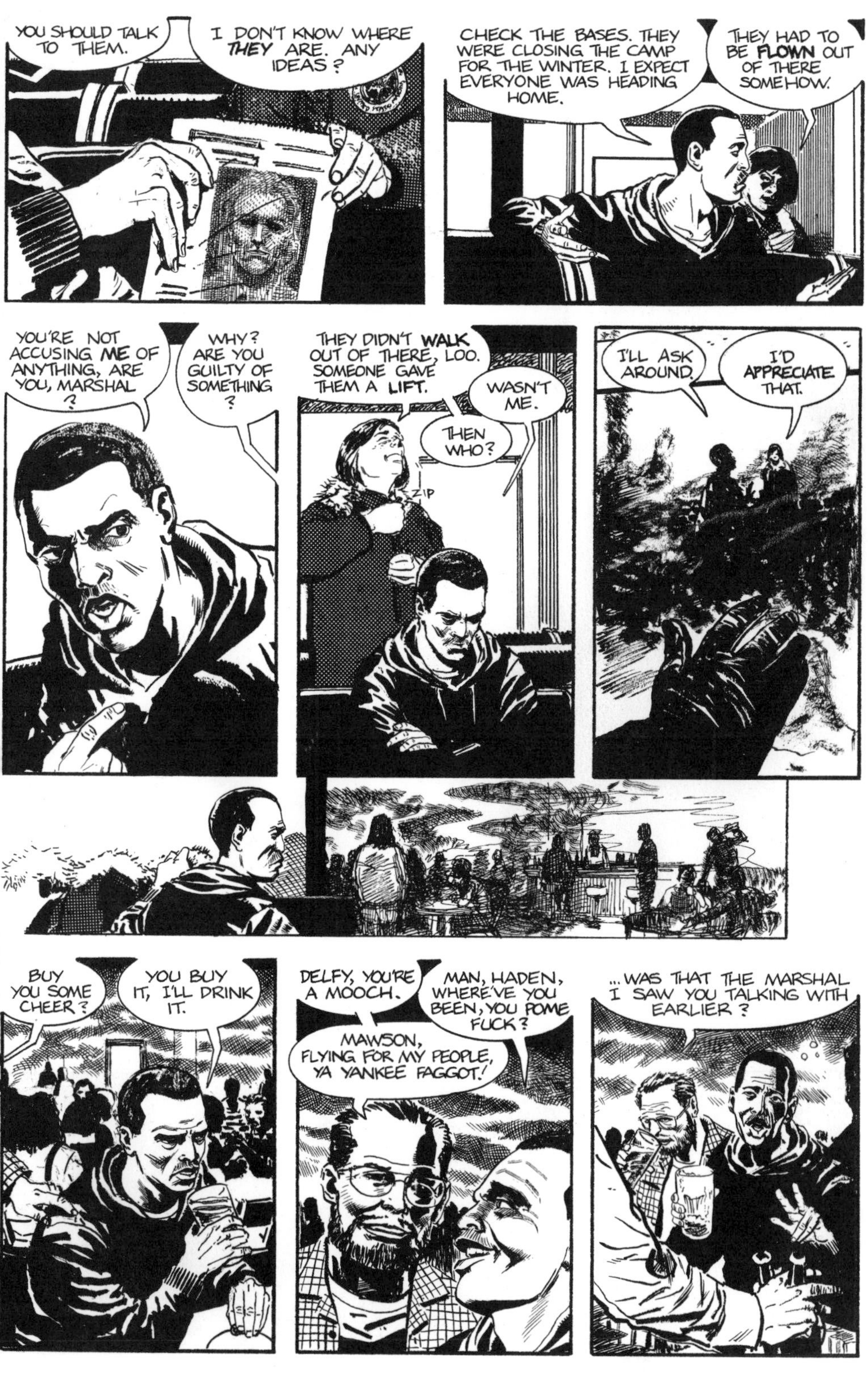
YOU SHOULD TALK TO THEM.
I DON'T KNOW WHERE THEY ARE. ANY IDEAS?
CHECK THE BASES. THEY WERE CLOSING THE CAMP FOR THE WINTER. I EXPECT EVERYONE WAS HEADING HOME.
THEY HAD TO BE FLOWN OUT OF THERE SOMEHOW.
YOU'RE NOT ACCUSING ME OF ANYTHING, ARE YOU, MARSHAL?
WHY? ARE YOU GUILTY OF SOMETHING?
THEY DIDN'T WALK OUT OF THERE, LOO. SOMEONE GAVE THEM A LIFT.
THEN WHO?
WASN'T ME.
ZIP
I'LL ASK AROUND.
I'D APPRECIATE THAT.
BUY YOU SOME CHEER?
YOU BUY IT, I'LL DRINK IT.
DELFY, YOU'RE A MOOCH.
MAN, HADEN, WHERE'VE YOU BEEN, YOU POME FUCK?
MAWSON, FLYING FOR MY PEOPLE, YA YANKEE FAGGOT!
...WAS THAT THE MARSHAL I SAW YOU TALKING WITH EARLIER?

I spend the next **two days** on the radio trying to find my missing men.

Waiting for a call back from someone, **anyone**, who knows what I'm talking about.

I get fucking nowhere.

I dream of a memory four years old...

I don't like how it makes me feel...

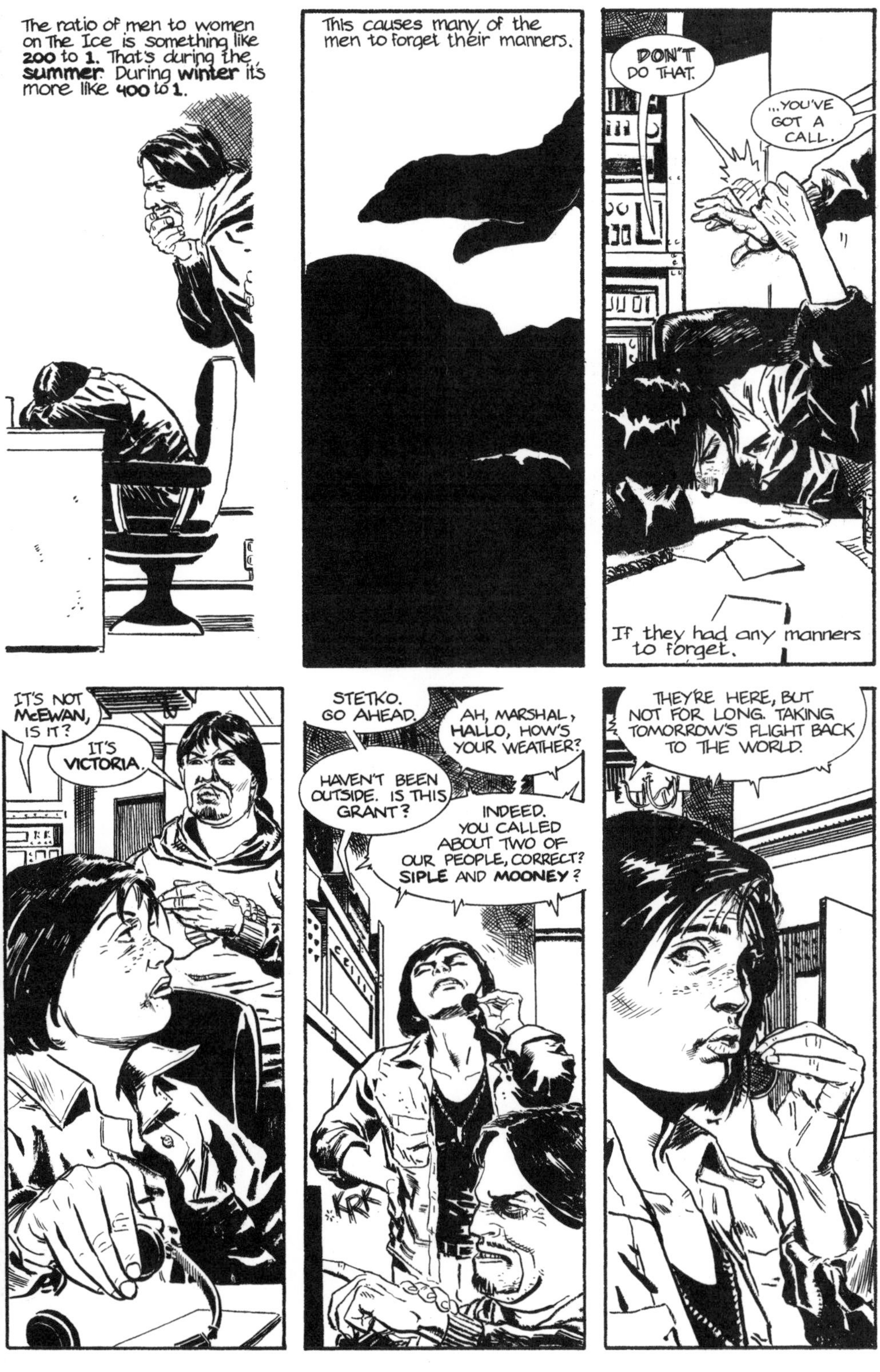

The ratio of men to women on The Ice is something like **200** to **1**. That's during the **summer**. During **winter** it's more like **400** to **1**.
This causes many of the men to forget their manners.
DON'T DO THAT.
...YOU'VE GOT A CALL.
If they had any manners to forget.
IT'S NOT **McEWAN**, IS IT?
IT'S **VICTORIA**.
STETKO. GO AHEAD.
AH, MARSHAL, **HALLO**, HOW'S YOUR WEATHER?
HAVEN'T BEEN OUTSIDE. IS THIS GRANT?
INDEED. YOU CALLED ABOUT TWO OF OUR PEOPLE, CORRECT? **SIPLE** AND **MOONEY**?
KRK
THEY'RE HERE, BUT NOT FOR LONG. TAKING TOMORROW'S FLIGHT BACK TO THE WORLD.

I can't trust Grant, but he'll keep his mouth shut.

He knows London *isn't* an idle threat.

It does no good telling him that I share his reservations.

I just remember that there are *rules*, after all...

...that's how it's all supposed to *work*.

And when it *doesn't* work----when the rules are *broken*...

...I do my job. I *fix* it.

TALK.

SHE'LL BE HERE IN TWENTY MINUTES.

THANK YOU.

It's *simple*, really.

simple.

21

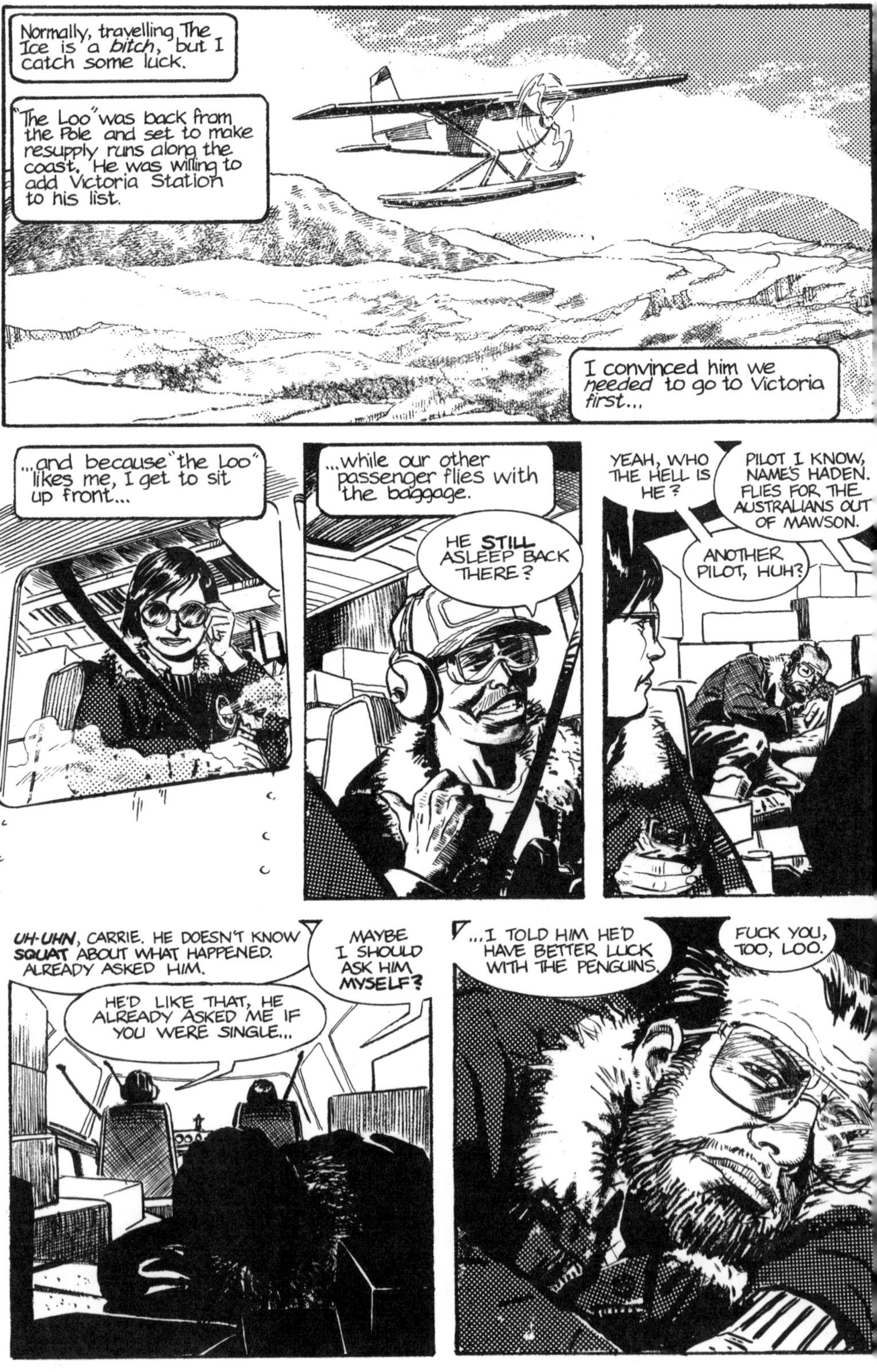

Normally, travelling The Ice is a *bitch*, but I catch some luck.
"The Loo" was back from the Pole and set to make resupply runs along the coast. He was willing to add Victoria Station to his list.
I convinced him we *needed* to go to Victoria *first*...
...and because "the Loo" likes me, I get to sit up front...
...while our other passenger flies with the baggage.
HE **STILL** ASLEEP BACK THERE?
YEAH, WHO THE HELL IS HE?
PILOT I KNOW, NAME'S HADEN. FLIES FOR THE AUSTRALIANS OUT OF MAWSON.
ANOTHER PILOT, HUH?
UH-UHN, CARRIE. HE DOESN'T KNOW **SQUAT** ABOUT WHAT HAPPENED. ALREADY ASKED HIM.
MAYBE I SHOULD ASK HIM **MYSELF?**
HE'D LIKE THAT, HE ALREADY ASKED ME IF YOU WERE SINGLE...
...I TOLD HIM HE'D HAVE BETTER LUCK WITH THE PENGUINS.
FUCK YOU, TOO, LOO.

VICTORIA UK, *THIS* IS CHARLIE HOTEL EIGHT-NINER OUT OF McMURDO. **HOW'S** YOUR WEATHER? OVER.

...**WIND** AT SEVEN KNOTS FROM **SSE**... GOOD LANDING CONDITIONS **BUT** BE ADVISED...

...SITUATION **UNSTABLE**... WINDS FORECAST TO REACH **60 PLUS** KNOTS IN NEXT **FOUR** HOURS. OVER.

ROGER **THAT**, VICTORIA...

...WE'RE ON FINAL APPROACH NOW.

BE ADVISED THAT HER MAJESTY'S GOVERNMENT **CANNOT** GRANT PERMISSION FOR LANDING OR ASSISTANCE DURING YOUR STAY, **AND** THAT YOU VISIT VICTORIA STATION AT YOUR OWN RISK. OVER.

CONFIRMED. OVER AND OUT.

DON'T YOU LOVE IT WHEN THEY COVER THEIR ASSES LIKE THAT? WHAT THEY'RE REALLY SAYING IS, "IF YOU GET YOUR TITS IN THE WRINGER, YOU'RE ON YOUR OWN."

YOU HAVE SUCH A WAY WITH WORDS, HADEN.

WE **COULD** HAVE A PROBLEM, THOUGH...

...THE WINDS KICK UP, WE'LL BE GROUNDED, GOD *KNOWS* FOR HOW LONG.

...NOT THAT YOU'D MIND.

...

SORRY, WHAT?

NOTHING.

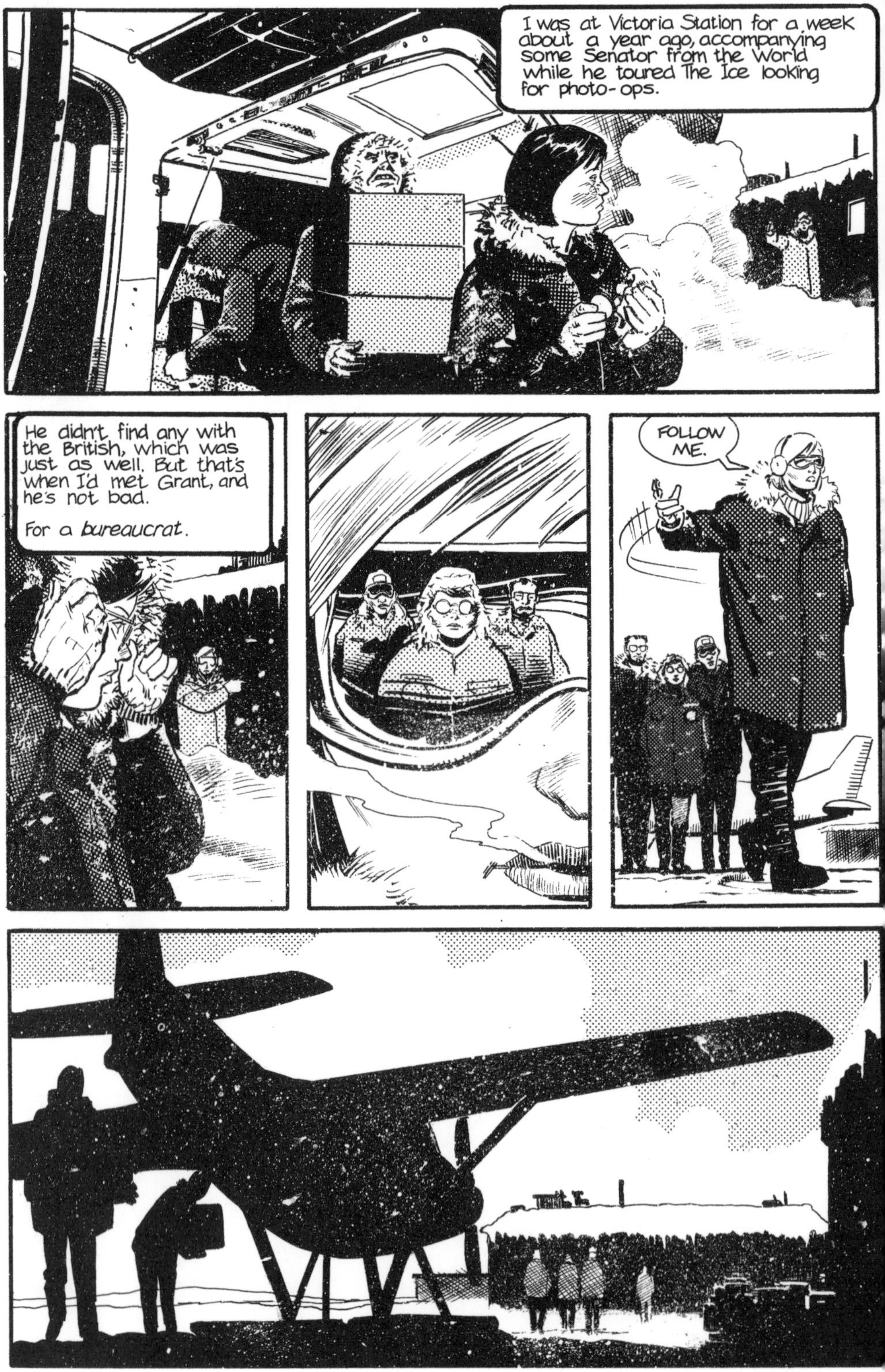

I was at Victoria Station for a week about a year ago, accompanying some Senator from the World while he toured The Ice looking for photo-ops.
He didn't find any with the British, which was just as well. But that's when I'd met Grant, and he's not bad.
For a *bureaucrat*.
FOLLOW ME.

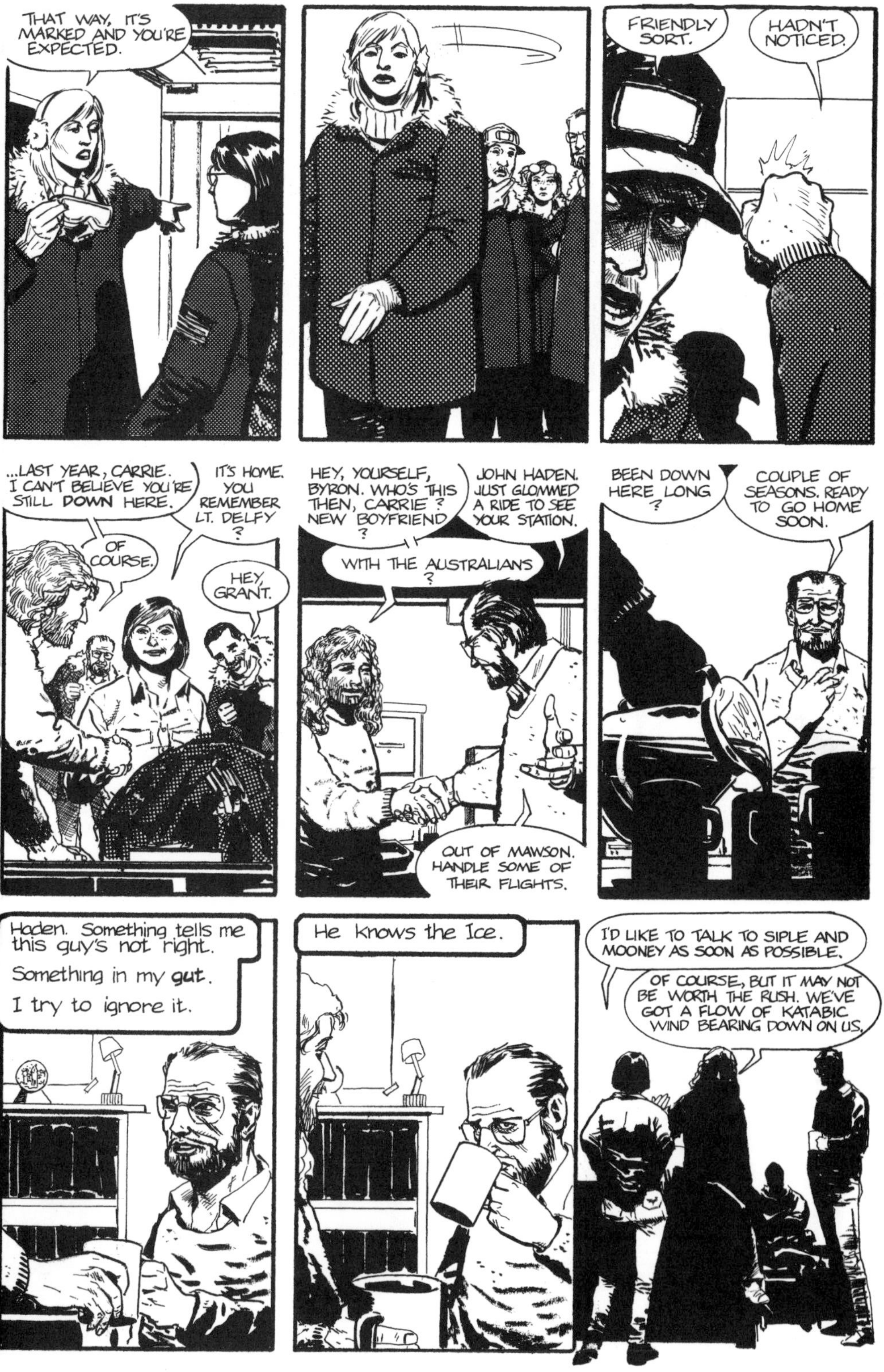
THAT WAY, IT'S MARKED AND YOU'RE EXPECTED.
FRIENDLY SORT.
HADN'T NOTICED.
...LAST YEAR, CARRIE. I CAN'T BELIEVE YOU'RE STILL **DOWN** HERE.
OF COURSE.
IT'S HOME. YOU REMEMBER LT. DELFY?
HEY, GRANT.
HEY, YOURSELF, BYRON. WHO'S THIS THEN, CARRIE? NEW BOYFRIEND?
WITH THE AUSTRALIANS?
JOHN HADEN. JUST GLOMMED A RIDE TO SEE YOUR STATION.
OUT OF MAWSON. HANDLE SOME OF THEIR FLIGHTS.
BEEN DOWN HERE LONG?
COUPLE OF SEASONS. READY TO GO HOME SOON.
Haden. Something tells me this guy's not right.
Something in my **gut**.
I try to ignore it.
He knows the Ice.
I'D LIKE TO TALK TO SIPLE AND MOONEY AS SOON AS POSSIBLE.
OF COURSE, BUT IT MAY NOT BE WORTH THE RUSH. WE'VE GOT A FLOW OF KATABIC WIND BEARING DOWN ON US.

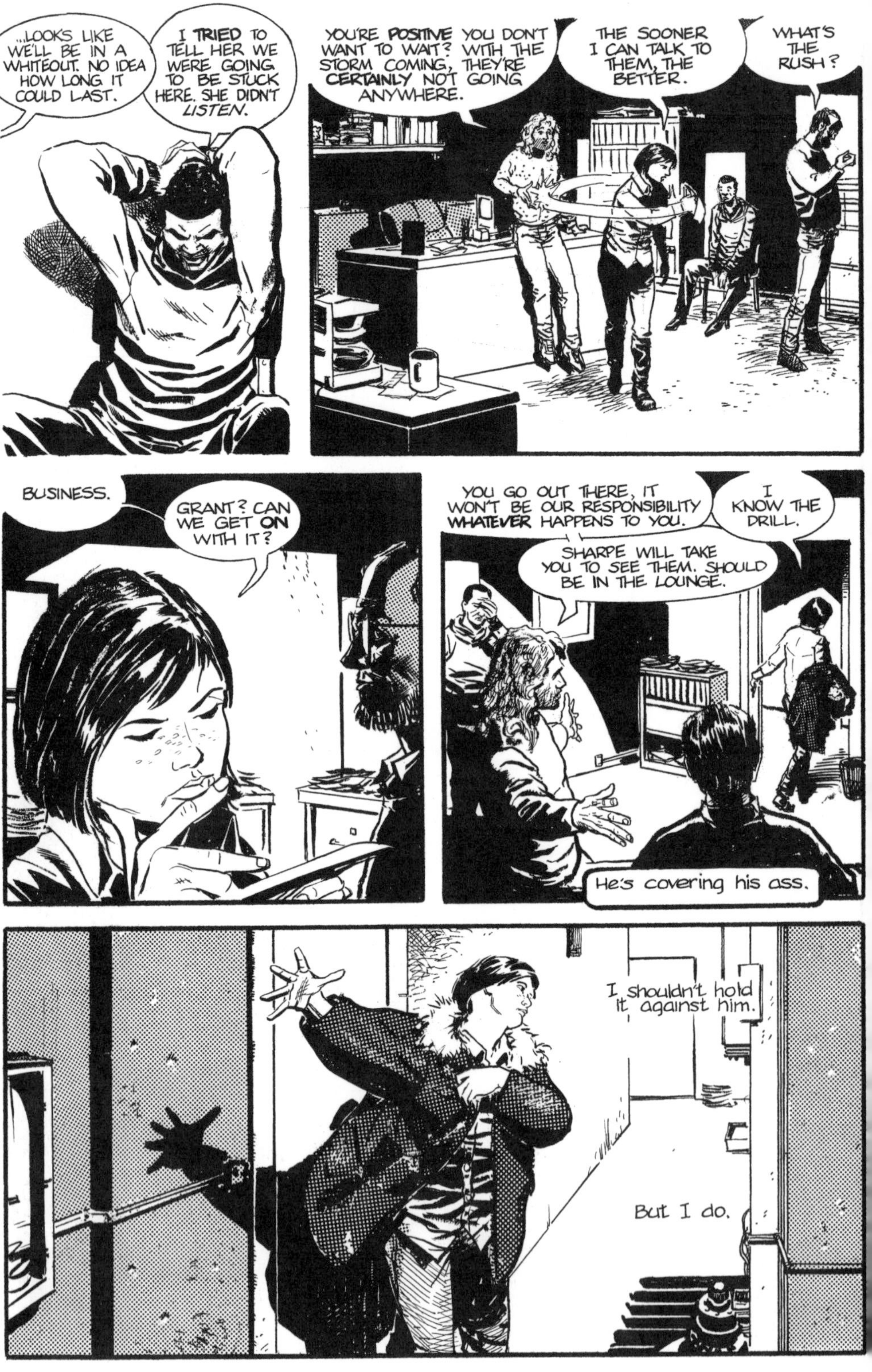
...LOOKS LIKE WE'LL BE IN A WHITEOUT. NO IDEA HOW LONG IT COULD LAST.
I TRIED TO TELL HER WE WERE GOING TO BE STUCK HERE. SHE DIDN'T LISTEN.
YOU'RE POSITIVE YOU DON'T WANT TO WAIT? WITH THE STORM COMING, THEY'RE CERTAINLY NOT GOING ANYWHERE.
THE SOONER I CAN TALK TO THEM, THE BETTER.
WHAT'S THE RUSH?
BUSINESS.
GRANT? CAN WE GET ON WITH IT?
YOU GO OUT THERE, IT WON'T BE OUR RESPONSIBILITY WHATEVER HAPPENS TO YOU.
I KNOW THE DRILL.
SHARPE WILL TAKE YOU TO SEE THEM. SHOULD BE IN THE LOUNGE.
He's covering his ass.
I shouldn't hold it against him.
But I do.

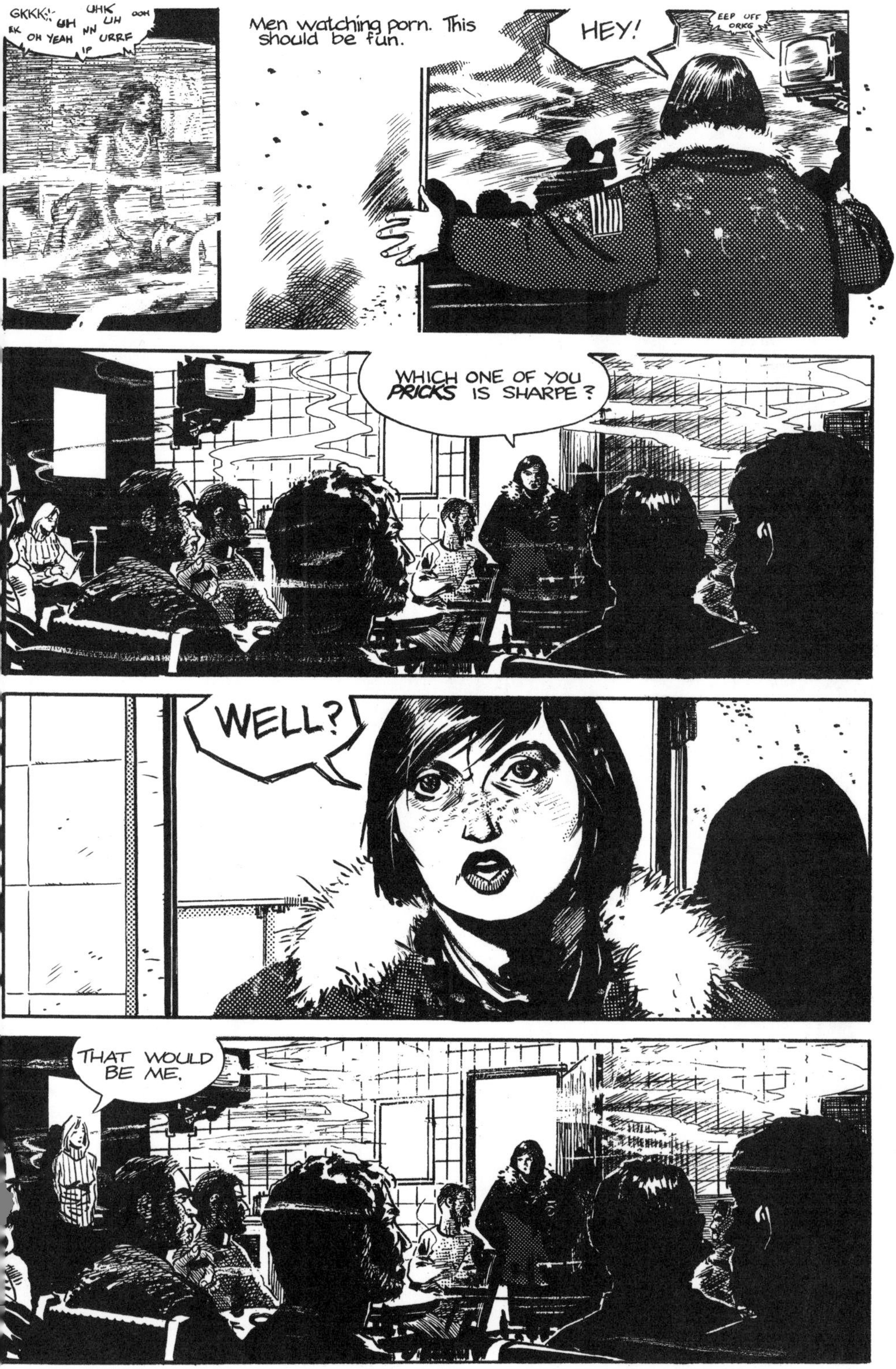
GKKK!
EK
UH
OH YEAH
UHK
NN
IP
UH
URRF
OOH
Men watching porn. This should be fun.
HEY!
EEP UFF ORKG
WHICH ONE OF YOU PRICKS IS SHARPE?
WELL?
THAT WOULD BE ME.

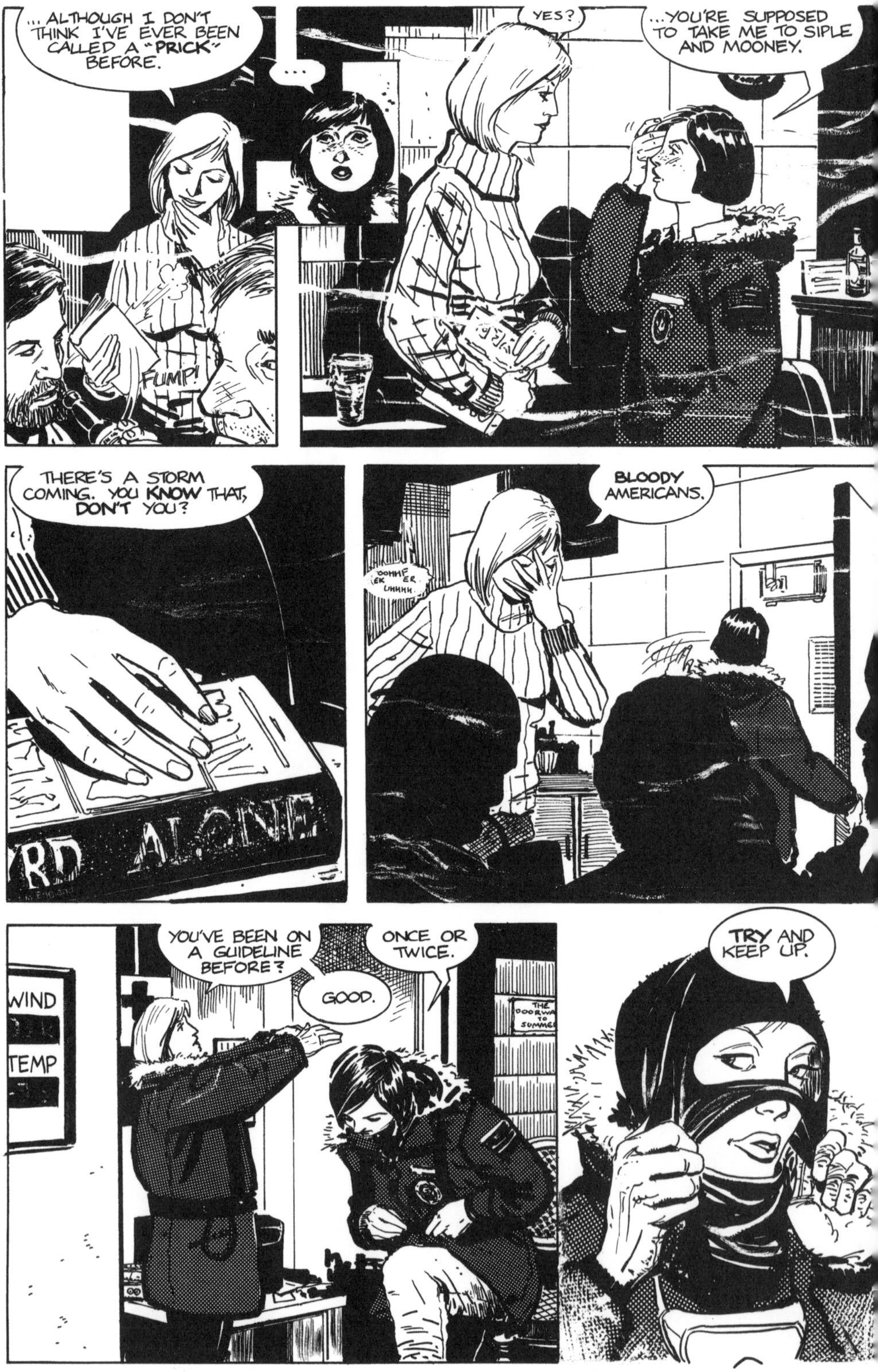

... ALTHOUGH I DON'T THINK I'VE EVER BEEN CALLED A "PRICK" BEFORE.
FUMP!
...
YES?
...YOU'RE SUPPOSED TO TAKE ME TO SIPLE AND MOONEY.
THERE'S A STORM COMING. YOU KNOW THAT, DON'T YOU?
RD ALONE
BLOODY AMERICANS.
OOHHF EK ER UHHHH
YOU'VE BEEN ON A GUIDELINE BEFORE?
ONCE OR TWICE.
GOOD.
WIND
TEMP
TRY AND KEEP UP.

Wind chill...

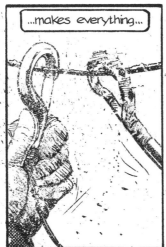

...makes everything...

...harder.

The **third** time the wind almost lifts me off the ground, I start reconsidering...

Why am I doing this?

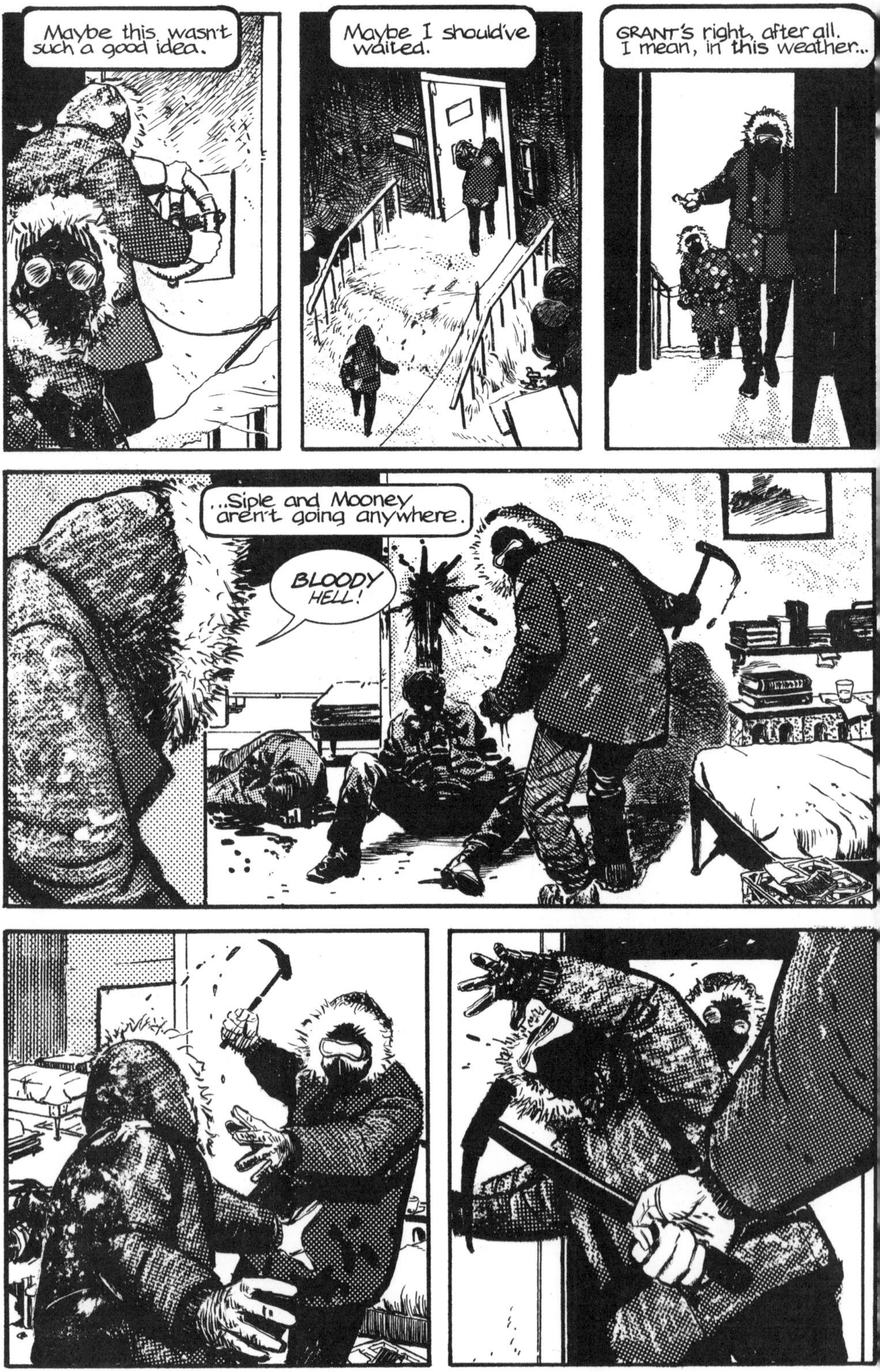
Maybe this wasn't such a good idea.
Maybe I should've waited.
GRANT'S right, after all. I mean, in this weather...
...Siple and Mooney aren't going anywhere.
BLOODY HELL!

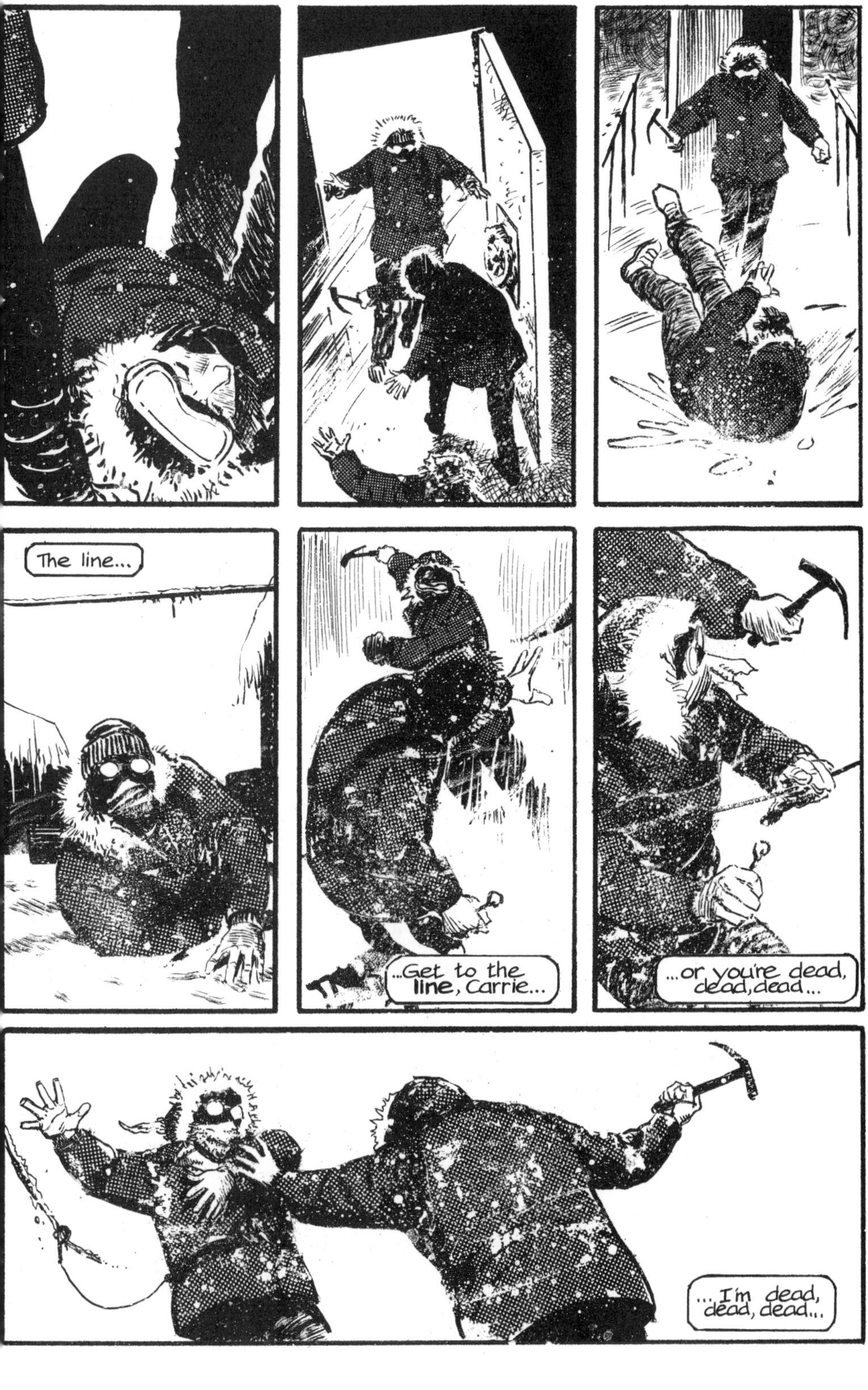
The line...
...Get to the line, Carrie...
...or you're dead, dead, dead...
...I'm dead, dead, dead...

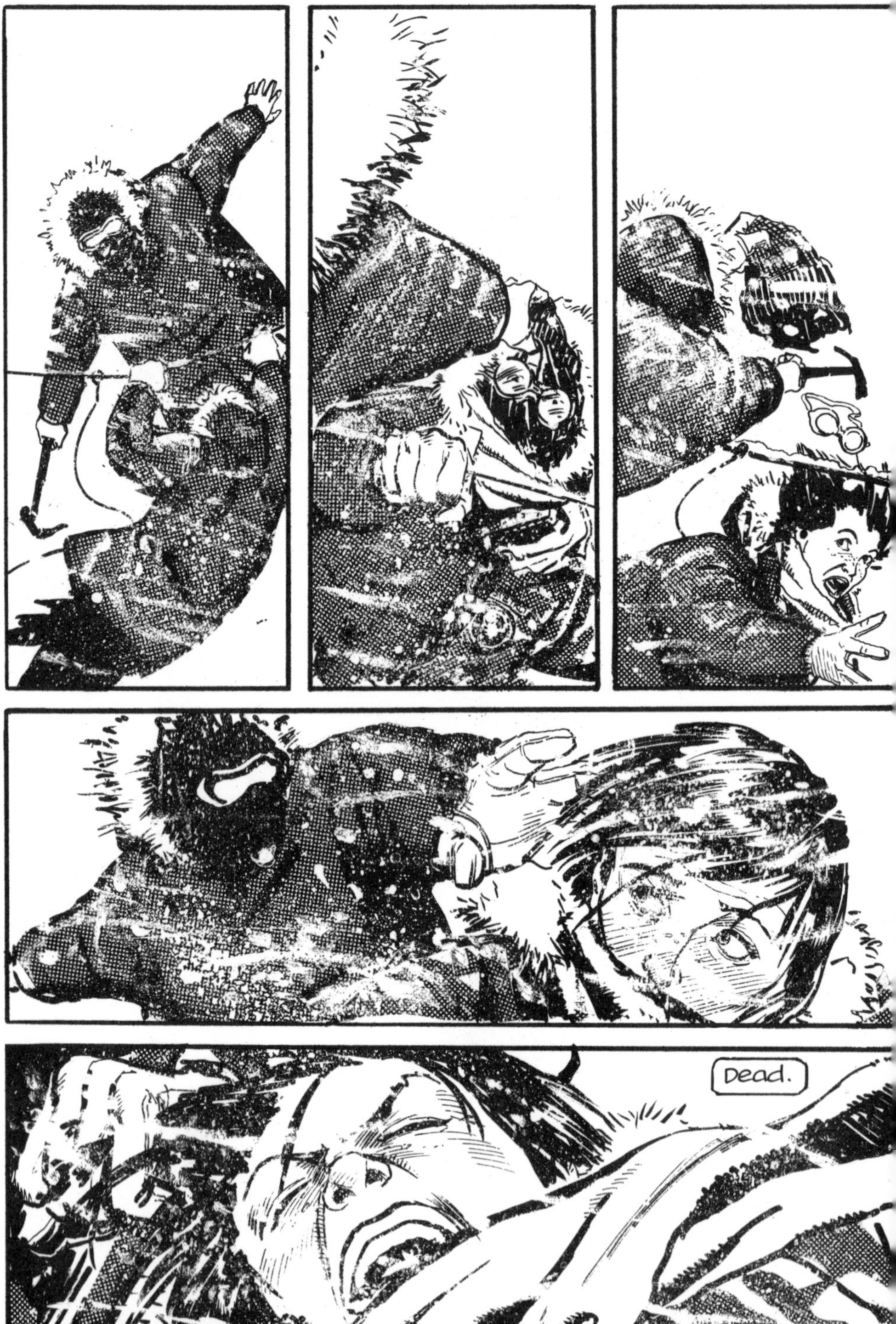
Dead.

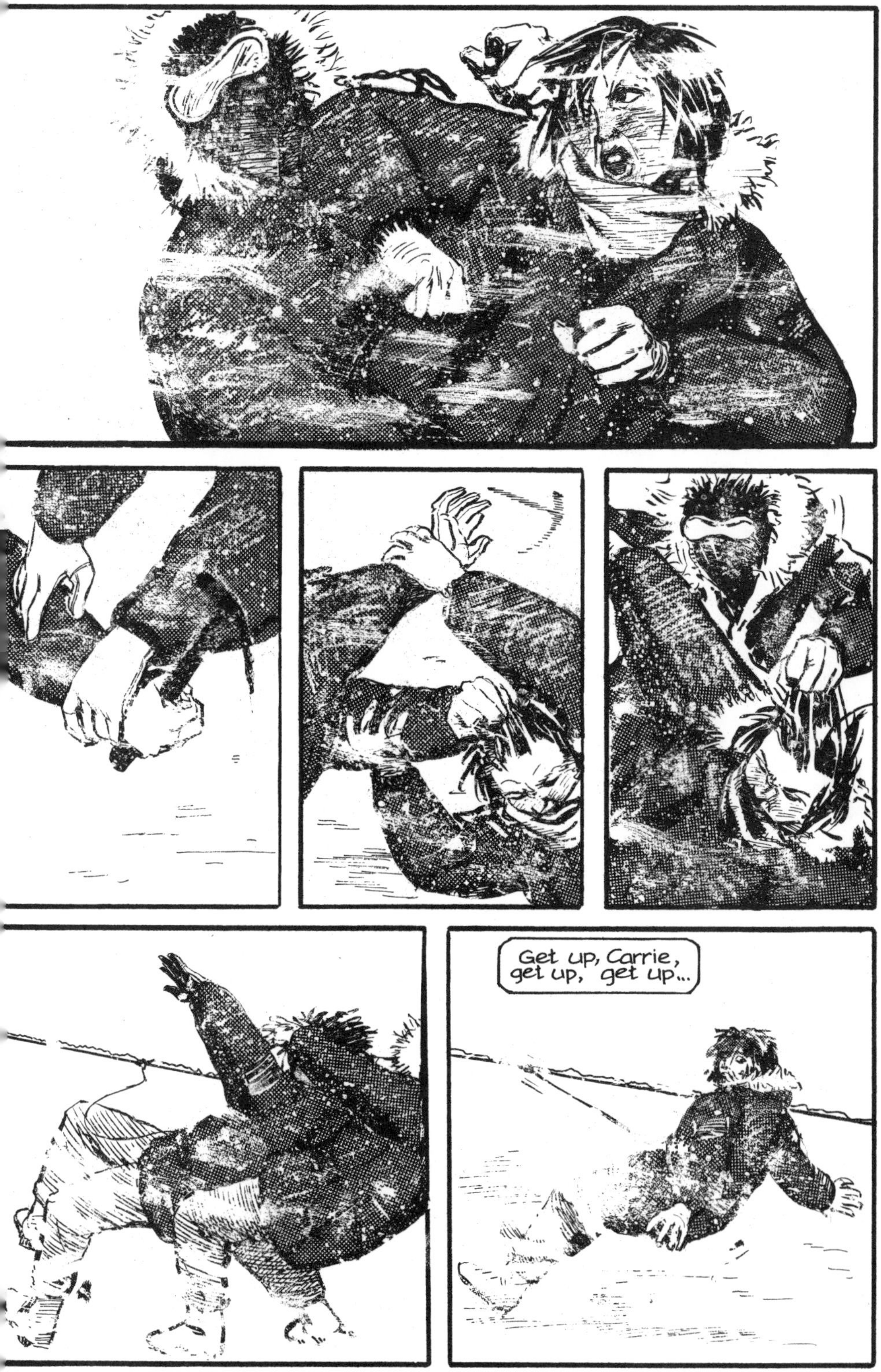
Get up, Carrie, get up, get up...

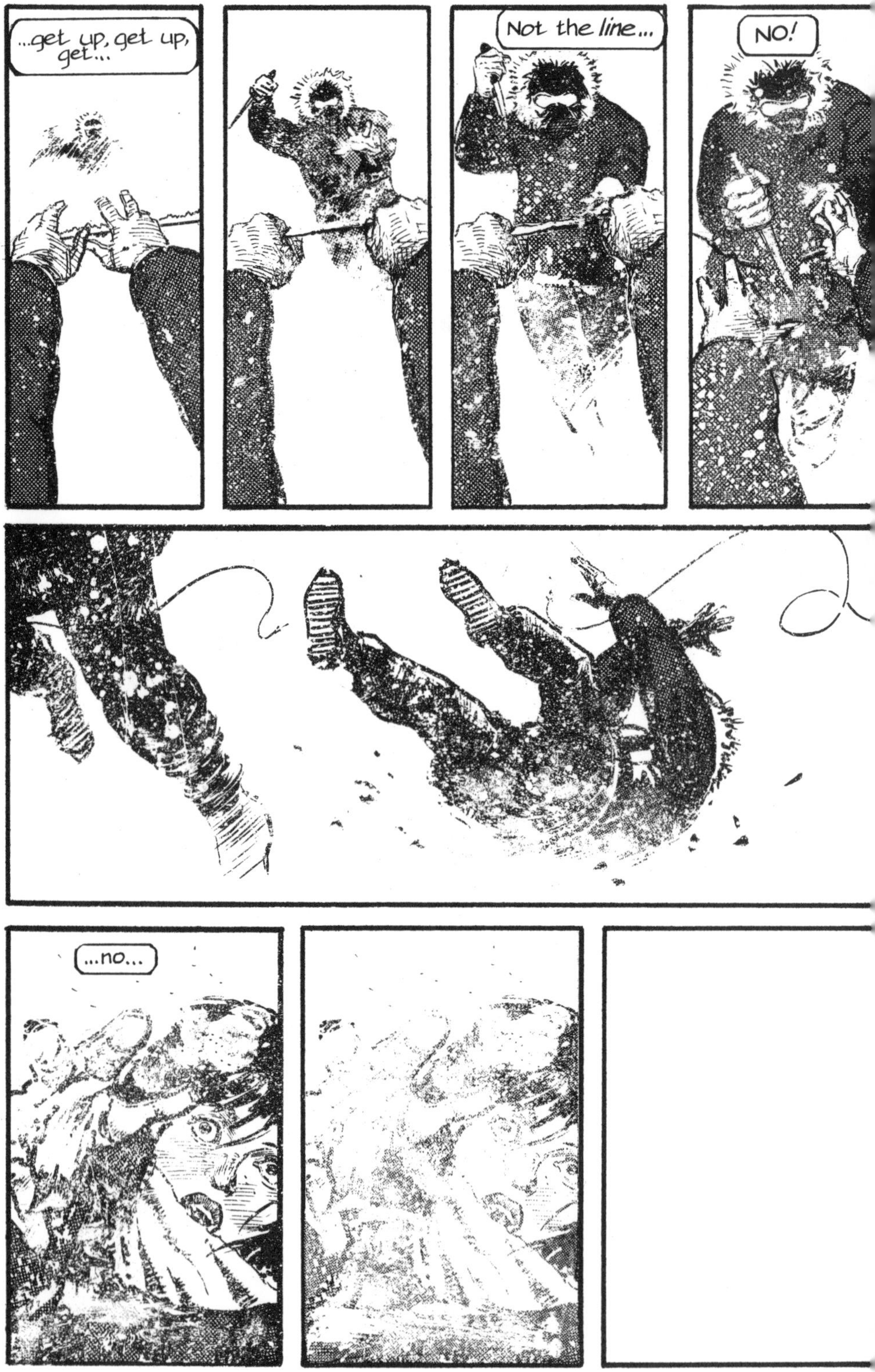
...get up, get up, get...
Not the *line*...
NO!
...no...

CHAPTER TWO

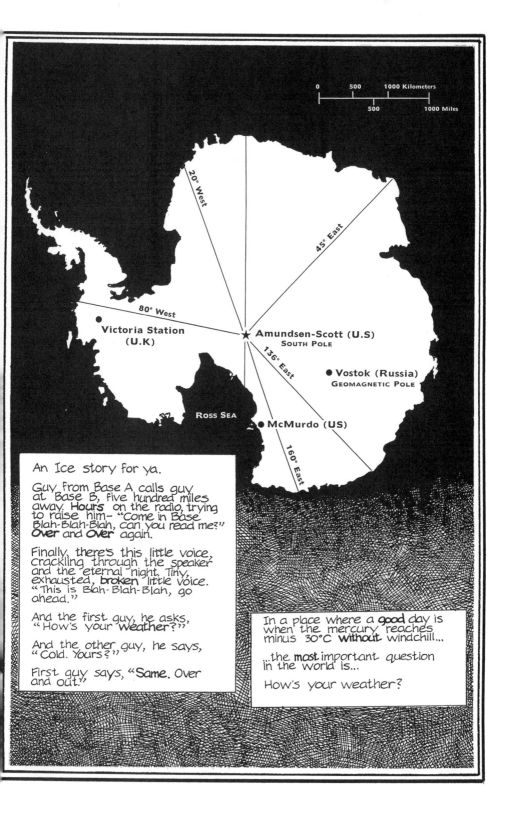

My weather sucks.

Tru Fax. Antarctica is about 14.2 million square kilometers, not counting the tail or the islands...

Rock covered with 30 million cubic kilometers of ice. It's the highest continent, average elevation 2320 meters above sea level. That's 7380 feet, for those of you who never learned metric...

Think about how cold it has to be to keep 30 million cubic kilometers frozen.

Pretty fucking cold.

On the coast, at McMurdo, it's a balmy minus 5°C...

Survivable. Life exists to prove the point. Penguins, seals, insects, other birds, some particularly masochistic fish...

In the interior though, temperatures are much lower. Minus 70°C during the winter. Not counting windchill...

It's so fucking cold that **nothing** survives on it's own. No seals. No birds. No bugs. Not even bacteria...

Piece of trivia.— coldest temperature ever recorded on Earth was by the Russians at Vostok Station. Get this— minus 89.6°C, recorded July 21, 1983.

Cold like that kills. Water vapor in your lungs freezes instantly, bursts cells...

Kind of like exploding from within...

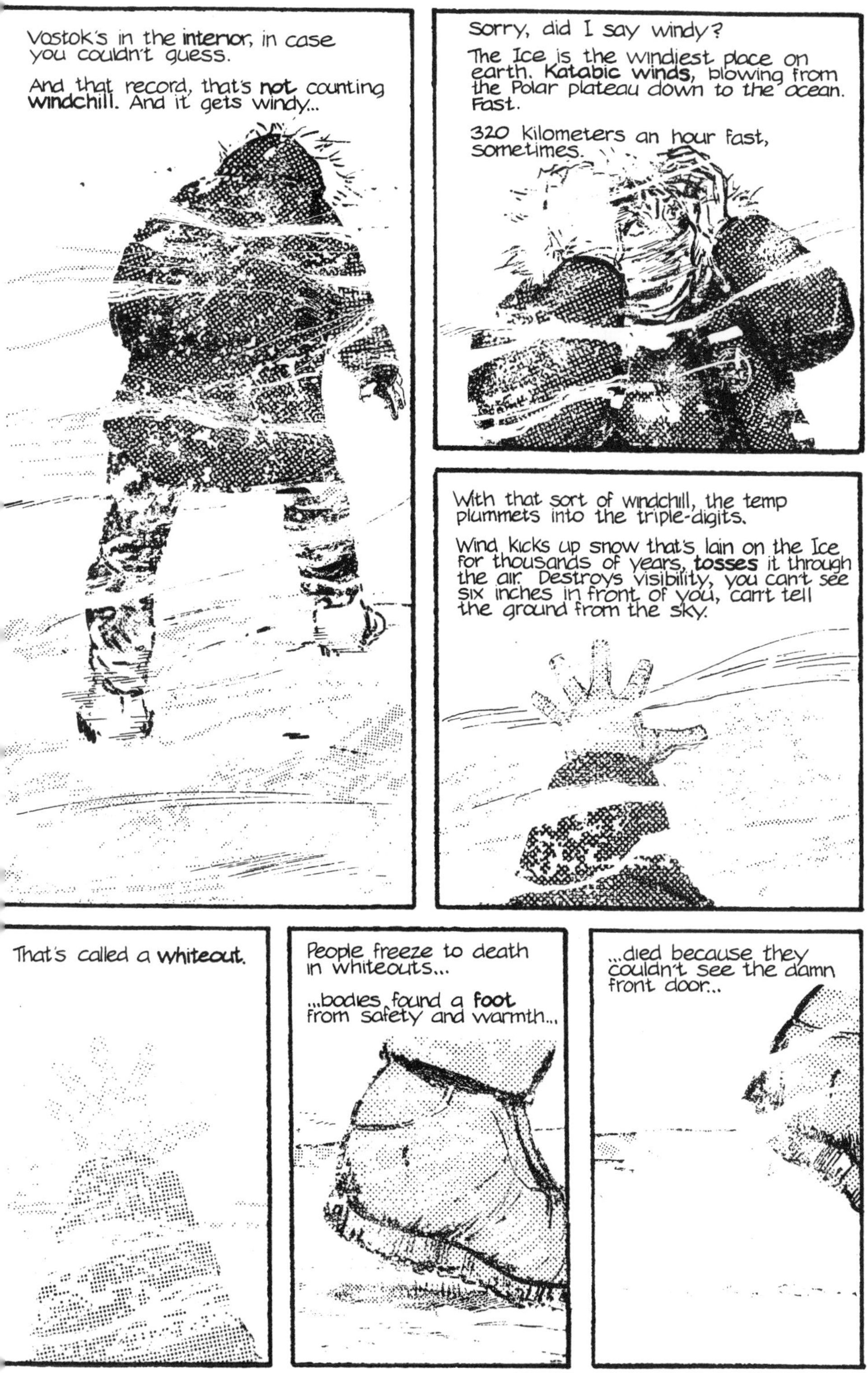
Vostok's in the **interior**, in case you couldn't guess.
And that record, that's **not** counting **windchill**. And it gets windy...
Sorry, did I say windy?
The Ice is the windiest place on earth. **Katabic winds**, blowing from the Polar plateau down to the ocean. **Fast**.
320 Kilometers an hour fast, sometimes.
With that sort of windchill, the temp plummets into the triple-digits.
Wind kicks up snow that's lain on the Ice for thousands of years, **tosses** it through the air. Destroys visibility, you can't see six inches in front of you, can't tell the ground from the sky.
That's called a **whiteout**.
People freeze to death in whiteouts...
...bodies found a **foot** from safety and warmth...
...died because they couldn't see the damn front door...

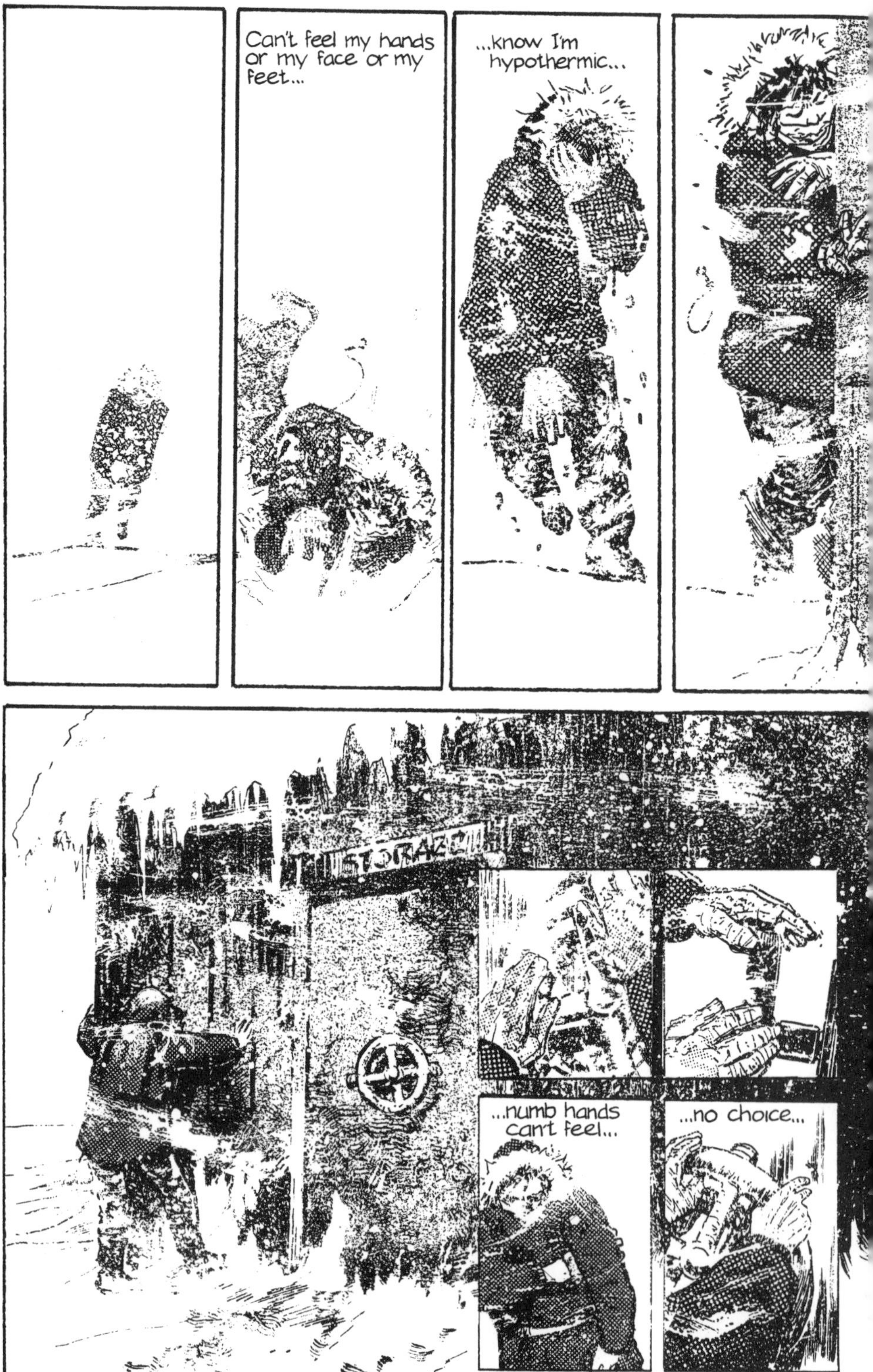
Can't feel my hands or my face or my feet...
...know I'm hypothermic...
...numb hands can't feel...
...no choice...

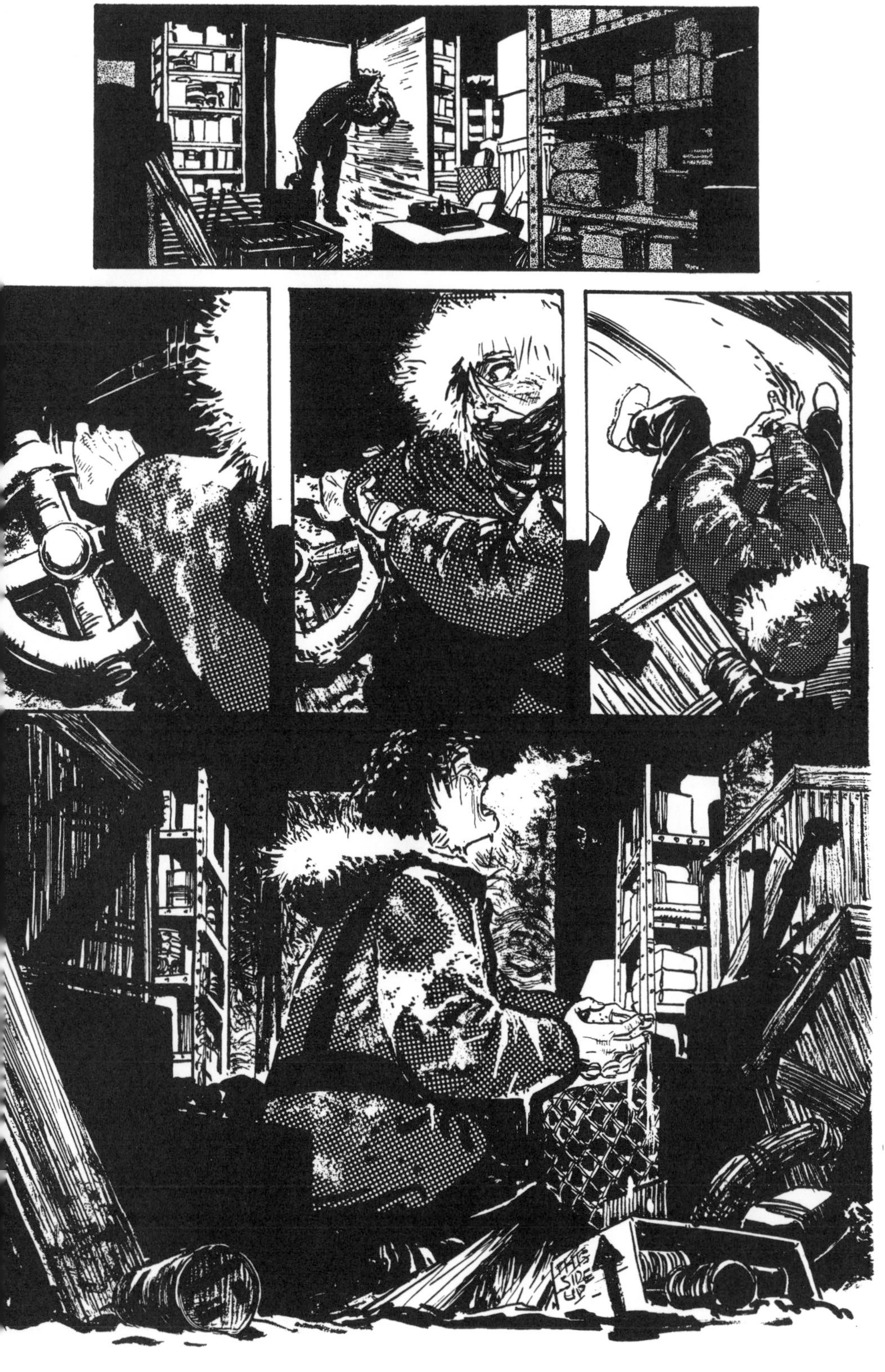
THIS SIDE UP

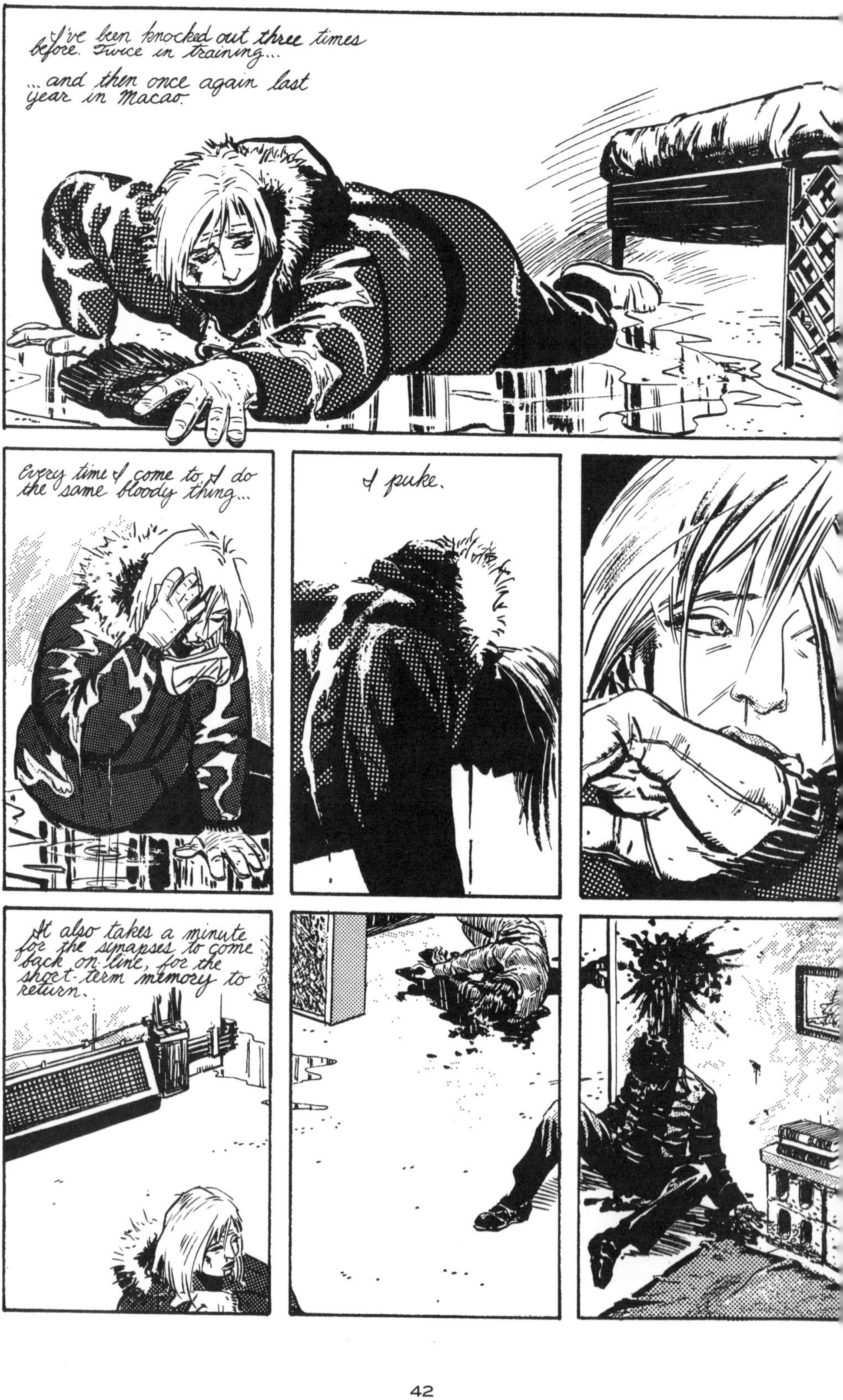
I've been knocked out three times before. Twice in training...
...and then once again last year in Macao.
Every time I come to I do the same bloody thing...
I puke.
It also takes a minute for the synapses to come back on-line, for the short-term memory to return.

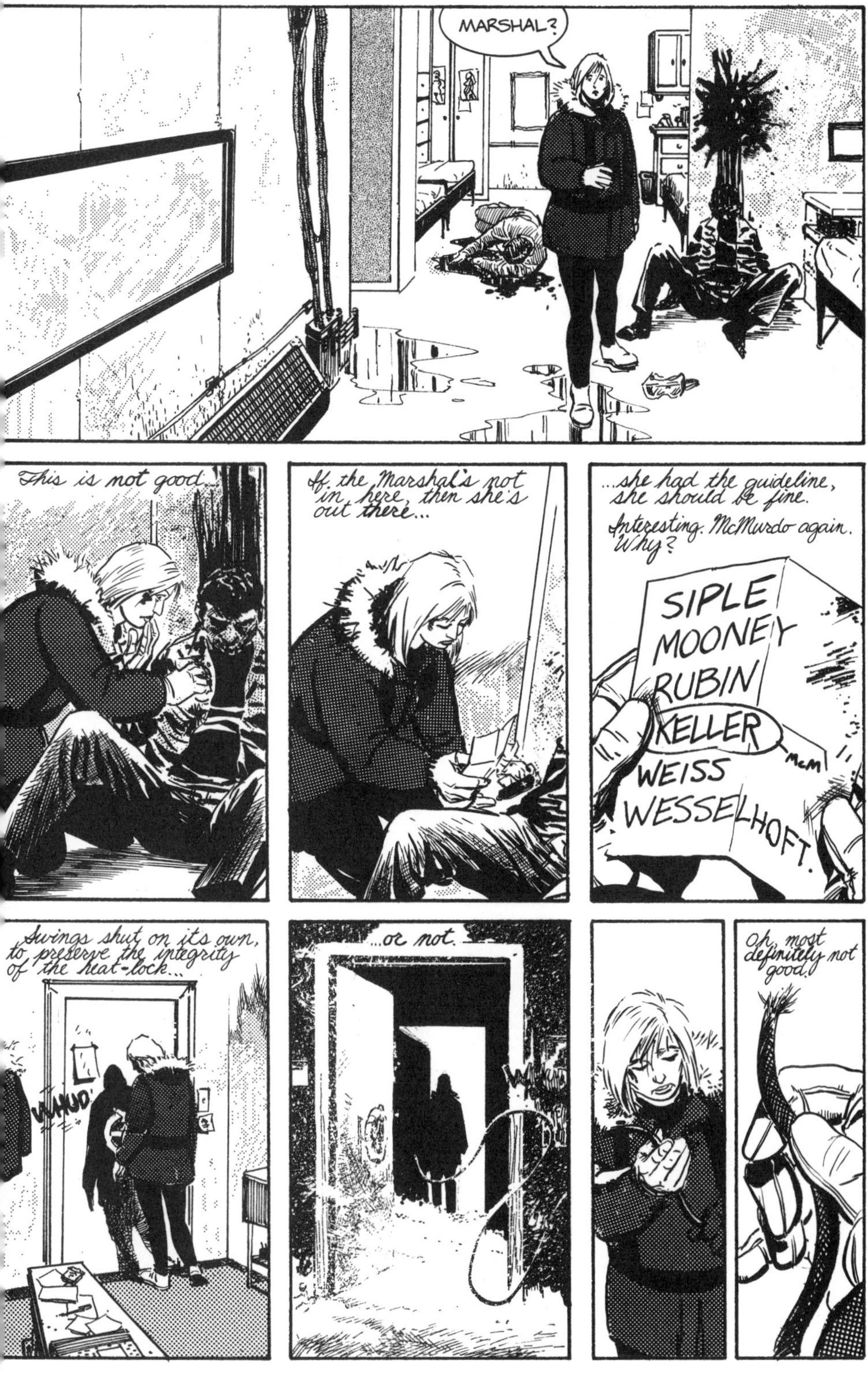
MARSHAL?
This is not good.
If the Marshal's not in here, then she's out there...
...she had the guideline, she should be fine.
Interesting. McMurdo again. Why?
SIPLE
MOONEY
RUBIN
KELLER
McM
WEISS
WESSELHOFT.
Swings shut on its own, to preserve the integrity of the heat-lock...
WHUD
...or not.
Oh, most definitely not good.

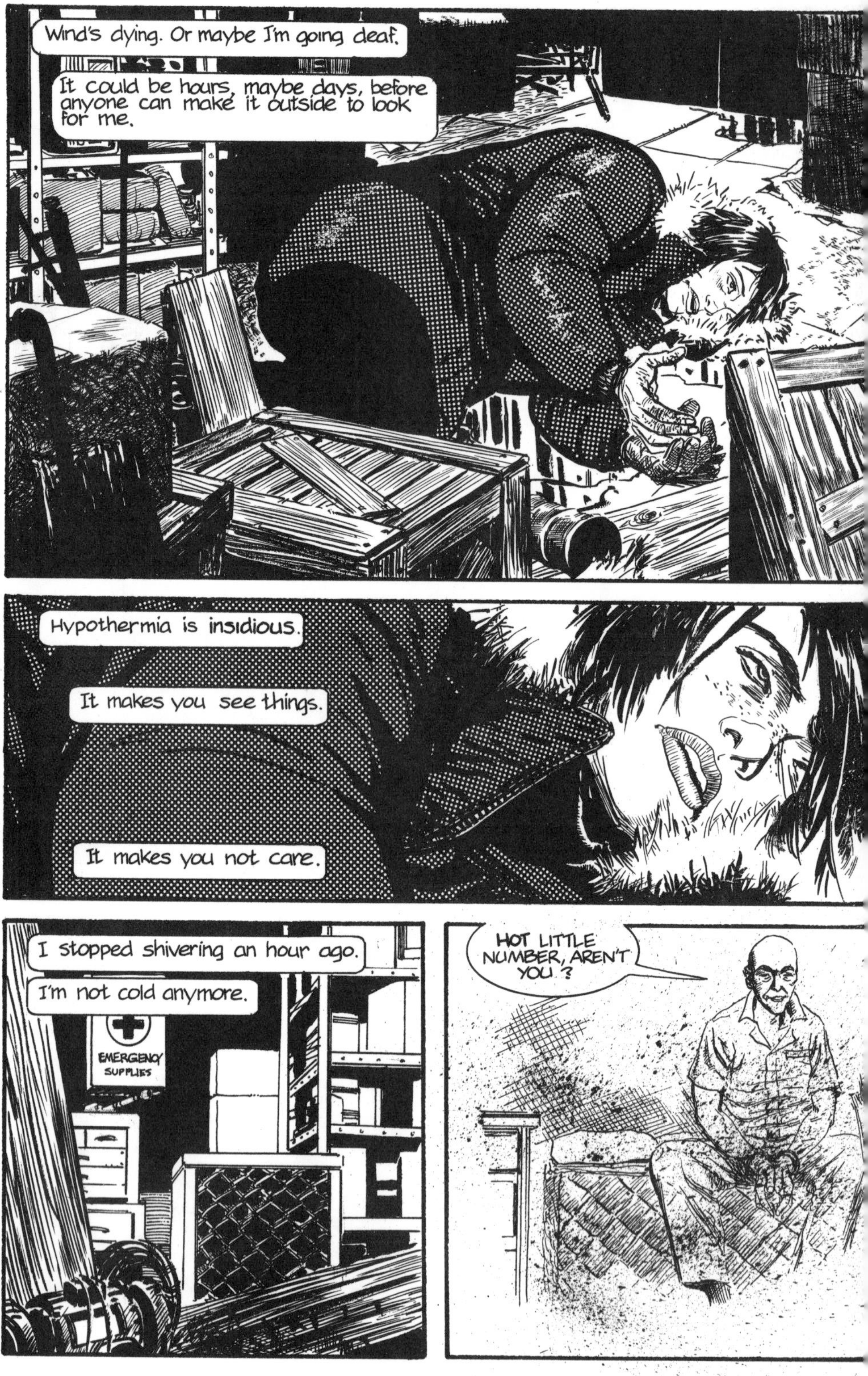
Wind's dying. Or maybe I'm going deaf.
It could be hours, maybe days, before anyone can make it outside to look for me.
Hypothermia is insidious.
It makes you see things.
It makes you not care.
I stopped shivering an hour ago.
I'm not cold anymore.
EMERGENCY SUPPLIES
HOT LITTLE NUMBER, AREN'T YOU ?

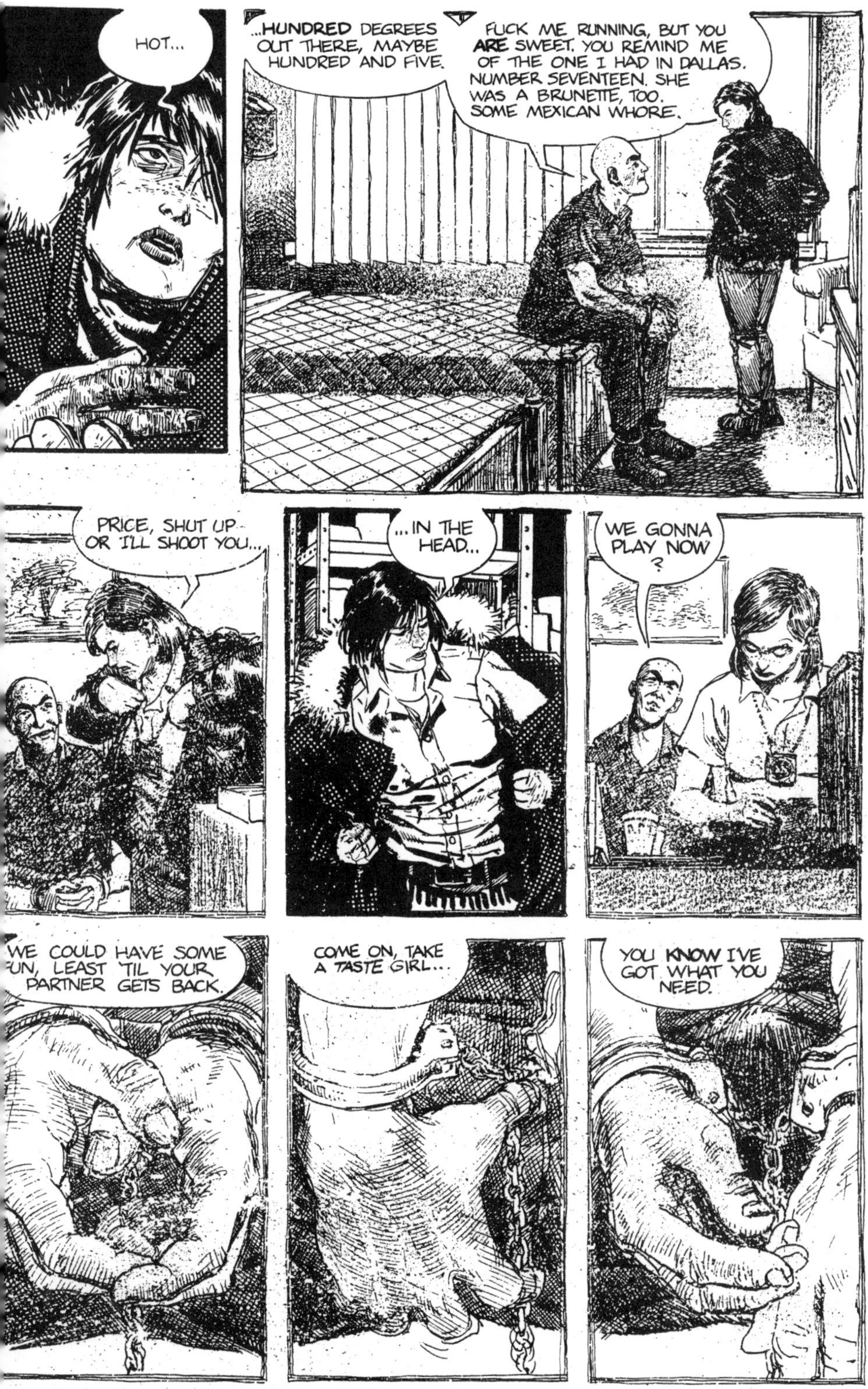
HOT...
...HUNDRED DEGREES OUT THERE, MAYBE HUNDRED AND FIVE.
FUCK ME RUNNING, BUT YOU ARE SWEET. YOU REMIND ME OF THE ONE I HAD IN DALLAS. NUMBER SEVENTEEN. SHE WAS A BRUNETTE, TOO. SOME MEXICAN WHORE.
PRICE, SHUT UP OR I'LL SHOOT YOU...
...IN THE HEAD...
WE GONNA PLAY NOW ?
WE COULD HAVE SOME FUN, LEAST 'TIL YOUR PARTNER GETS BACK.
COME ON, TAKE A TASTE GIRL...
YOU KNOW I'VE GOT WHAT YOU NEED.

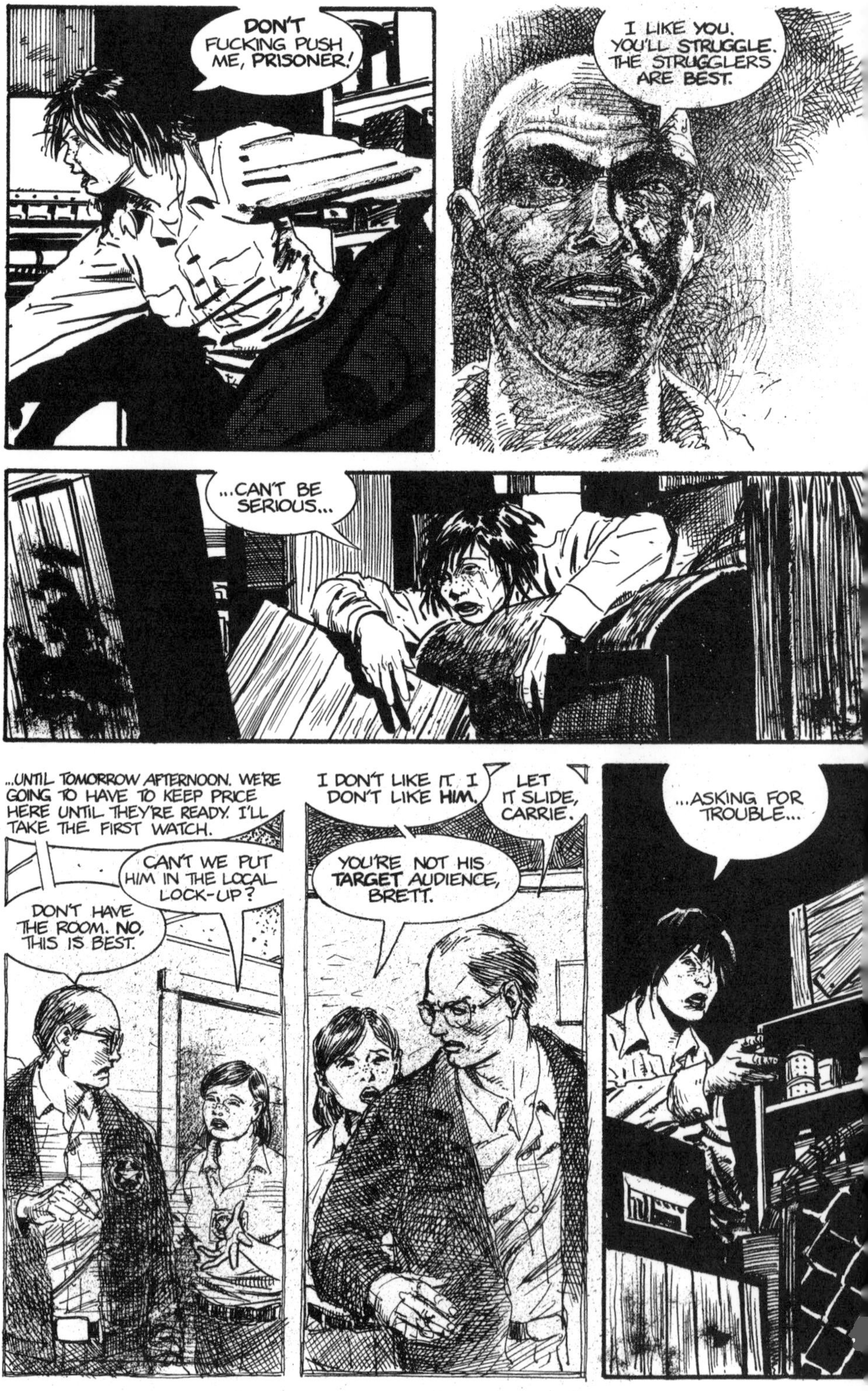
DON'T FUCKING PUSH ME, PRISONER!
I LIKE YOU. YOU'LL STRUGGLE. THE STRUGGLERS ARE BEST.
...CAN'T BE SERIOUS...
...UNTIL TOMORROW AFTERNOON. WE'RE GOING TO HAVE TO KEEP PRICE HERE UNTIL THEY'RE READY. I'LL TAKE THE FIRST WATCH.
CAN'T WE PUT HIM IN THE LOCAL LOCK-UP?
DON'T HAVE THE ROOM. NO, THIS IS BEST.
I DON'T LIKE IT. I DON'T LIKE HIM.
LET IT SLIDE, CARRIE.
YOU'RE NOT HIS TARGET AUDIENCE, BRETT.
...ASKING FOR TROUBLE...

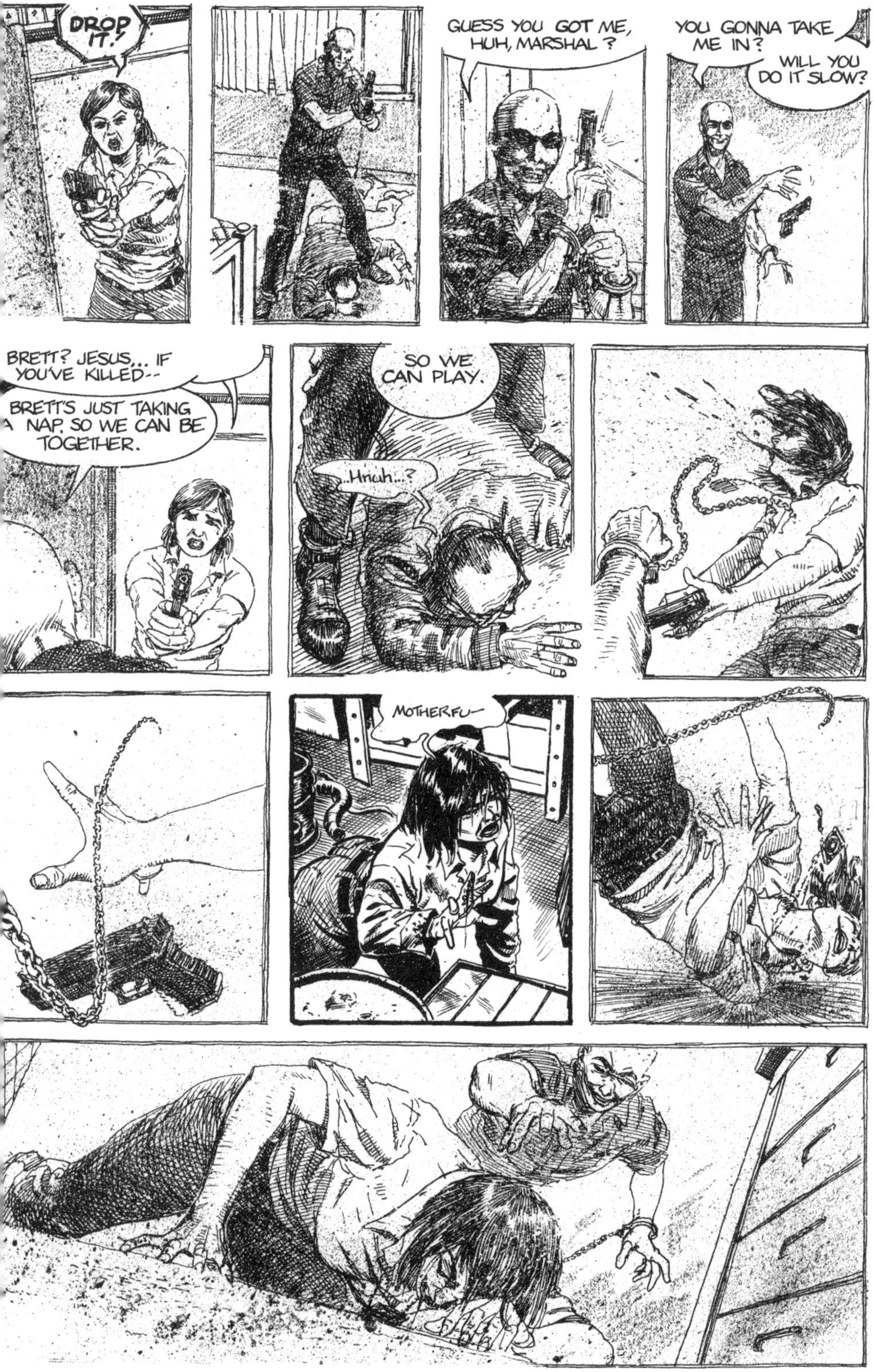
DROP IT.'
GUESS YOU GOT ME, HUH, MARSHAL ?
YOU GONNA TAKE ME IN ?
WILL YOU DO IT SLOW?
BRETT? JESUS,... IF YOU'VE KILLED--
BRETT'S JUST TAKING A NAP, SO WE CAN BE TOGETHER.
SO WE CAN PLAY.
...Hnuh...?
MOTHERFU—

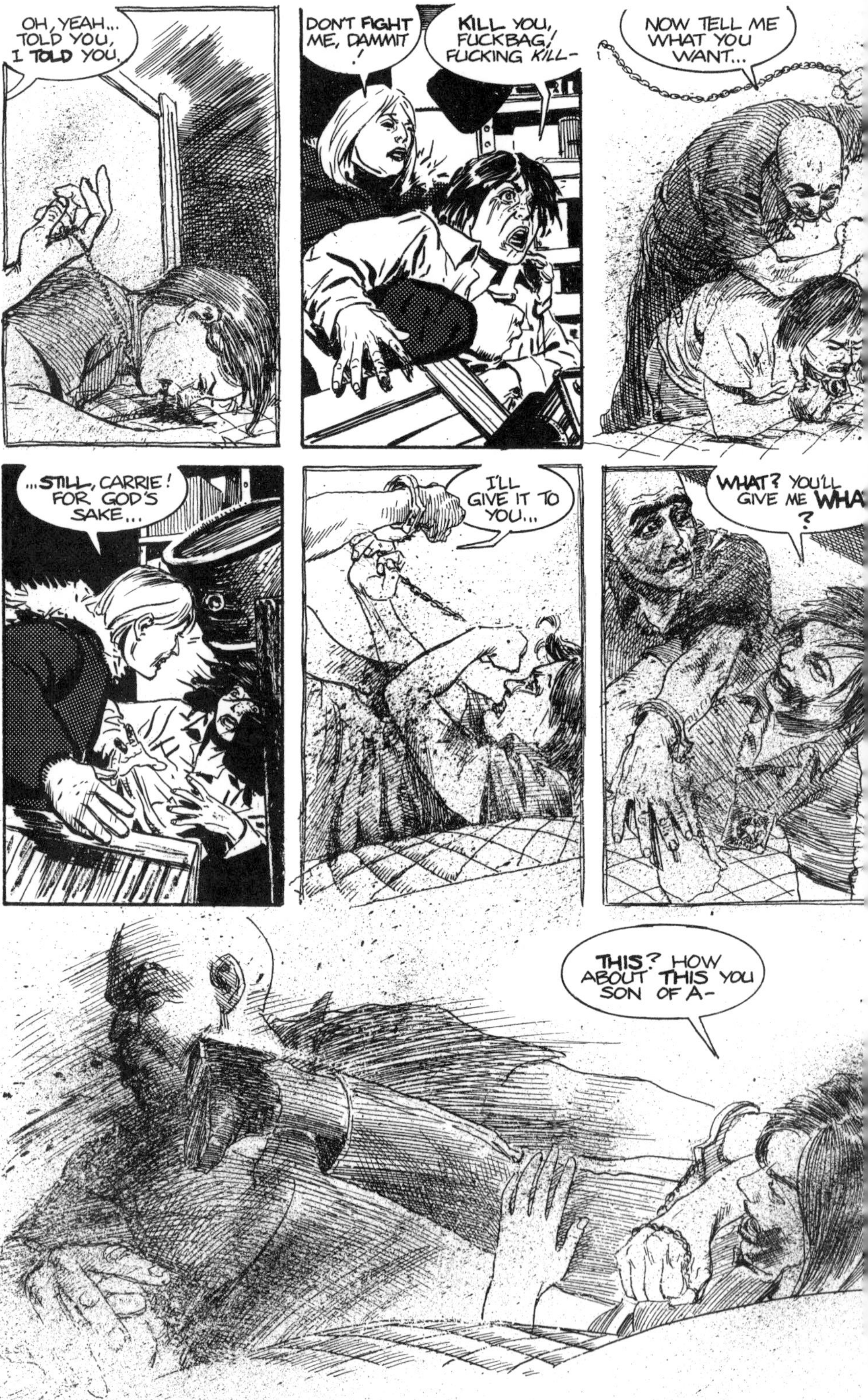

OH, YEAH... TOLD YOU, I TOLD YOU.
DON'T FIGHT ME, DAMMIT!
KILL YOU, FUCKBAG! FUCKING KILL-
NOW TELL ME WHAT YOU WANT...
...STILL, CARRIE! FOR GOD'S SAKE...
I'LL GIVE IT TO YOU...
WHAT? YOU'LL GIVE ME WHA ?
THIS? HOW ABOUT THIS YOU SON OF A-

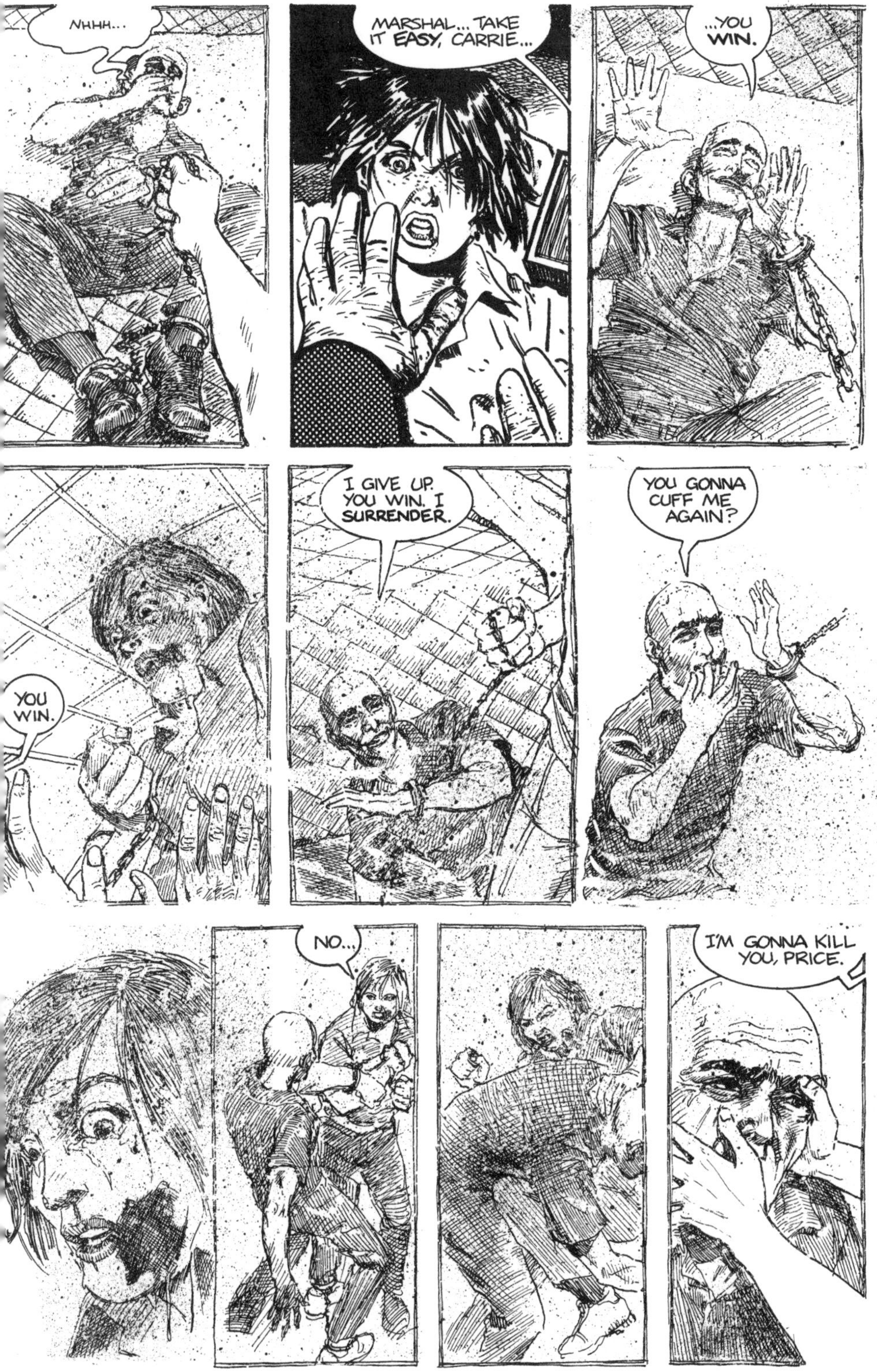
NHHH...
MARSHAL... TAKE IT EASY, CARRIE...
...YOU WIN.
YOU WIN.
I GIVE UP. YOU WIN. I SURRENDER.
YOU GONNA CUFF ME AGAIN?
NO...
I'M GONNA KILL YOU, PRICE.

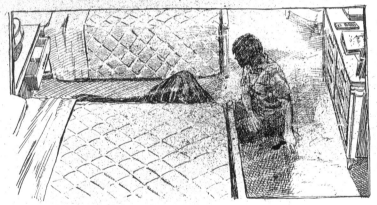

...WIND STARTED DYING. THEN I CHECKED THE SURROUNDING SHEDS. SHE LEFT A PORTION OF HER **HAND** ON ONE OF THE DOORS.

DAMN LUCKY. ANY LONGER AND HER CORE TEMPERATURE WOULD HAVE HIT THE POINT OF NO RETURN.

BUT SHE'LL MAKE IT?

SHE WILL. I CAN'T SPEAK FOR THE **FINGERS** ON HER HAND, THOUGH.

I'LL LET HER PEOPLE KNOW.

YOU'VE GOT TWO BODIES IN YOUR ACCOMMODATION BARRACKS.

GIFT FROM YOU?

ALAS, NO...

...THEY WERE THAT WAY WHEN WE ARRIVED. THE BASTARD WHO DID THEM IS **ALSO** THE MAN WHO CUT HER LINE.

OR SOMEBODY SHE BROUGHT WITH HER.

SOMEBODY HERE, YOU THINK?

YOU'RE SENDING STETKO BACK TO McMURDO?

ALL OF THEM. HRH'S GOVERNMENT DOESN'T HAVE THE **RESOURCES** TO OFFER COMFORT TO A FOREIGNER. WE **CAN'T** GIVE HER ANY MORE TREATMENT. THE AMERICANS CAN WATCH OUT FOR THEIR OWN.

I'M GOING WITH THEM.

TRY NOT TO LOOK **TOO** DELIGHTED, MARK.

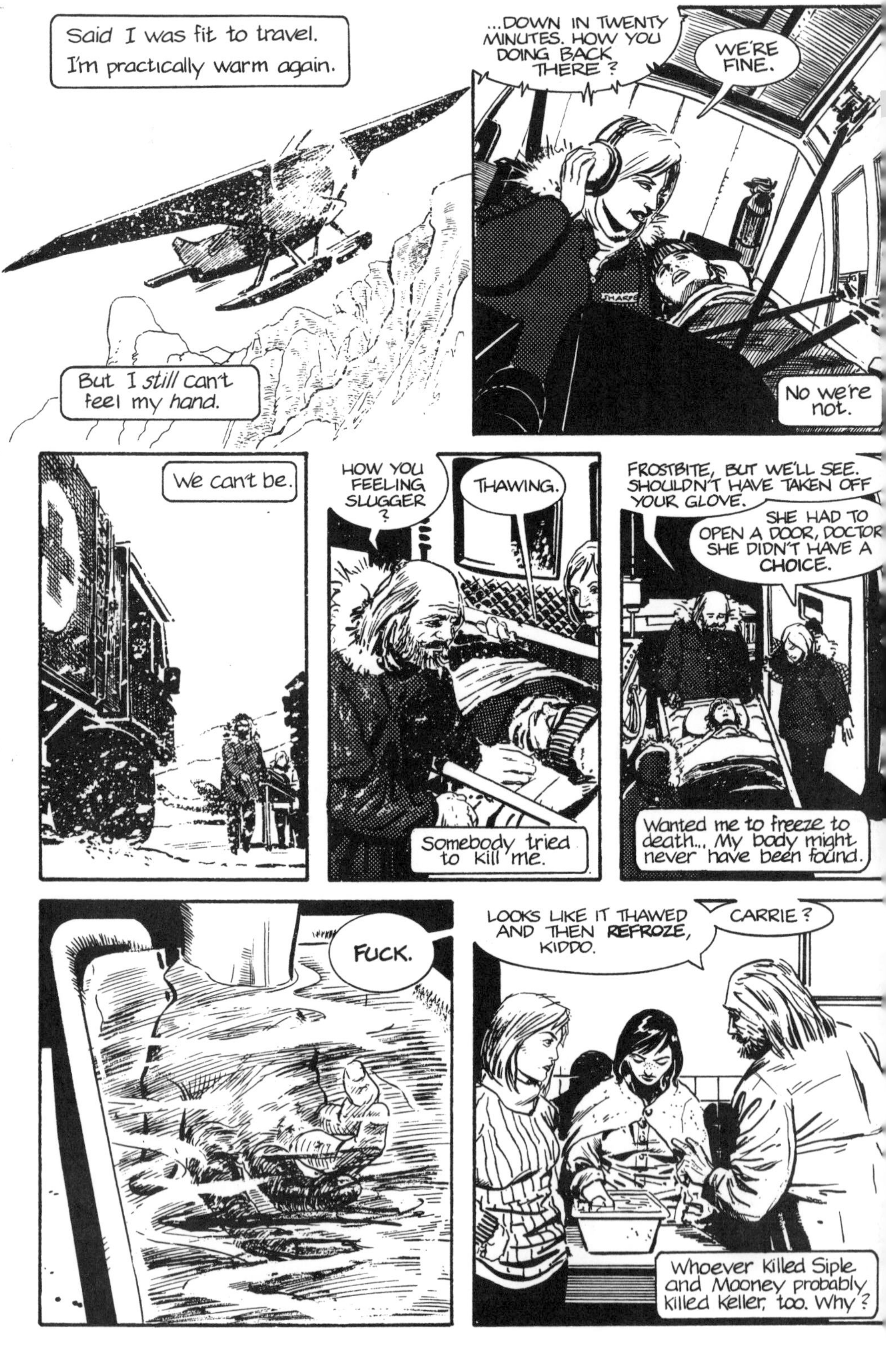
Said I was fit to travel. I'm practically warm again.
But I still can't feel my hand.
...DOWN IN TWENTY MINUTES. HOW YOU DOING BACK THERE ?
WE'RE FINE.
No we're not.
We can't be.
HOW YOU FEELING SLUGGER ?
THAWING.
Somebody tried to kill me.
FROSTBITE, BUT WE'LL SEE. SHOULDN'T HAVE TAKEN OFF YOUR GLOVE.
SHE HAD TO OPEN A DOOR, DOCTOR SHE DIDN'T HAVE A CHOICE.
Wanted me to freeze to death... My body might never have been found.
FUCK.
LOOKS LIKE IT THAWED AND THEN REFROZE, KIDDO.
CARRIE ?
Whoever killed Siple and Mooney probably killed Keller, too. Why ?

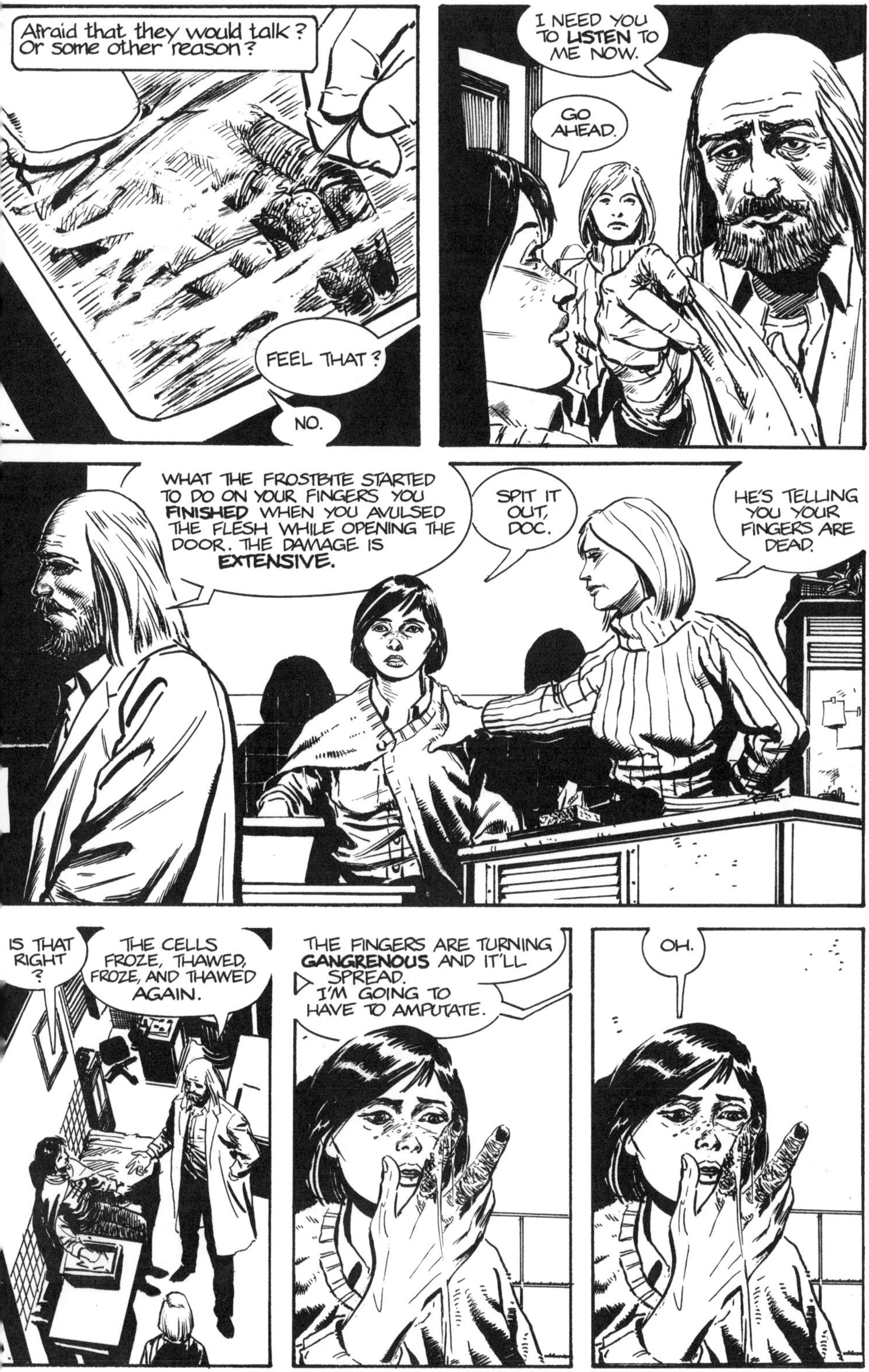
Afraid that they would talk? Or some other reason?
FEEL THAT?
NO.
I NEED YOU TO LISTEN TO ME NOW.
GO AHEAD.
WHAT THE FROSTBITE STARTED TO DO ON YOUR FINGERS YOU FINISHED WHEN YOU AVULSED THE FLESH WHILE OPENING THE DOOR. THE DAMAGE IS EXTENSIVE.
SPIT IT OUT, DOC.
HE'S TELLING YOU YOUR FINGERS ARE DEAD.
IS THAT RIGHT?
THE CELLS FROZE, THAWED, FROZE, AND THAWED AGAIN.
THE FINGERS ARE TURNING GANGRENOUS AND IT'LL SPREAD.
I'M GOING TO HAVE TO AMPUTATE.
OH.

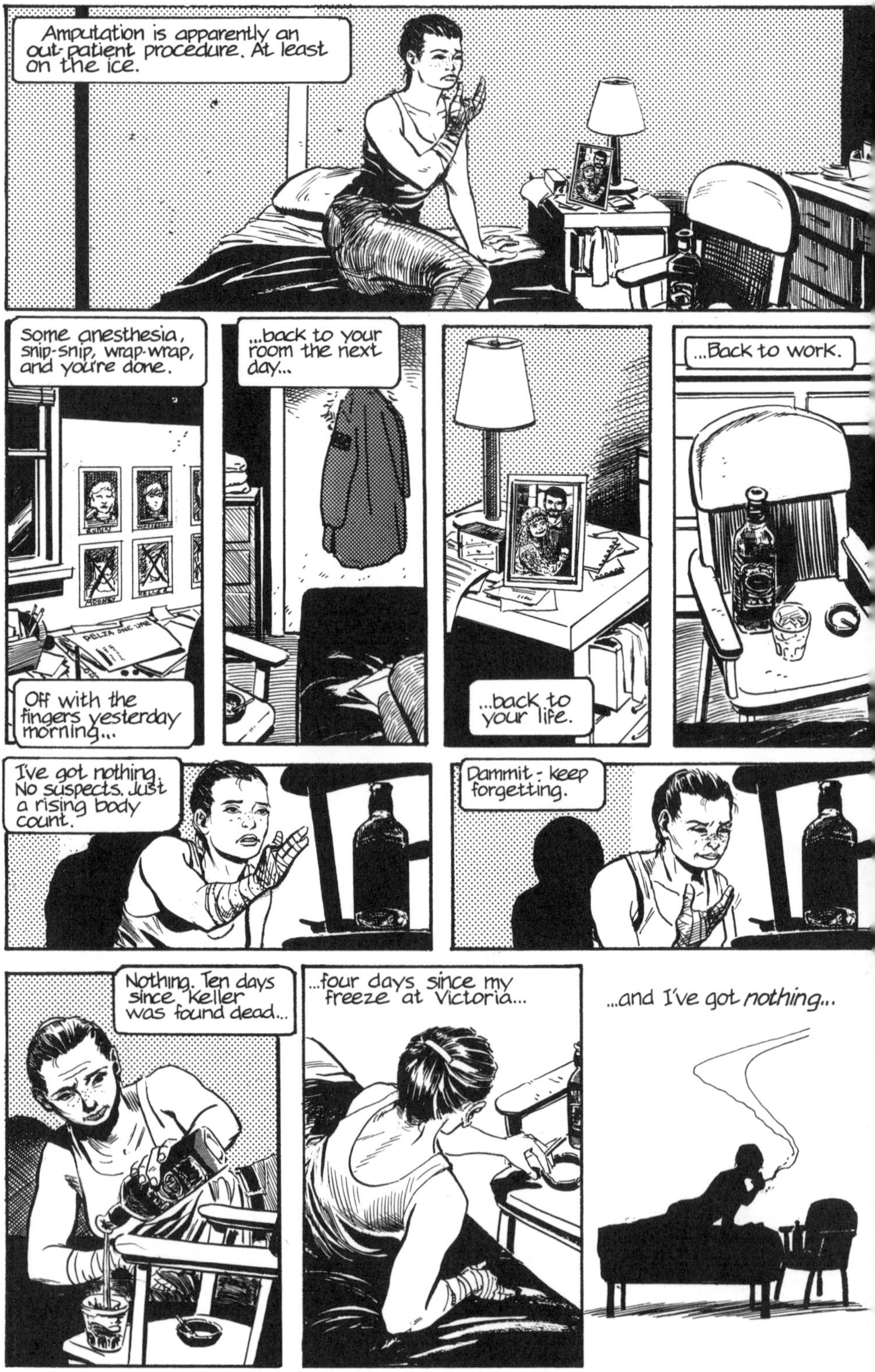
Amputation is apparently an out-patient procedure. At least on the ice.
Some anesthesia, snip-snip, wrap-wrap, and you're done.
Off with the fingers yesterday morning...
...back to your room the next day...
...back to your life.
...Back to work.
I've got nothing. No suspects. Just a rising body count.
Dammit - keep forgetting.
Nothing. Ten days since Keller was found dead...
...four days since my freeze at Victoria...
...and I've got *nothing*...

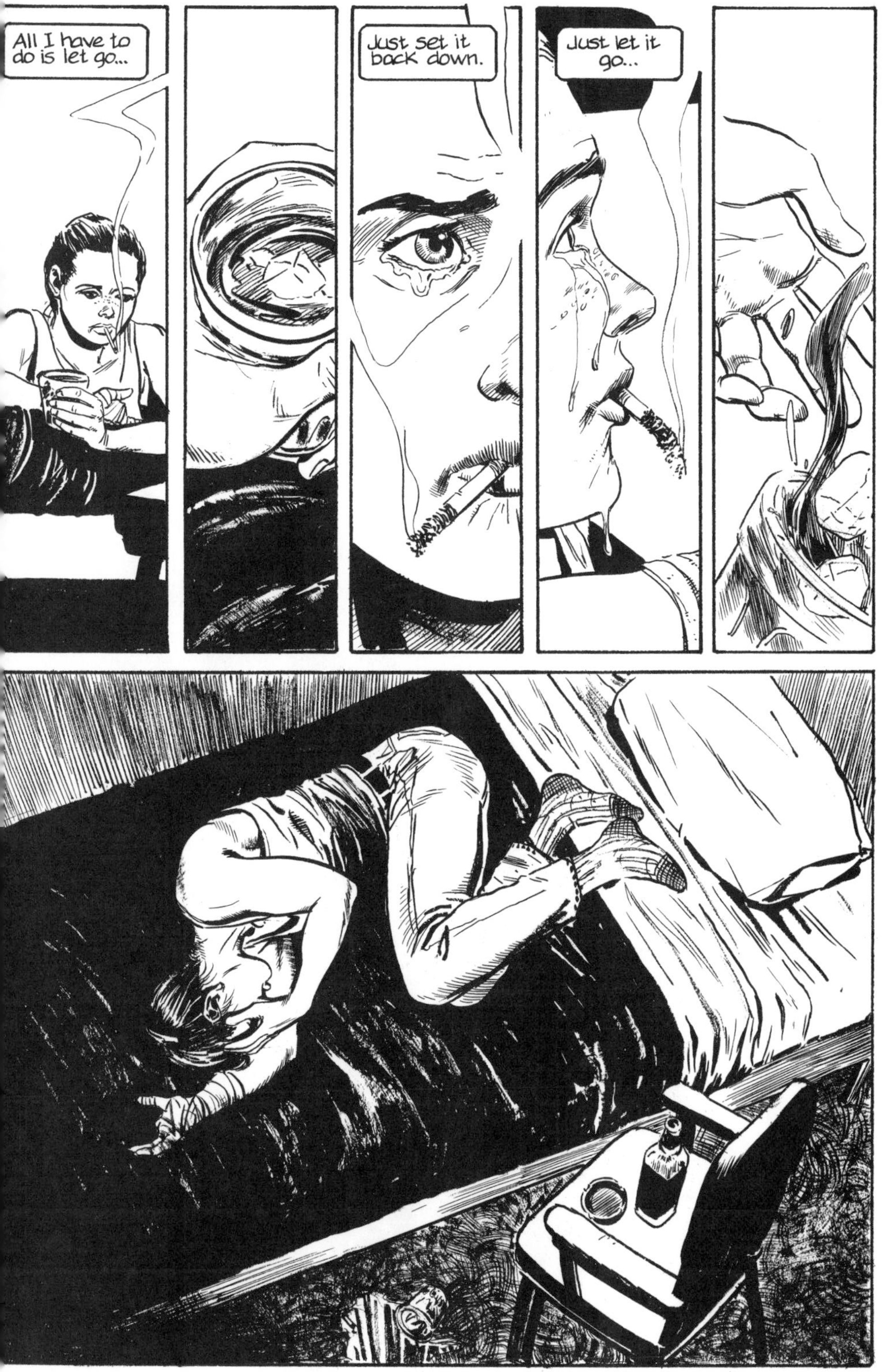
All I have to do is let go...
Just set it back down.
Just let it go...

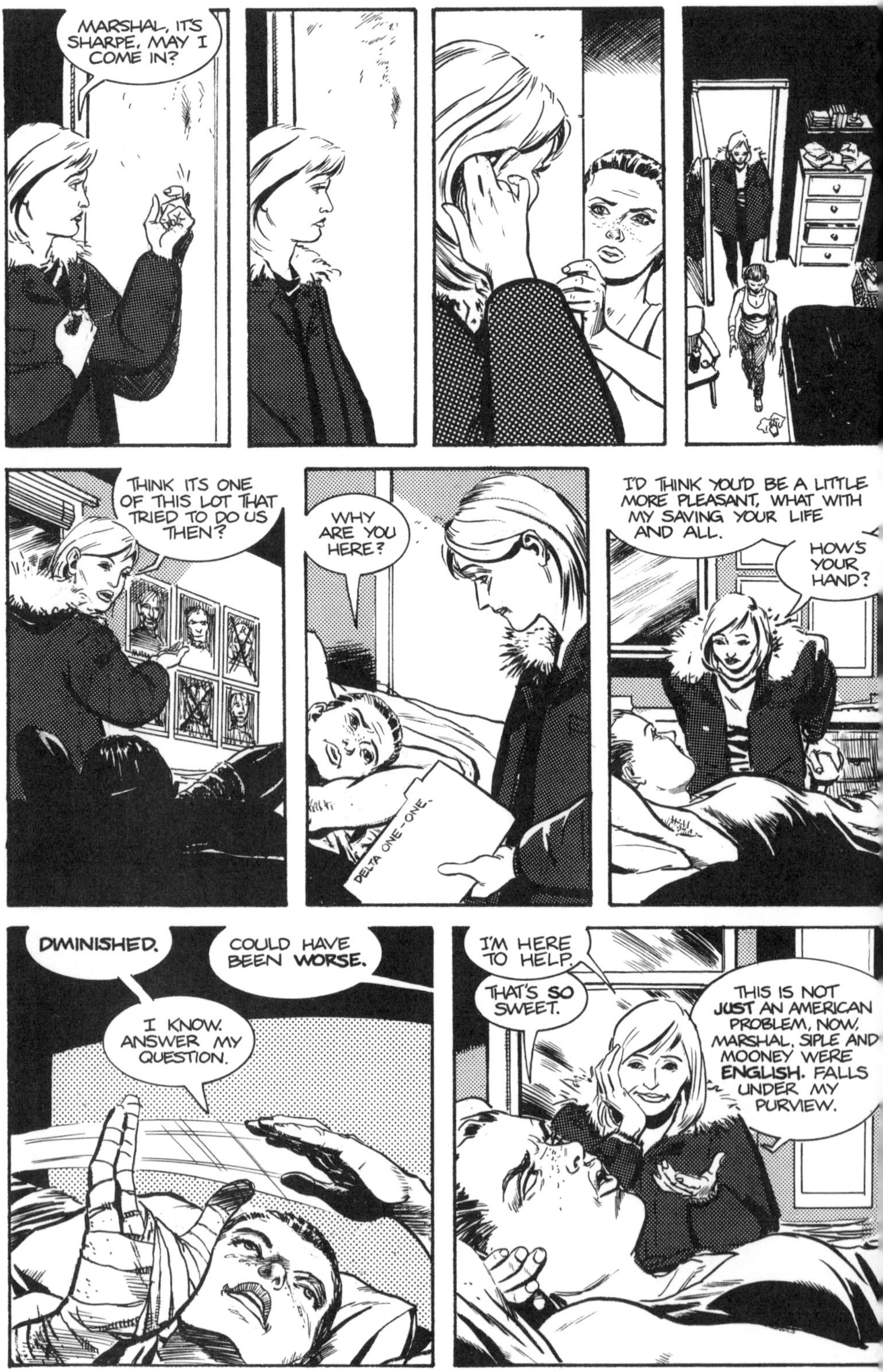
MARSHAL, IT'S SHARPE. MAY I COME IN?
THINK ITS ONE OF THIS LOT THAT TRIED TO DO US THEN?
WHY ARE YOU HERE?
DELTA ONE-ONE
I'D THINK YOU'D BE A LITTLE MORE PLEASANT, WHAT WITH MY SAVING YOUR LIFE AND ALL.
HOW'S YOUR HAND?
DIMINISHED.
COULD HAVE BEEN WORSE.
I KNOW. ANSWER MY QUESTION.
I'M HERE TO HELP.
THAT'S SO SWEET.
THIS IS NOT JUST AN AMERICAN PROBLEM, NOW, MARSHAL. SIPLE AND MOONEY WERE ENGLISH. FALLS UNDER MY PURVIEW.

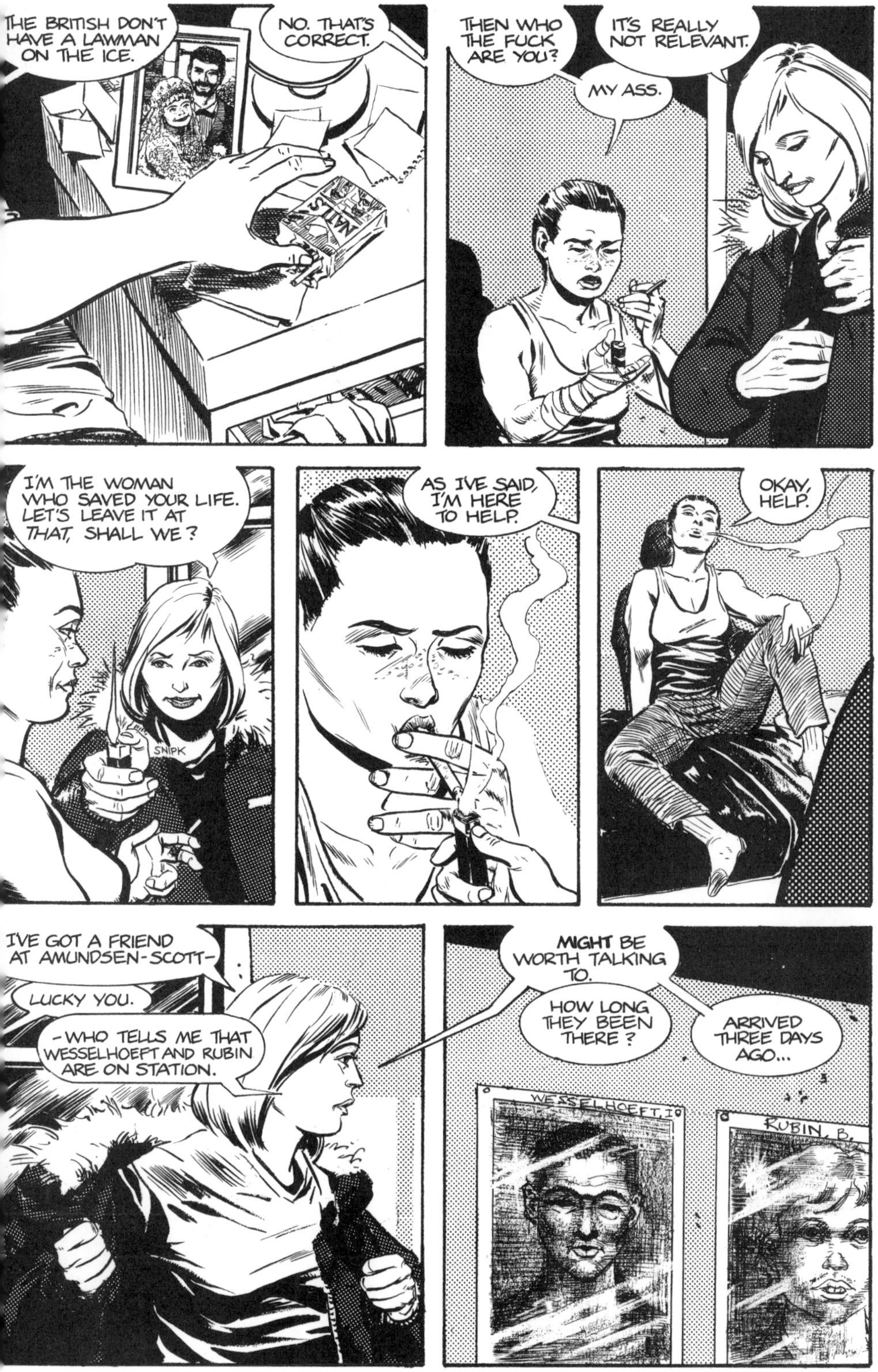

THE BRITISH DON'T HAVE A LAWMAN ON THE ICE.
NO. THAT'S CORRECT.
THEN WHO THE FUCK ARE YOU?
IT'S REALLY NOT RELEVANT.
MY ASS.
I'M THE WOMAN WHO SAVED YOUR LIFE. LET'S LEAVE IT AT *THAT*, SHALL WE?
SNIPK
AS I'VE SAID, I'M HERE TO HELP.
OKAY, HELP.
I'VE GOT A FRIEND AT AMUNDSEN-SCOTT-
LUCKY YOU.
-WHO TELLS ME THAT WESSELHOEFT AND RUBIN ARE ON STATION.
MIGHT BE WORTH TALKING TO.
HOW LONG THEY BEEN THERE?
ARRIVED THREE DAYS AGO...
WESSELHOEFT, I.
RUBIN, B.

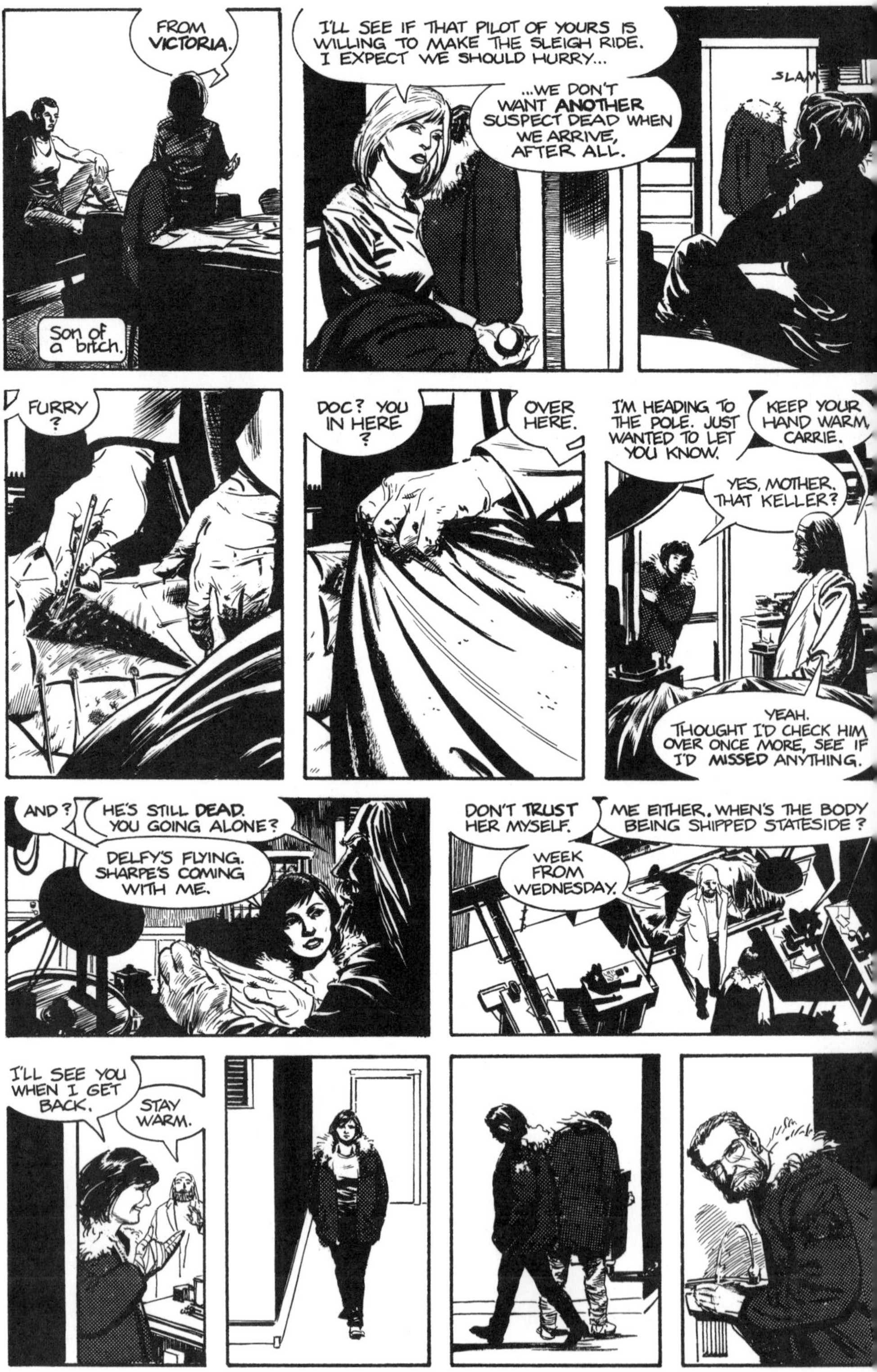

FROM VICTORIA.
Son of a bitch.
I'LL SEE IF THAT PILOT OF YOURS IS WILLING TO MAKE THE SLEIGH RIDE. I EXPECT WE SHOULD HURRY...
...WE DON'T WANT ANOTHER SUSPECT DEAD WHEN WE ARRIVE, AFTER ALL.
SLAM
FURRY?
DOC? YOU IN HERE?
OVER HERE.
I'M HEADING TO THE POLE. JUST WANTED TO LET YOU KNOW.
KEEP YOUR HAND WARM, CARRIE.
YES, MOTHER. THAT KELLER?
YEAH. THOUGHT I'D CHECK HIM OVER ONCE MORE, SEE IF I'D MISSED ANYTHING.
AND?
HE'S STILL DEAD. YOU GOING ALONE?
DELFY'S FLYING. SHARPE'S COMING WITH ME.
DON'T TRUST HER MYSELF.
ME EITHER. WHEN'S THE BODY BEING SHIPPED STATESIDE?
WEEK FROM WEDNESDAY.
I'LL SEE YOU WHEN I GET BACK.
STAY WARM.

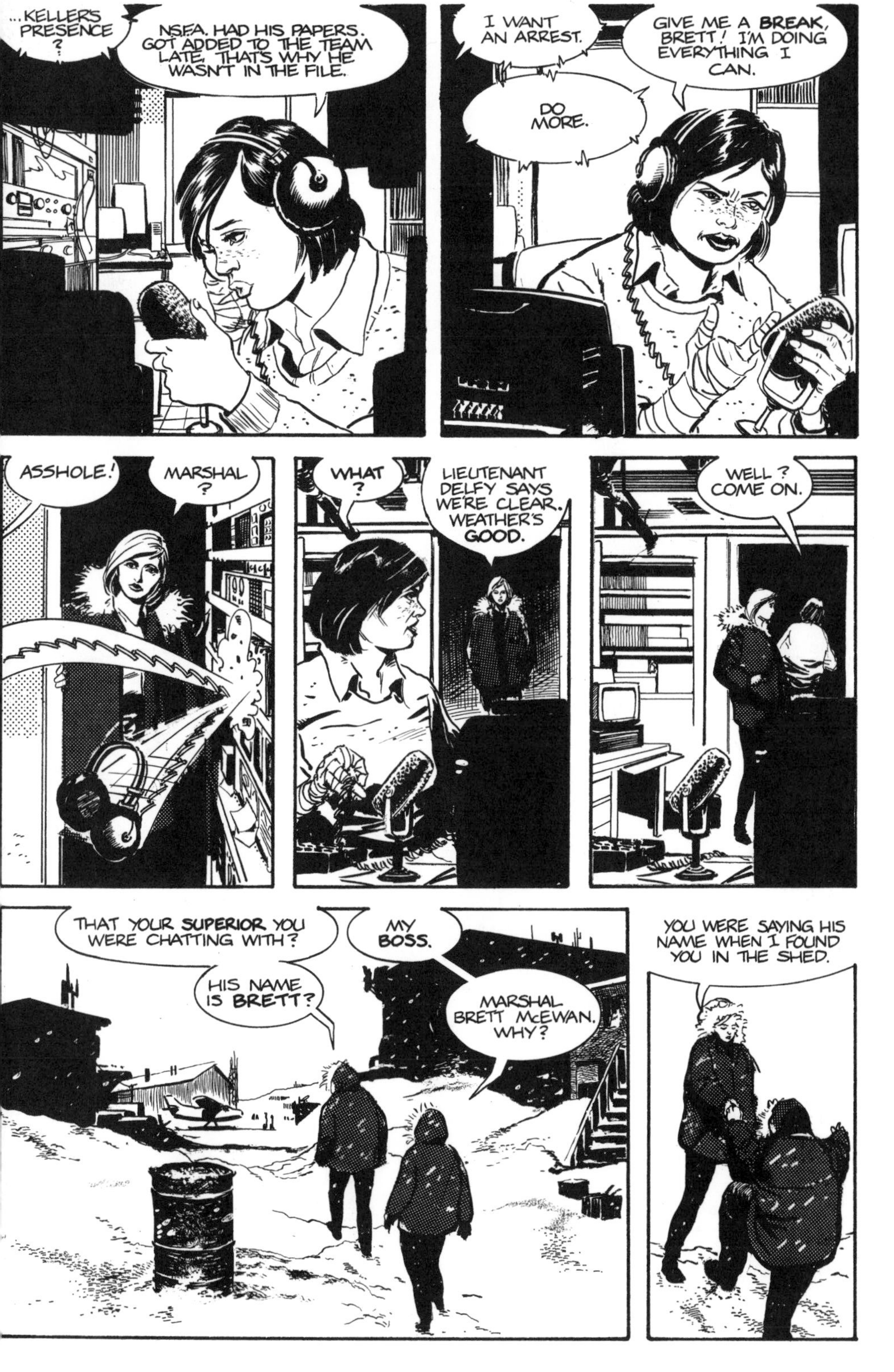

...KELLER'S PRESENCE ?
N.S.F.A. HAD HIS PAPERS. GOT ADDED TO THE TEAM LATE. THAT'S WHY HE WASN'T IN THE FILE.
I WANT AN ARREST.
GIVE ME A BREAK, BRETT! I'M DOING EVERYTHING I CAN.
DO MORE.
ASSHOLE!
MARSHAL ?
WHAT ?
LIEUTENANT DELFY SAYS WE'RE CLEAR. WEATHER'S GOOD.
WELL ? COME ON.
THAT YOUR SUPERIOR YOU WERE CHATTING WITH?
MY BOSS.
HIS NAME IS BRETT?
MARSHAL BRETT McEWAN. WHY?
YOU WERE SAYING HIS NAME WHEN I FOUND YOU IN THE SHED.

YOU ALSO MENTIONED A MAN NAMED PRICE. I THOUGHT YOU WERE HALLUCINATING.

DIDN'T THINK ANYTHING OF IT AT THE TIME.

WELL, THERE ARE RUMORS. I'M SURE YOU'VE HEARD THEM. THAT YOU'RE IN EXILE, DOWN HERE BECAUSE THE U.S. MARSHAL'S SERVICE DIDN'T KNOW WHAT TO DO WITH YOU.

AND NOW?

I DON'T CARE. WHETHER OR NOT YOU'RE QUEER DOESN'T MATTER TO ME IN THE LEAST, FOR EXAMPLE. BUT IF THERE'S A CHANCE YOU'LL KILL THE SUSPECTS RATHER THAN ARREST THEM... THAT CONCERNS ME.

CONCERNS ME, TOO.

More than you know.

60

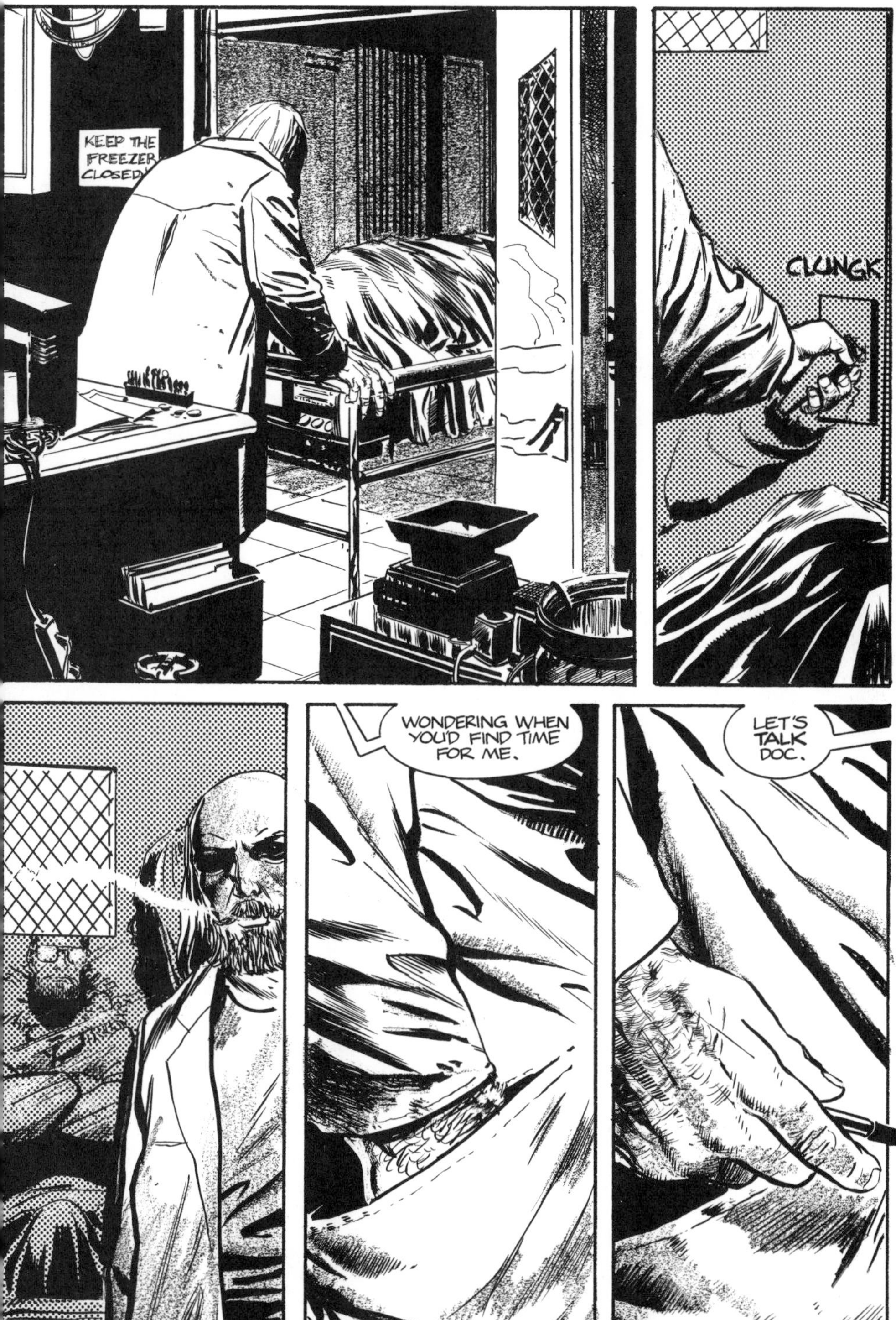
KEEP THE FREEZER CLOSED!
CLUNGK
WONDERING WHEN YOU'D FIND TIME FOR ME.
LET'S TALK DOC.

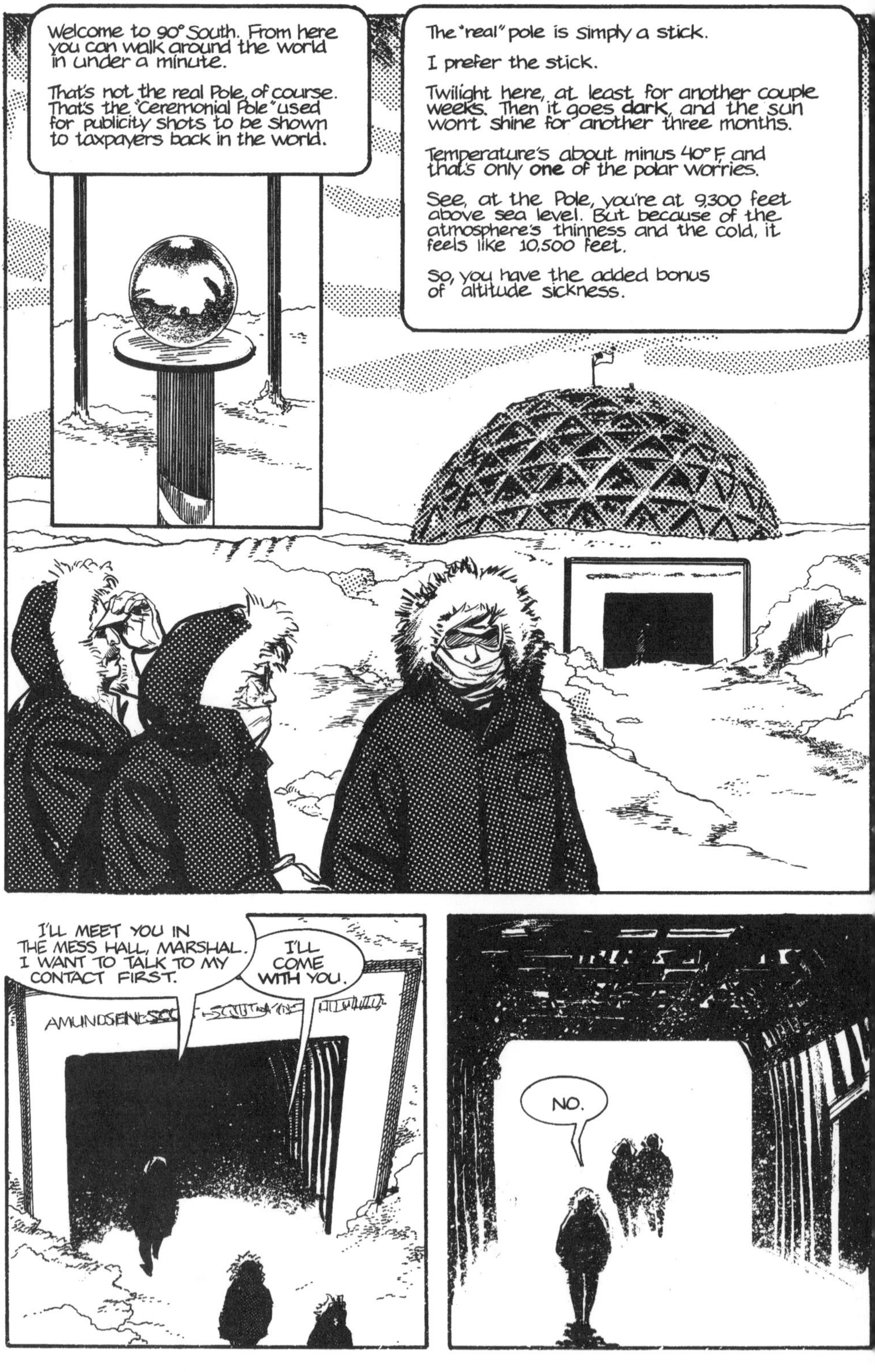
Welcome to 90° South. From here you can walk around the world in under a minute.
That's not the real Pole, of course. That's the "Ceremonial Pole" used for publicity shots to be shown to taxpayers back in the world.
The "real" pole is simply a stick.
I prefer the stick.
Twilight here, at least for another couple weeks. Then it goes **dark**, and the sun won't shine for another three months.
Temperature's about minus 40° F, and that's only **one** of the polar worries.
See, at the Pole, you're at 9,300 feet above sea level. But because of the atmosphere's thinness and the cold, it feels like 10,500 feet.
So, you have the added bonus of altitude sickness.
I'LL MEET YOU IN THE MESS HALL, MARSHAL. I WANT TO TALK TO MY CONTACT FIRST.
I'LL COME WITH YOU.
NO.

SO, WHO IS SHE?

SHE'S A SPOOK.

NOT A SCIENTIST?

NOPE. MAYBE MILITARY INTELLIGENCE.

REMINDS ME OF YOU, KIND OF.

YOU'RE BOTH BITCHY.

YOU CAN'T TELL, BUT I'M GIVING YOU THE FINGER.

GETTING A REFILL. WANT ONE?

SURE.

ALEXANDER KELLER
AGE 28 UNIVERSITY of CHICAGO
Dept. of Geology & Geophysics 1966

63

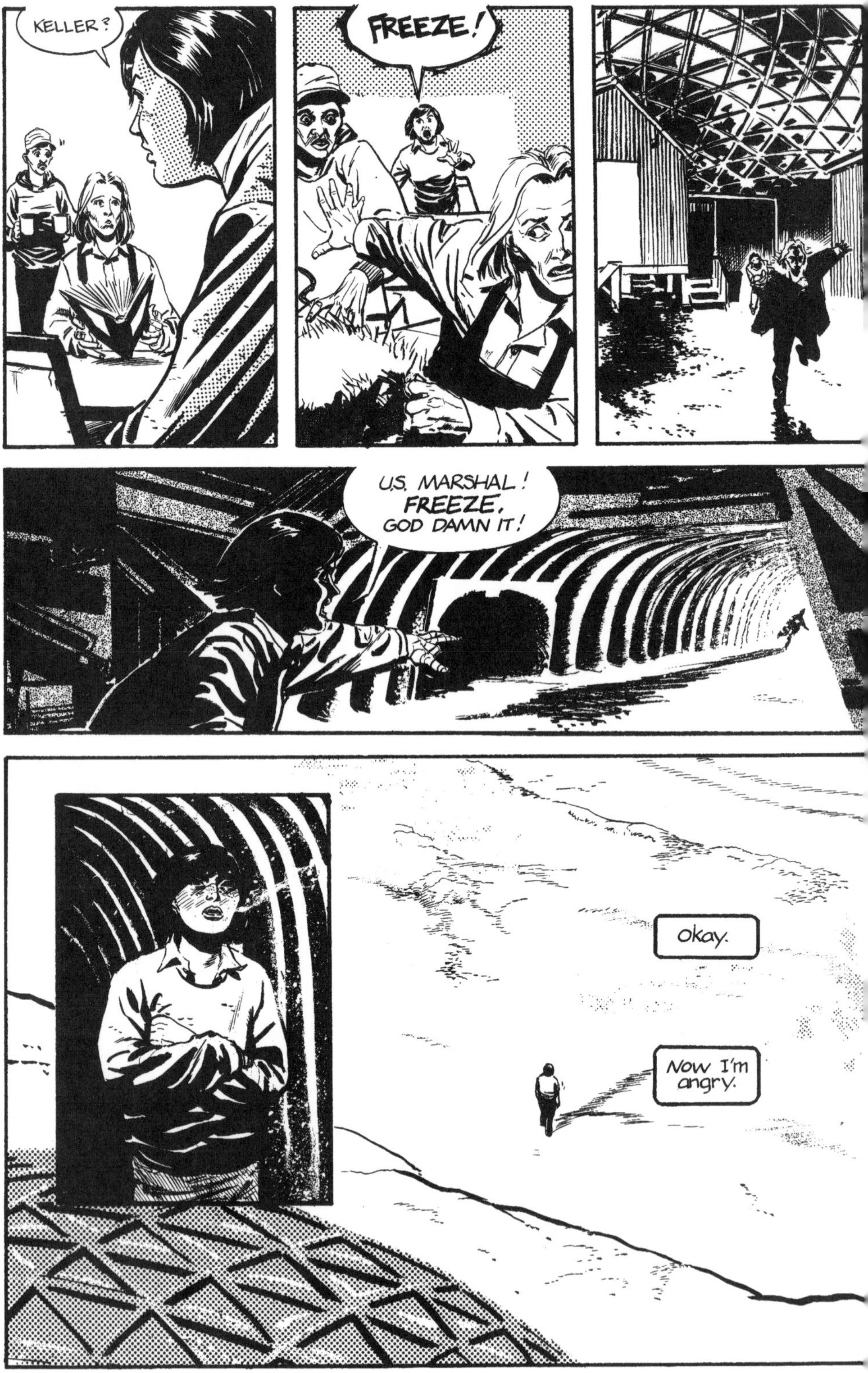
KELLER?
FREEZE!
U.S. MARSHAL! FREEZE, GOD DAMN IT!
Okay.
Now I'm angry.

CHAPTER THREE

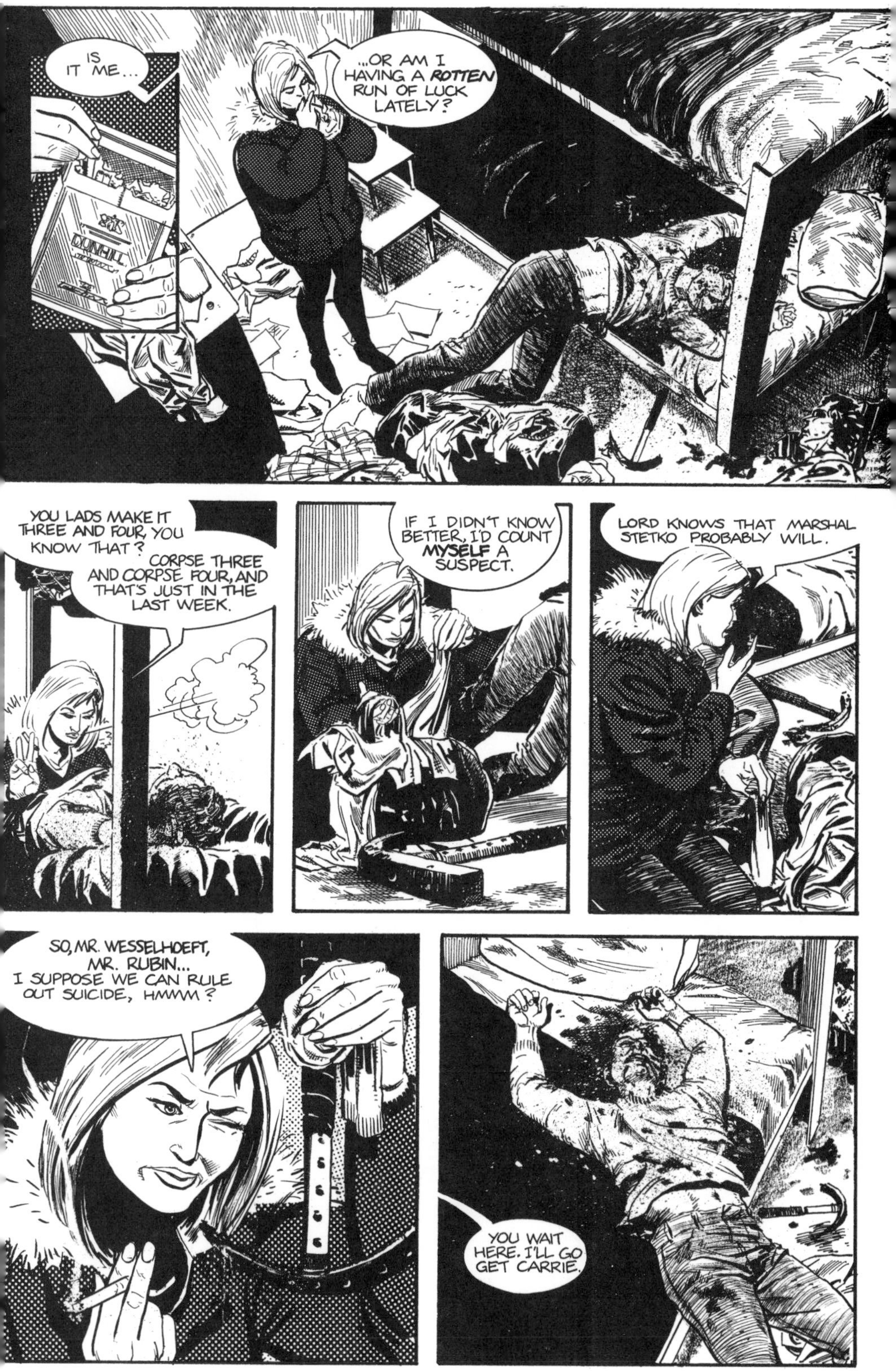
IS IT ME...
...OR AM I HAVING A *ROTTEN* RUN OF LUCK LATELY?
YOU LADS MAKE IT THREE AND FOUR, YOU KNOW THAT?
CORPSE THREE AND CORPSE FOUR, AND THAT'S JUST IN THE LAST WEEK.
IF I DIDN'T KNOW BETTER, I'D COUNT **MYSELF** A SUSPECT.
LORD KNOWS THAT MARSHAL STETKO PROBABLY WILL.
SO, MR. WESSELHOEFT, MR. RUBIN... I SUPPOSE WE CAN RULE OUT SUICIDE, HMMM?
YOU WAIT HERE. I'LL GO GET CARRIE.

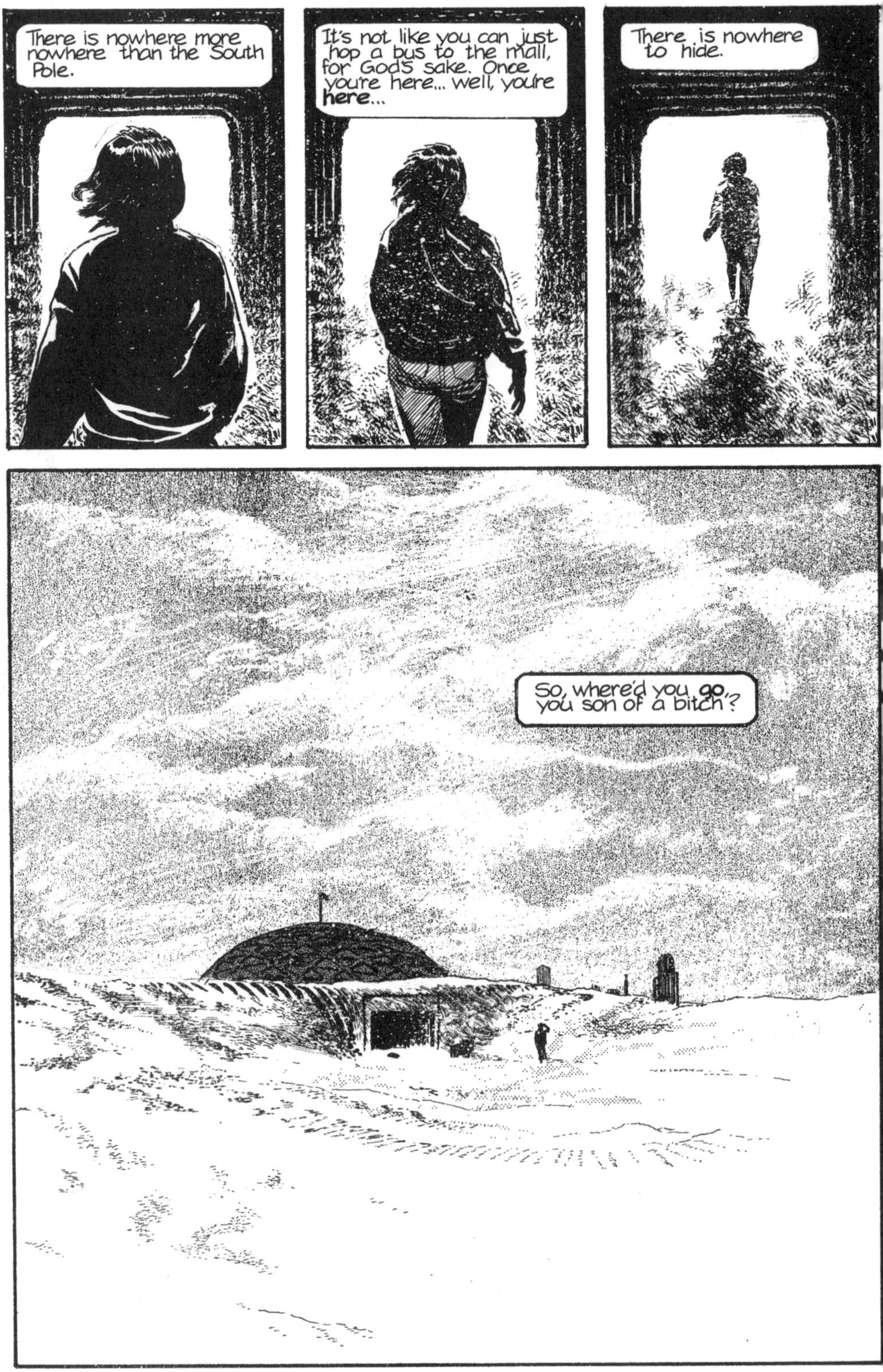

There is nowhere more nowhere than the South Pole.
It's not like you can just hop a bus to the mall, for God's sake. Once you're here... well, you're **here**...
There is nowhere to hide.
So, where'd you **go**, you son of a bitch?

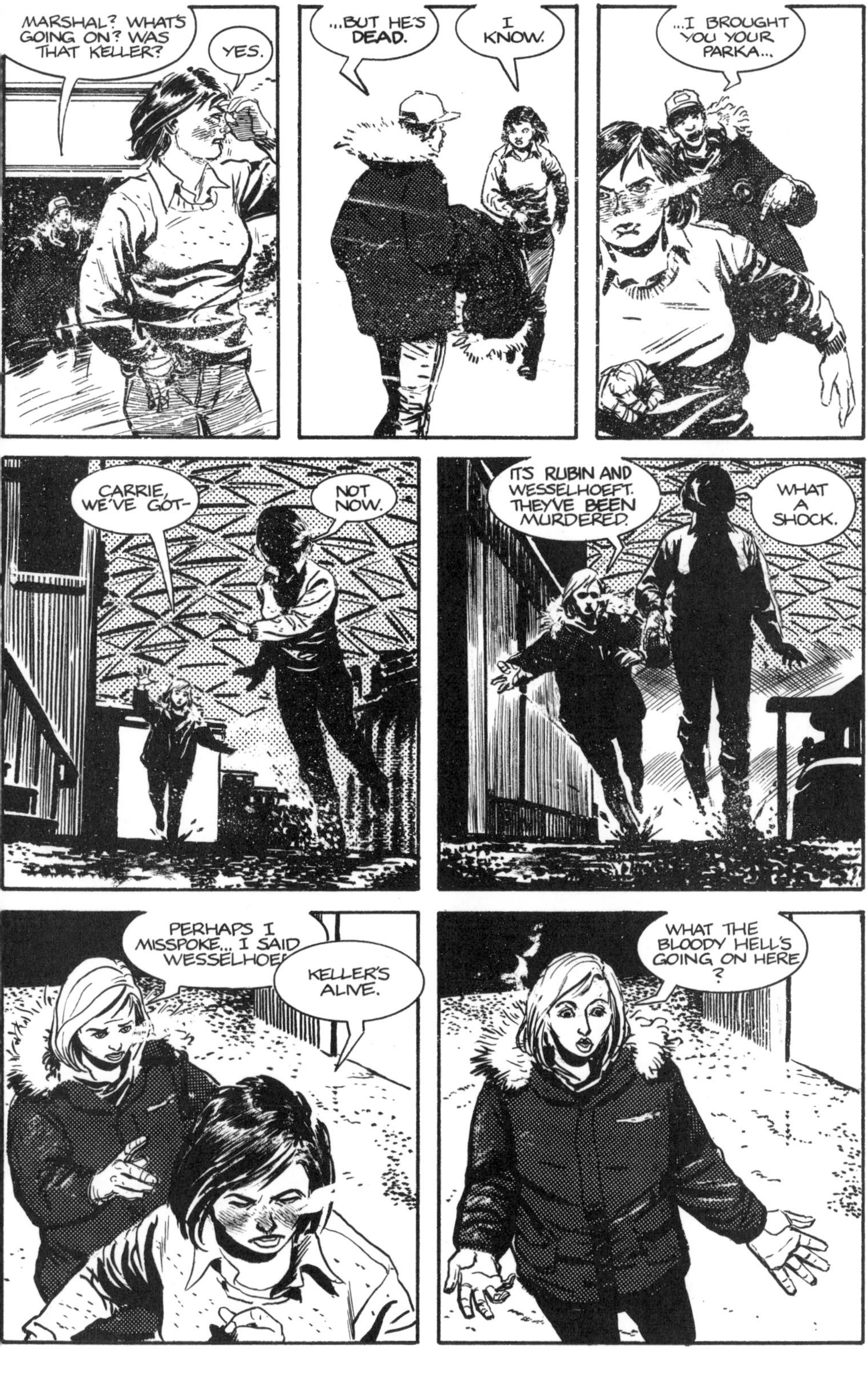
MARSHAL? WHAT'S GOING ON? WAS THAT KELLER?
YES.
...BUT HE'S DEAD.
I KNOW.
...I BROUGHT YOU YOUR PARKA...
CARRIE, WE'VE GOT-
NOT NOW.
IT'S RUBIN AND WESSELHOEFT. THEY'VE BEEN MURDERED.
WHAT A SHOCK.
PERHAPS I MISSPOKE... I SAID WESSELHOE
KELLER'S ALIVE.
WHAT THE BLOODY HELL'S GOING ON HERE ?

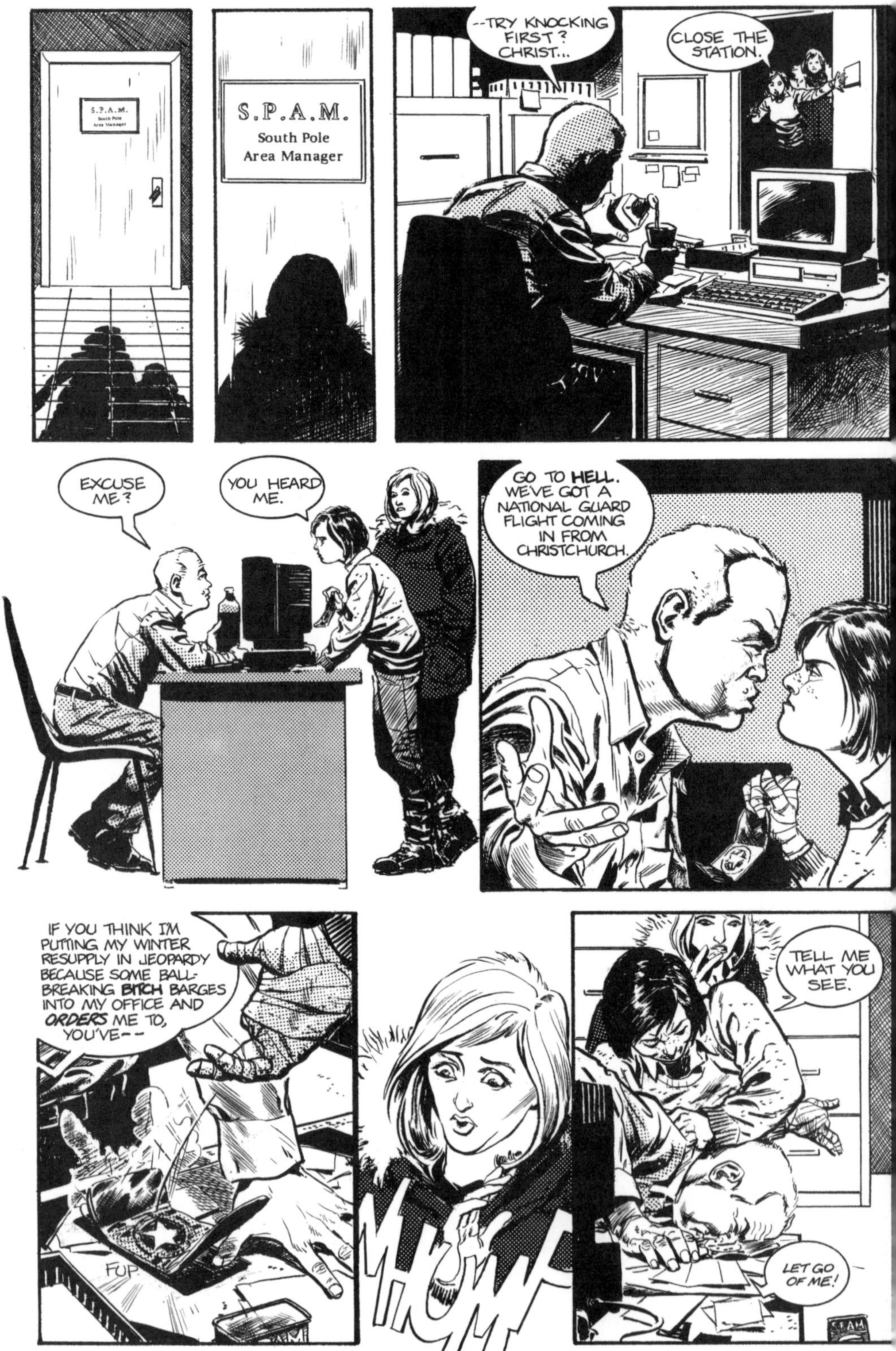
S.P.A.M.
South Pole
Area Manager
S.P.A.M.
South Pole
Area Manager
--TRY KNOCKING FIRST? CHRIST...
CLOSE THE STATION.
EXCUSE ME?
YOU HEARD ME.
GO TO **HELL**. WE'VE GOT A NATIONAL GUARD FLIGHT COMING IN FROM CHRISTCHURCH.
IF YOU THINK I'M PUTTING MY WINTER RESUPPLY IN JEOPARDY BECAUSE SOME BALL-BREAKING **BITCH** BARGES INTO MY OFFICE AND ***ORDERS*** ME TO, YOU'VE--
FUP
WHUMP
TELL ME WHAT YOU SEE.
LET GO OF ME!

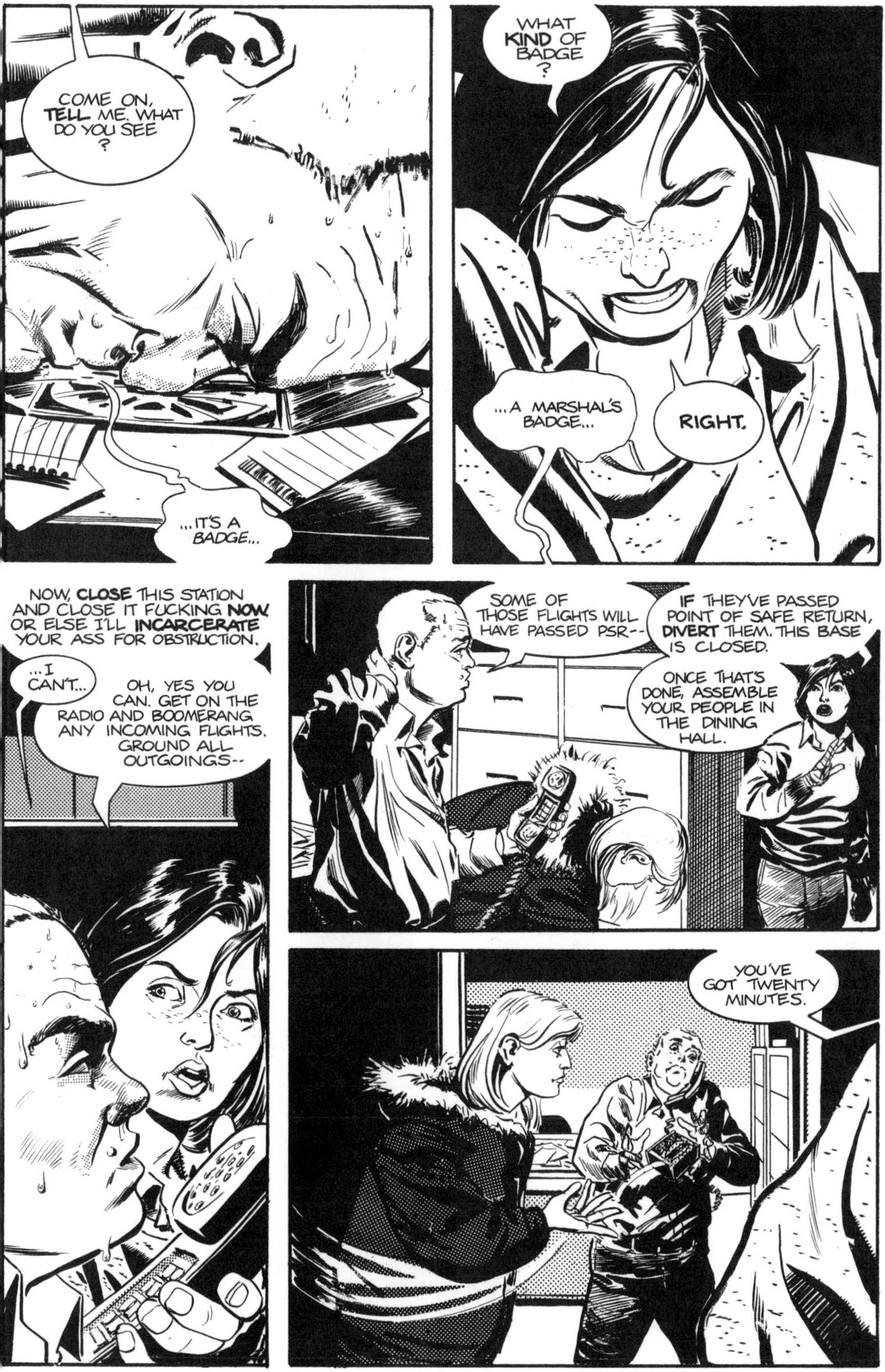
COME ON, TELL ME. WHAT DO YOU SEE ?
...IT'S A BADGE...
WHAT KIND OF BADGE ?
...A MARSHAL'S BADGE...
RIGHT.
NOW, CLOSE THIS STATION AND CLOSE IT FUCKING NOW. OR ELSE I'LL INCARCERATE YOUR ASS FOR OBSTRUCTION.
...I CAN'T...
OH, YES YOU CAN. GET ON THE RADIO AND BOOMERANG ANY INCOMING FLIGHTS. GROUND ALL OUTGOINGS--
SOME OF THOSE FLIGHTS WILL HAVE PASSED PSR--
IF THEY'VE PASSED POINT OF SAFE RETURN, DIVERT THEM. THIS BASE IS CLOSED.
ONCE THAT'S DONE, ASSEMBLE YOUR PEOPLE IN THE DINING HALL.
YOU'VE GOT TWENTY MINUTES.

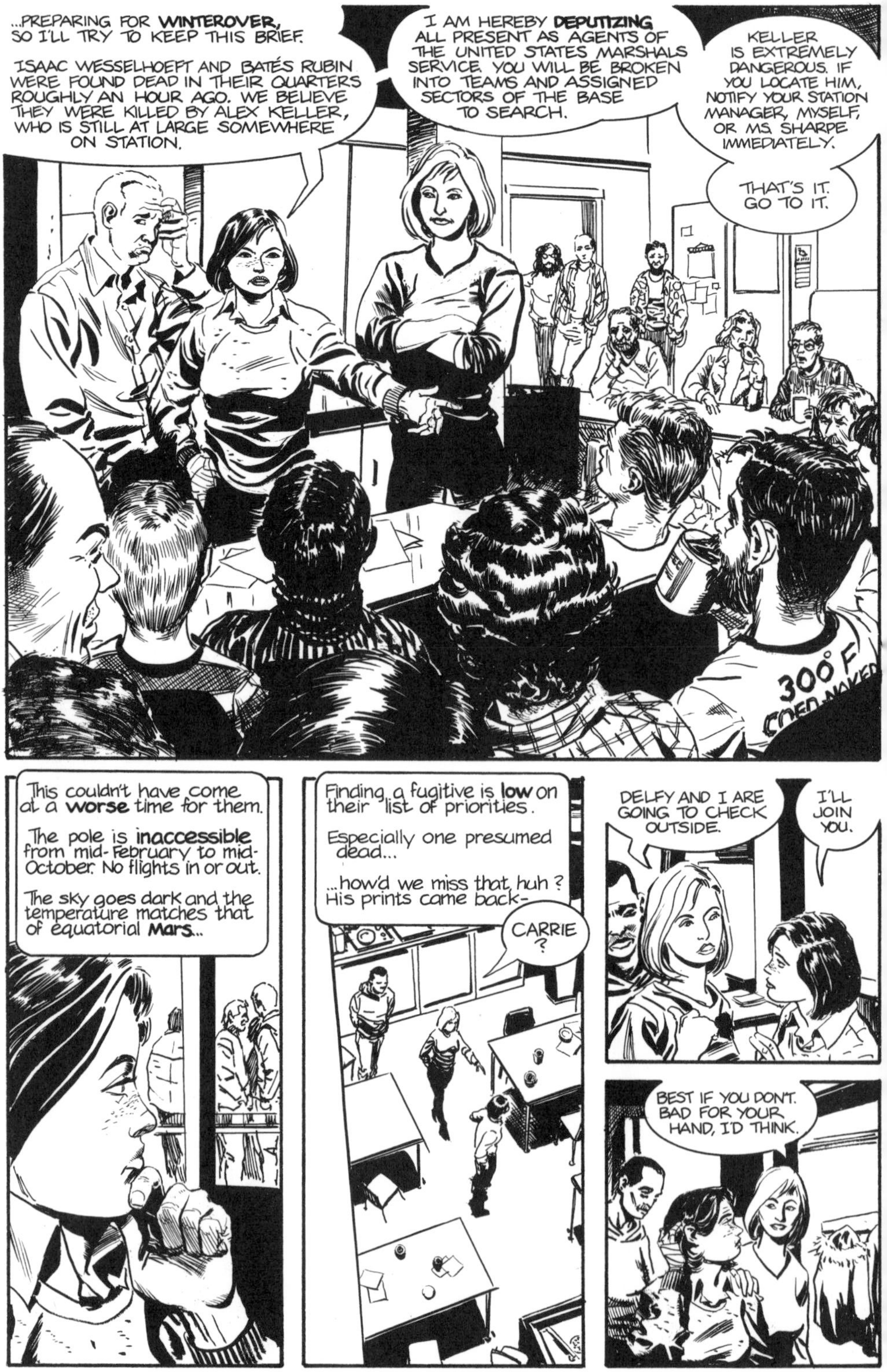
...PREPARING FOR **WINTEROVER**, SO I'LL TRY TO KEEP THIS BRIEF.
ISAAC WESSELHOEFT AND BATÉS RUBIN WERE FOUND DEAD IN THEIR QUARTERS ROUGHLY AN HOUR AGO. WE BELIEVE THEY WERE KILLED BY ALEX KELLER, WHO IS STILL AT LARGE SOMEWHERE ON STATION.
I AM HEREBY **DEPUTIZING** ALL PRESENT AS AGENTS OF THE UNITED STATES MARSHALS SERVICE. YOU WILL BE BROKEN INTO TEAMS AND ASSIGNED SECTORS OF THE BASE TO SEARCH.
KELLER IS EXTREMELY DANGEROUS. IF YOU LOCATE HIM, NOTIFY YOUR STATION MANAGER, MYSELF, OR MS. SHARPE IMMEDIATELY.
THAT'S IT. GO TO IT.
This couldn't have come at a **worse** time for them.
The pole is **inaccessible** from mid-February to mid-October. No flights in or out.
The sky goes dark and the temperature matches that of equatorial **Mars**...
Finding a fugitive is **low** on their list of priorities.
Especially one presumed dead...
...how'd we miss that, huh? His prints came back-
CARRIE?
DELFY AND I ARE GOING TO CHECK OUTSIDE.
I'LL JOIN YOU.
BEST IF YOU DON'T. BAD FOR YOUR HAND, I'D THINK.

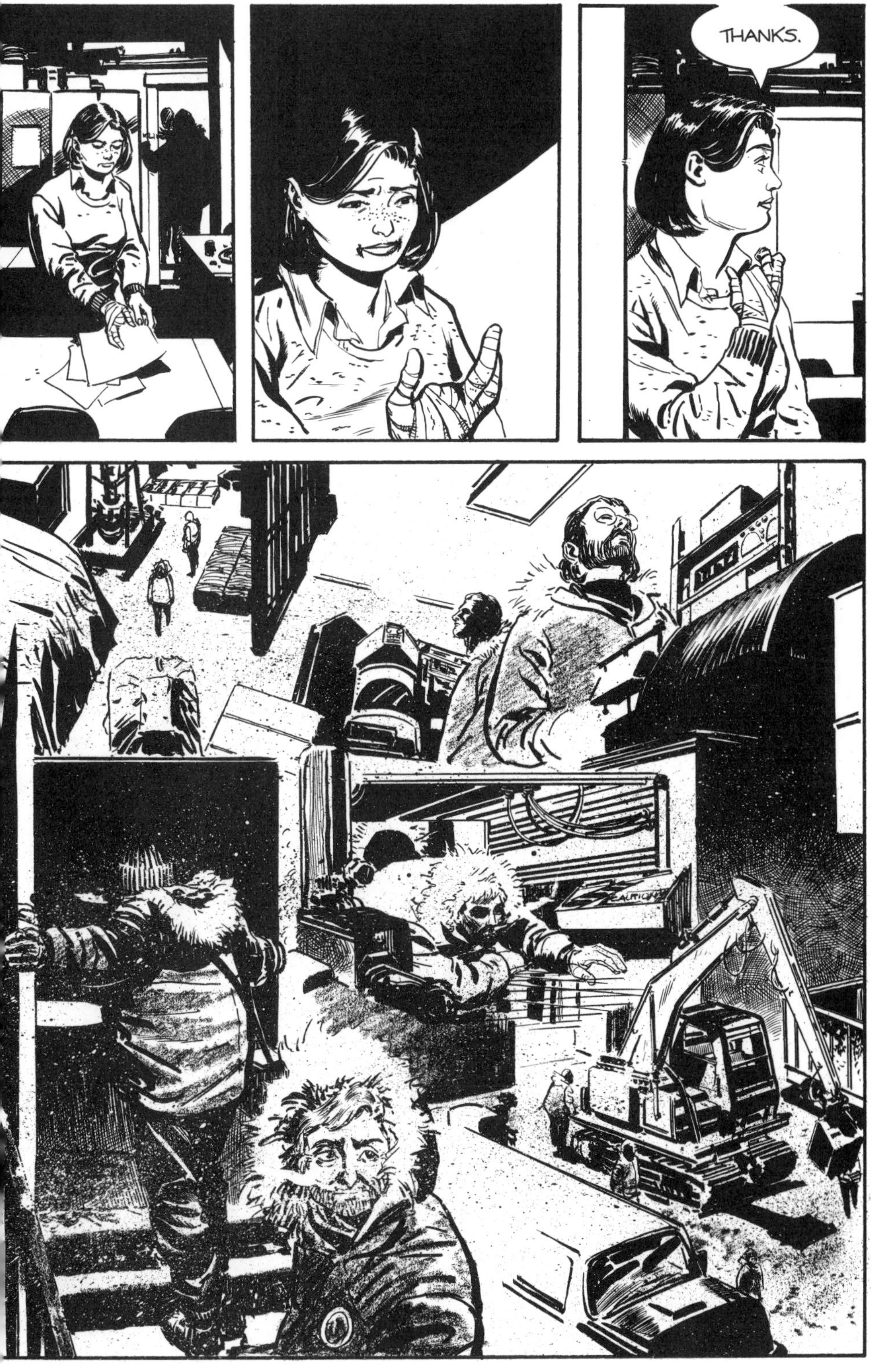
THANKS.

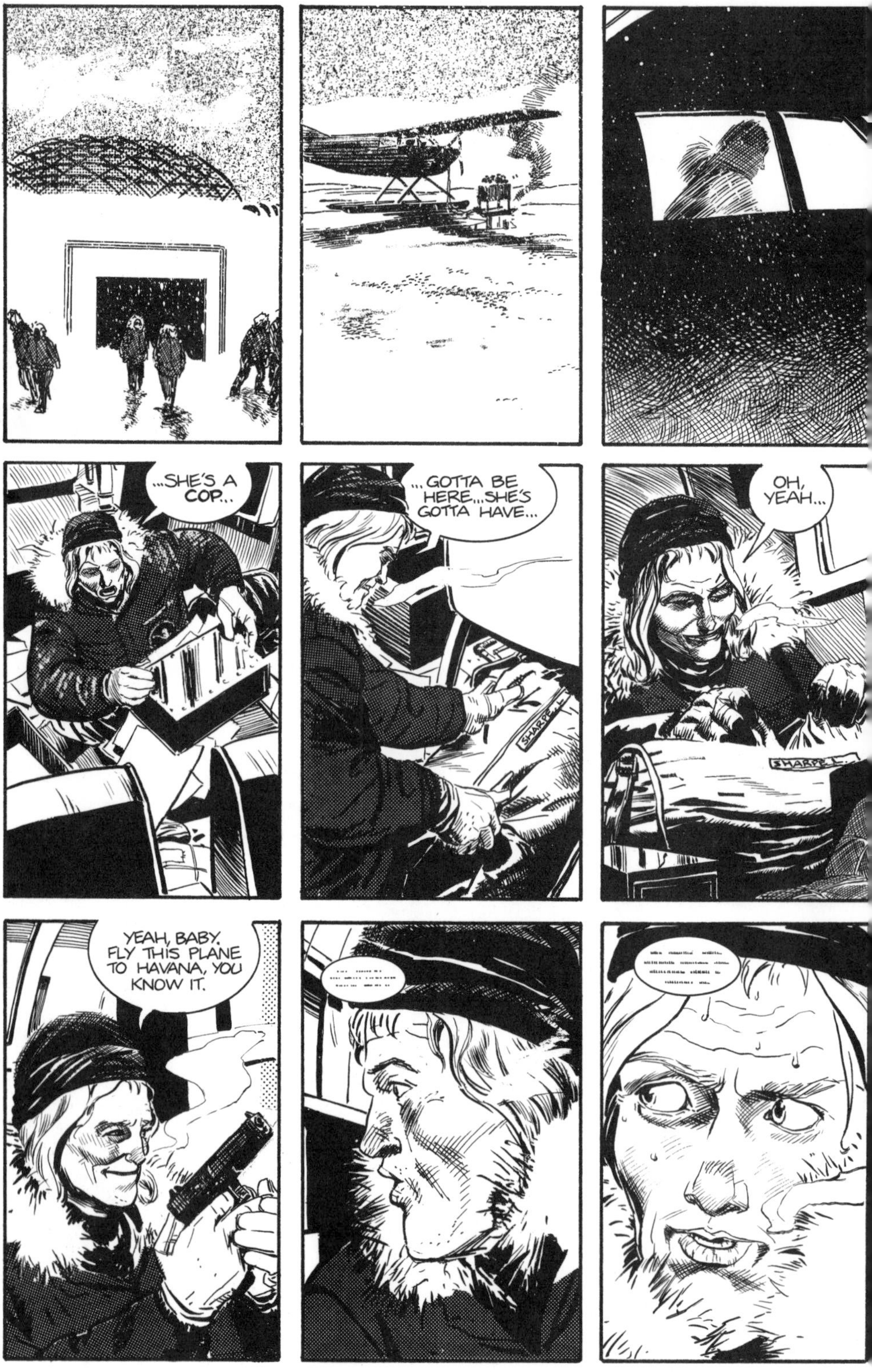
...SHE'S A COP...
...GOTTA BE HERE...SHE'S GOTTA HAVE...
OH, YEAH...
YEAH, BABY. FLY THIS PLANE TO HAVANA, YOU KNOW IT.

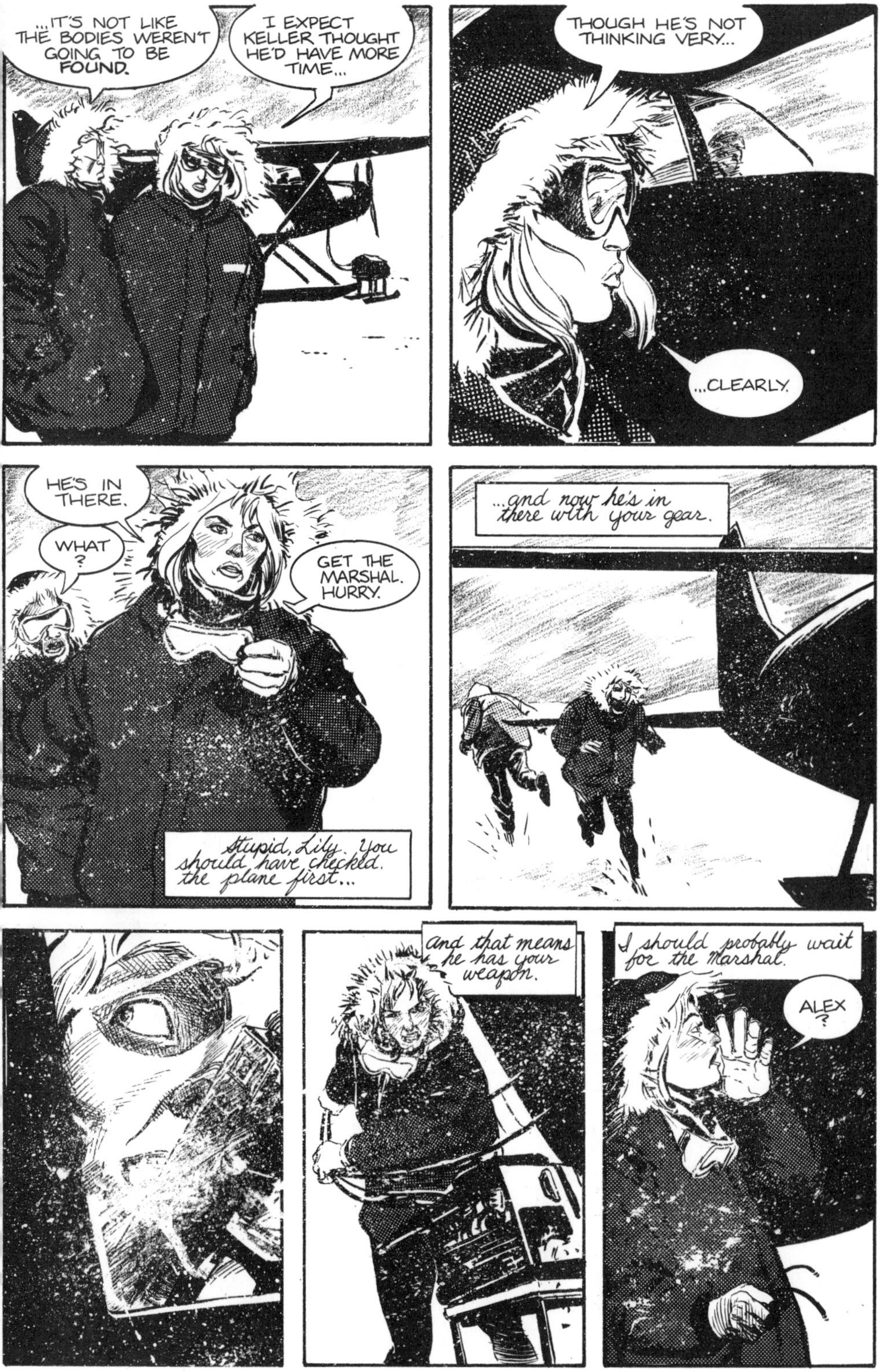
...IT'S NOT LIKE THE BODIES WEREN'T GOING TO BE FOUND.
I EXPECT KELLER THOUGHT HE'D HAVE MORE TIME...
THOUGH HE'S NOT THINKING VERY...
...CLEARLY.
HE'S IN THERE.
WHAT ?
GET THE MARSHAL. HURRY.
Stupid, Lily. You should have checked the plane first...
...and now he's in there with your gear.
and that means he has your weapon.
I should probably wait for the Marshal.
ALEX ?

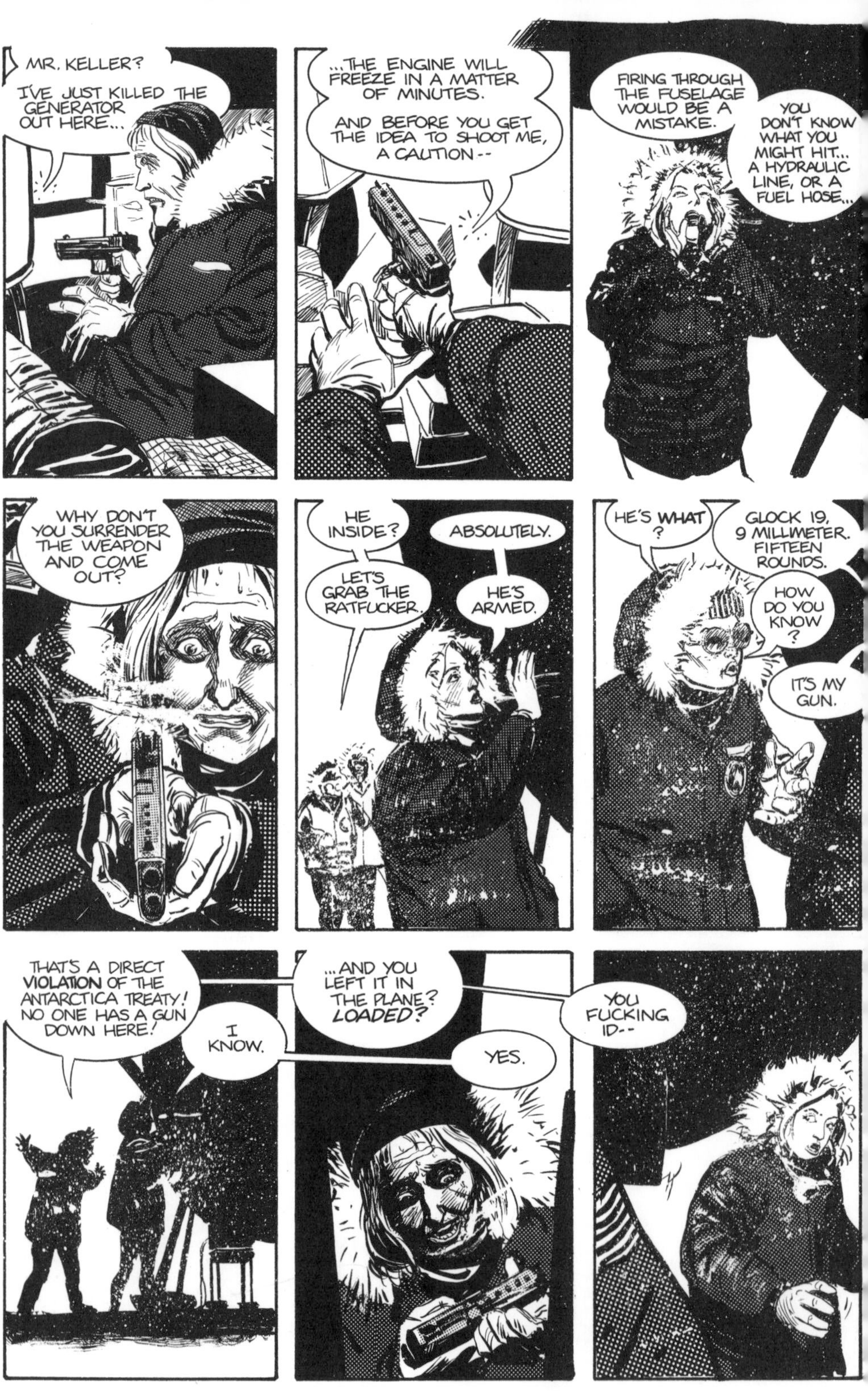
MR. KELLER?
I'VE JUST KILLED THE GENERATOR OUT HERE...
...THE ENGINE WILL FREEZE IN A MATTER OF MINUTES.
AND BEFORE YOU GET THE IDEA TO SHOOT ME, A CAUTION--
FIRING THROUGH THE FUSELAGE WOULD BE A MISTAKE.
YOU DON'T KNOW WHAT YOU MIGHT HIT... A HYDRAULIC LINE, OR A FUEL HOSE...
WHY DON'T YOU SURRENDER THE WEAPON AND COME OUT?
HE INSIDE?
ABSOLUTELY.
LET'S GRAB THE RATFUCKER.
HE'S ARMED.
HE'S WHAT?
GLOCK 19, 9 MILLIMETER. FIFTEEN ROUNDS.
HOW DO YOU KNOW?
IT'S MY GUN.
THAT'S A DIRECT VIOLATION OF THE ANTARCTICA TREATY! NO ONE HAS A GUN DOWN HERE!
I KNOW.
...AND YOU LEFT IT IN THE PLANE? LOADED?
YES.
YOU FUCKING ID--

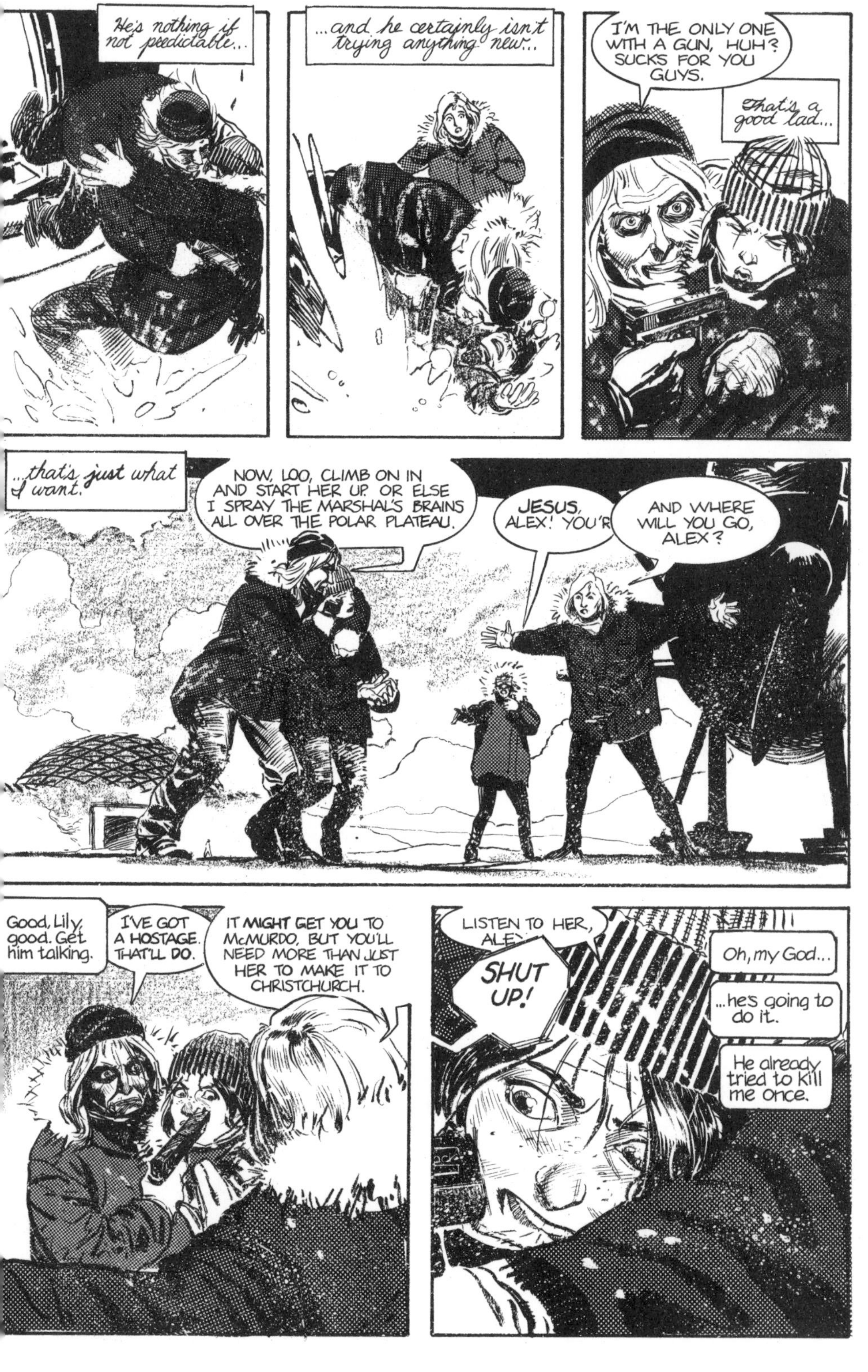
He's nothing if not predictable...
...and he certainly isn't trying anything new...
I'M THE ONLY ONE WITH A GUN, HUH? SUCKS FOR YOU GUYS.
That's a good lad...
...that's just what I want.
NOW, LOO, CLIMB ON IN AND START HER UP. OR ELSE I SPRAY THE MARSHAL'S BRAINS ALL OVER THE POLAR PLATEAU.
JESUS, ALEX! YOU'R
AND WHERE WILL YOU GO, ALEX?
Good, Lily, good. Get him talking.
I'VE GOT A HOSTAGE. THAT'LL DO.
IT MIGHT GET YOU TO McMURDO, BUT YOU'LL NEED MORE THAN JUST HER TO MAKE IT TO CHRISTCHURCH.
LISTEN TO HER, ALE
SHUT UP!
Oh, my God...
...he's going to do it.
He already tried to kill me once.

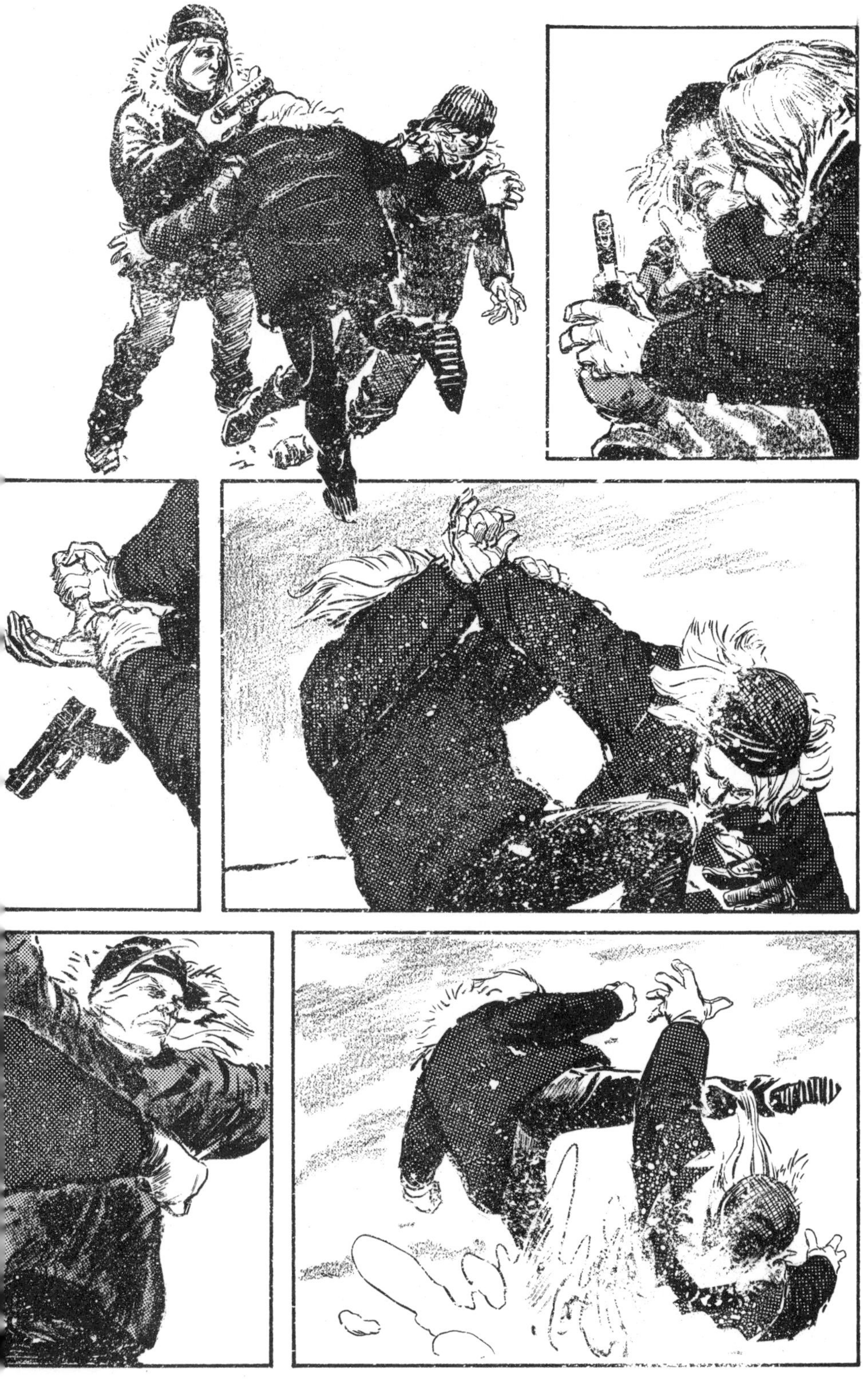

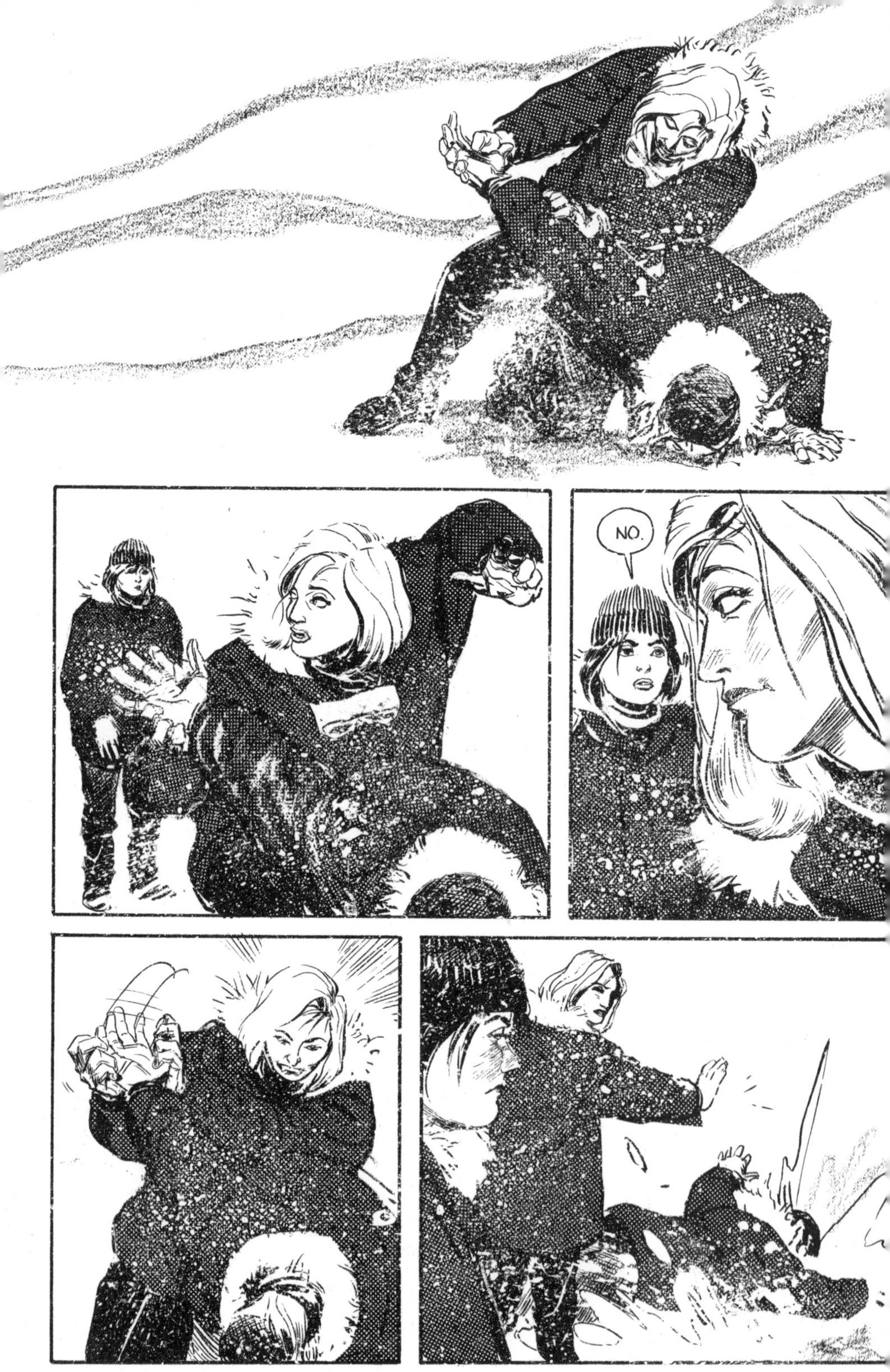
NO.

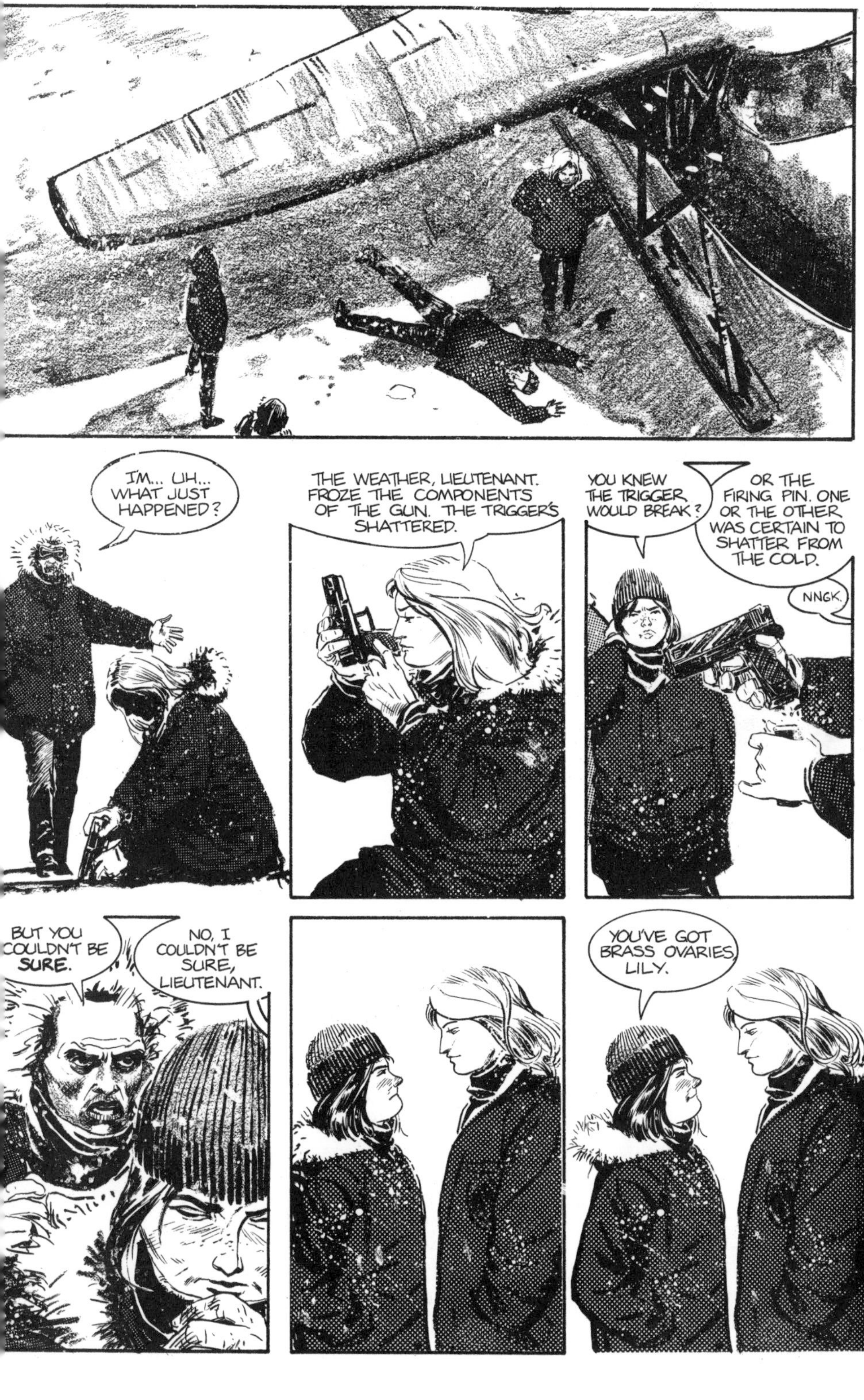
I'M... UH... WHAT JUST HAPPENED?
THE WEATHER, LIEUTENANT. FROZE THE COMPONENTS OF THE GUN. THE TRIGGER'S SHATTERED.
YOU KNEW THE TRIGGER WOULD BREAK?
OR THE FIRING PIN. ONE OR THE OTHER WAS CERTAIN TO SHATTER FROM THE COLD.
NNGK.
BUT YOU COULDN'T BE **SURE**.
NO, I COULDN'T BE SURE, LIEUTENANT.
YOU'VE GOT BRASS OVARIES, LILY.

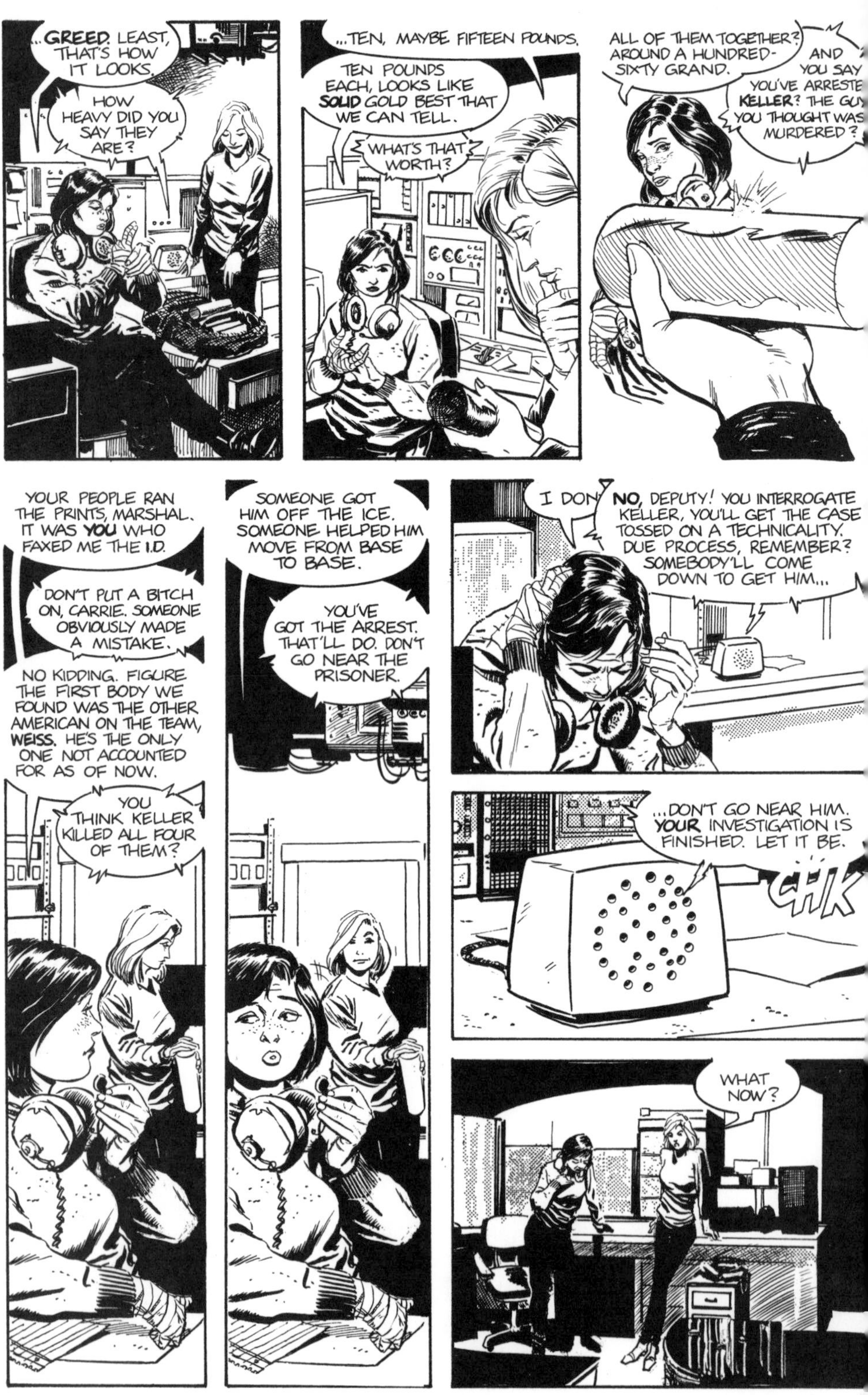
...GREED. LEAST, THAT'S HOW IT LOOKS.
HOW HEAVY DID YOU SAY THEY ARE?
...TEN, MAYBE FIFTEEN POUNDS.
TEN POUNDS EACH, LOOKS LIKE SOLID GOLD BEST THAT WE CAN TELL.
WHAT'S THAT WORTH?
ALL OF THEM TOGETHER? AROUND A HUNDRED-SIXTY GRAND.
AND YOU SAY YOU'VE ARRESTE KELLER? THE GU YOU THOUGHT WAS MURDERED?
YOUR PEOPLE RAN THE PRINTS, MARSHAL. IT WAS YOU WHO FAXED ME THE I.D.
DON'T PUT A BITCH ON, CARRIE. SOMEONE OBVIOUSLY MADE A MISTAKE.
NO KIDDING. FIGURE THE FIRST BODY WE FOUND WAS THE OTHER AMERICAN ON THE TEAM, WEISS. HE'S THE ONLY ONE NOT ACCOUNTED FOR AS OF NOW.
YOU THINK KELLER KILLED ALL FOUR OF THEM?
SOMEONE GOT HIM OFF THE ICE. SOMEONE HELPED HIM MOVE FROM BASE TO BASE.
YOU'VE GOT THE ARREST. THAT'LL DO. DON'T GO NEAR THE PRISONER.
I DON'
NO, DEPUTY! YOU INTERROGATE KELLER, YOU'LL GET THE CASE TOSSED ON A TECHNICALITY. DUE PROCESS, REMEMBER? SOMEBODY'LL COME DOWN TO GET HIM...
...DON'T GO NEAR HIM. YOUR INVESTIGATION IS FINISHED. LET IT BE.
CHK
WHAT NOW?

YOU'RE NOT GOING WHERE I THINK YOU'RE GOING.

WHERE DO YOU THINK I'M GOING?

DON'T. YOU'LL GET THE CASE TOSSED, YOU'LL GET REPRIMANDED, OR WORSE.

I'M NOT ASKING YOU TO HELP ME.

YOU'RE GOING TO LAND YOURSELF IN A WORLD OF TROUBLE WITH McEWAN.—

I DON'T CARE. I WANT ANSWERS.—

—HOW KELLER GOT OFF THE ICE. WHERE THIER GEAR WENT, WHO FLEW THEM...

...AND WHY. I WANT TO KNOW A WHOLE LOT OF WHY. IN FACT, I'VE GOT WHY COMING OUT MY EARS—HOLD ON—

KNOCK IT OFF

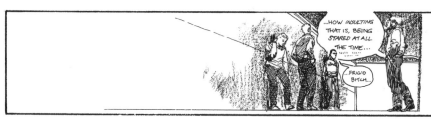

...HOW INSULTING THAT IS, BEING STARED AT ALL THE TIME...

...FRIGID BITCH...

...WAS I SAYING?

YOU WERE LISTING WHYS.

RIGHT. WHY, FOR INSTANCE...

...IS A BRITISH SPY CONCERNED WITH MY INVESTIGATION?

YOU MEAN, ME?

ON THE NOSE.

I'LL FIND OUT SOONER OR LATER, LILY.

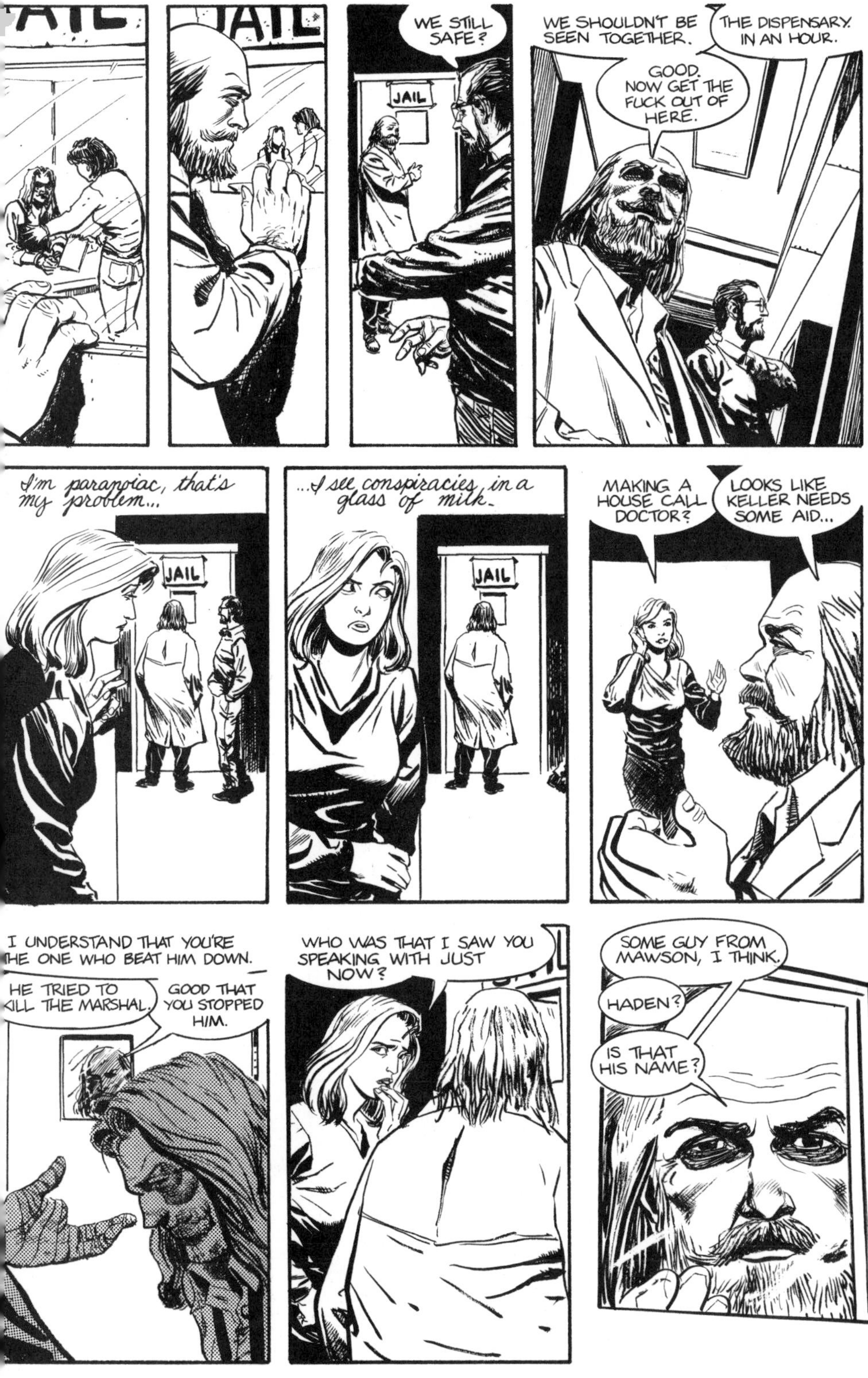

JAIL
WE STILL SAFE?
JAIL
WE SHOULDN'T BE SEEN TOGETHER.
THE DISPENSARY. IN AN HOUR.
GOOD. NOW GET THE FUCK OUT OF HERE.
I'm paranoiac, that's my problem...
JAIL
...I see conspiracies in a glass of milk.
JAIL
MAKING A HOUSE CALL DOCTOR?
LOOKS LIKE KELLER NEEDS SOME AID...
I UNDERSTAND THAT YOU'RE THE ONE WHO BEAT HIM DOWN.
HE TRIED TO KILL THE MARSHAL.
GOOD THAT YOU STOPPED HIM.
WHO WAS THAT I SAW YOU SPEAKING WITH JUST NOW?
SOME GUY FROM MAWSON, I THINK.
HADEN?
IS THAT HIS NAME?

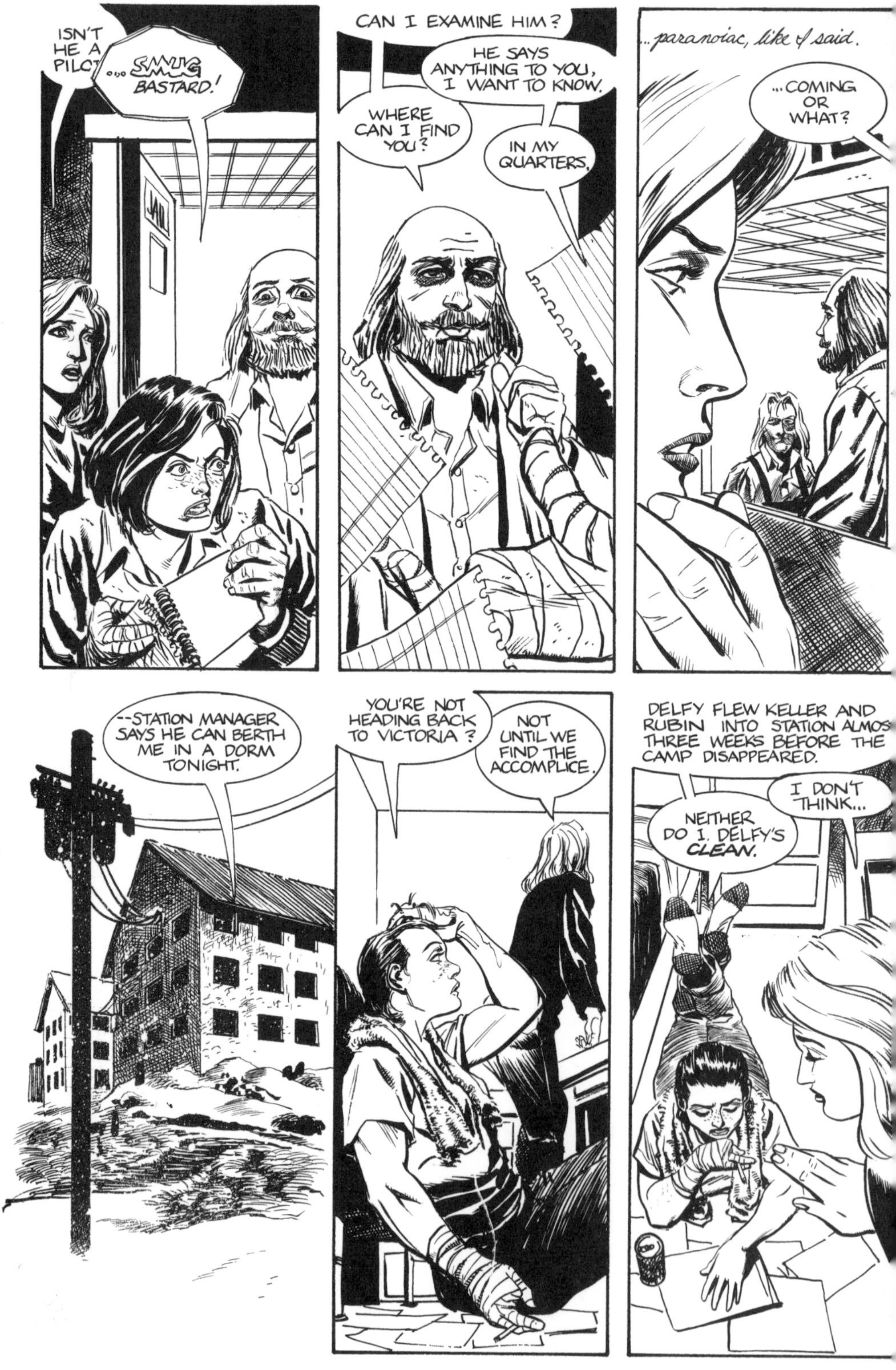
ISN'T HE A PILOT
...SMUG SMUG BASTARD!
CAN I EXAMINE HIM?
HE SAYS ANYTHING TO YOU, I WANT TO KNOW.
WHERE CAN I FIND YOU?
IN MY QUARTERS.
...paranoiac, like I said.
...COMING OR WHAT?
--STATION MANAGER SAYS HE CAN BERTH ME IN A DORM TONIGHT.
YOU'RE NOT HEADING BACK TO VICTORIA?
NOT UNTIL WE FIND THE ACCOMPLICE.
DELFY FLEW KELLER AND RUBIN INTO STATION ALMOS THREE WEEKS BEFORE THE CAMP DISAPPEARED.
I DON'T THINK...
NEITHER DO I. DELFY'S CLEAN.

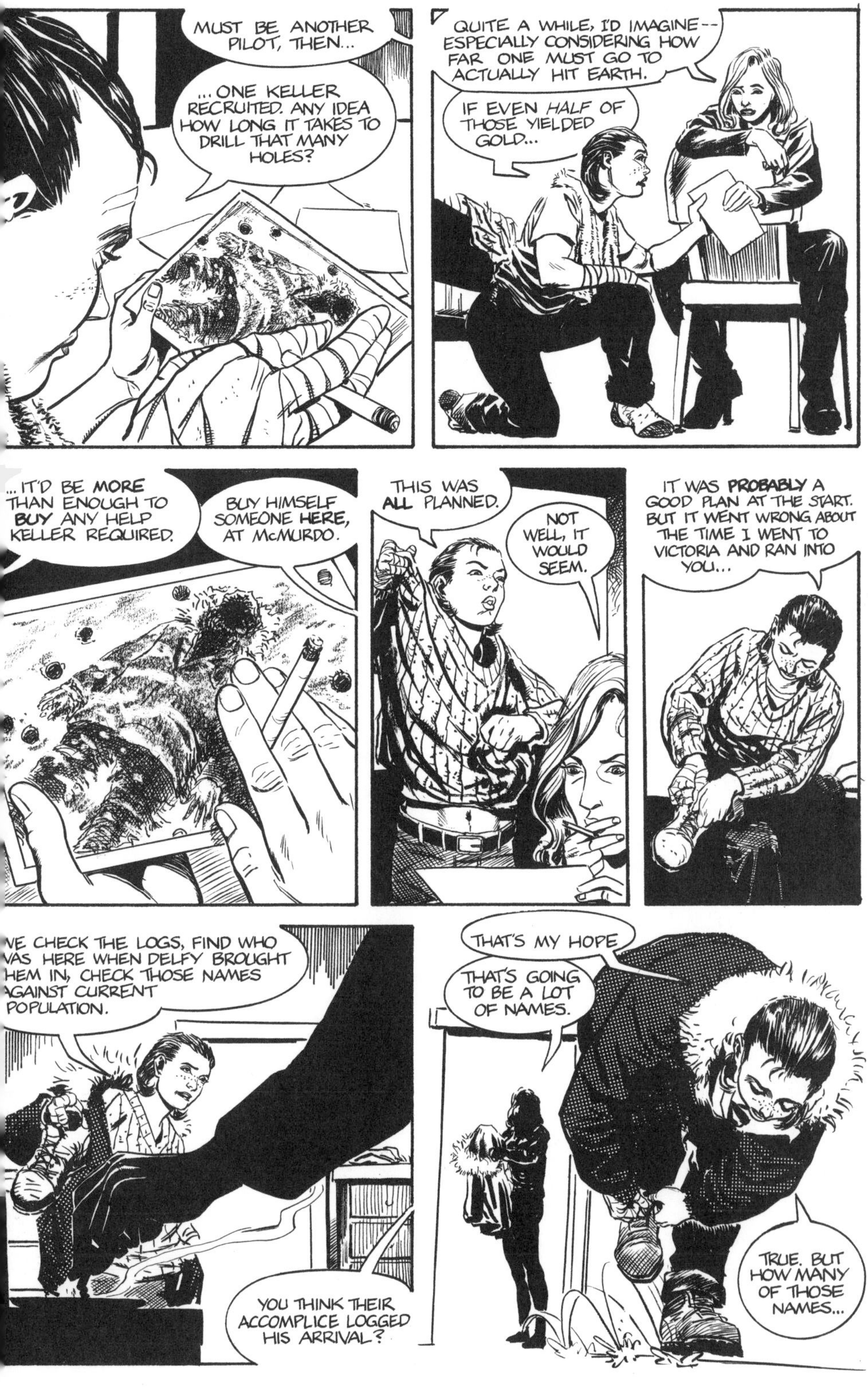
MUST BE ANOTHER PILOT, THEN...
...ONE KELLER RECRUITED. ANY IDEA HOW LONG IT TAKES TO DRILL THAT MANY HOLES?
QUITE A WHILE, I'D IMAGINE-- ESPECIALLY CONSIDERING HOW FAR ONE MUST GO TO ACTUALLY HIT EARTH.
IF EVEN *HALF* OF THOSE YIELDED GOLD...
...IT'D BE **MORE** THAN ENOUGH TO **BUY** ANY HELP KELLER REQUIRED.
BUY HIMSELF SOMEONE **HERE**, AT McMURDO.
THIS WAS **ALL** PLANNED.
NOT WELL, IT WOULD SEEM.
IT WAS **PROBABLY** A GOOD PLAN AT THE START. BUT IT WENT WRONG ABOUT THE TIME I WENT TO VICTORIA AND RAN INTO YOU...
VE CHECK THE LOGS, FIND WHO VAS HERE WHEN DELFY BROUGHT HEM IN, CHECK THOSE NAMES AGAINST CURRENT POPULATION.
YOU THINK THEIR ACCOMPLICE LOGGED HIS ARRIVAL?
THAT'S MY HOPE.
THAT'S GOING TO BE A LOT OF NAMES.
TRUE. BUT HOW MANY OF THOSE NAMES...

"...ARE REGISTERED PILOTS?"

WERE YOU SEEN?

NO, I MADE SURE.

BOUGHT DELFY A FEW DRINKS, GOT HIM TALKING. THE MARSHAL FOUND THE STICKS KELLER TOOK OFF WESSELHOEFT AND RUBIN.

HOW MANY?

SIXTEEN.

HE DIDN'T GET SUSPICIOUS?

DELFY? NAH HE'S THE TRUSTING SORT. THINKS WE'RE **MATES**.

SHARPE SAW YOU TALKING TO ME EARLIER.

DID SHE HEAR US?

NO. SHE KNOWS ABOUT **YOU** THOUGH... THAT YOU'RE A PILOT.

IF SHE'S TOLD THE MARSHAL, WE'RE FUCKED.

CARRIE HASN'T BEEN TO SEE ME... SO I DOUBT SHARPE'S TOLD HER ANYTHING, YET.

OR SHE'S WAITING FOR MORE EVIDENCE. OR MAYBE SHE'LL RUN AT KELLER AGAIN, AND THIS TIME HE COULD GO TITS UP ON US...

WE CAN'T LET HER...

I WON'T LET YOU TOUCH HER HADEN.

DON'T GET SENTIMENTAL.

I SAID NO!

NO MORE BODIES, HADEN. THIS ISN'T WHAT I SIGNED ON FOR.

RELAX, DOC. IF SHARPE'S KEPT QUIET, SHE'S THE ONLY ONE WE HAVE TO WORRY ABOUT--

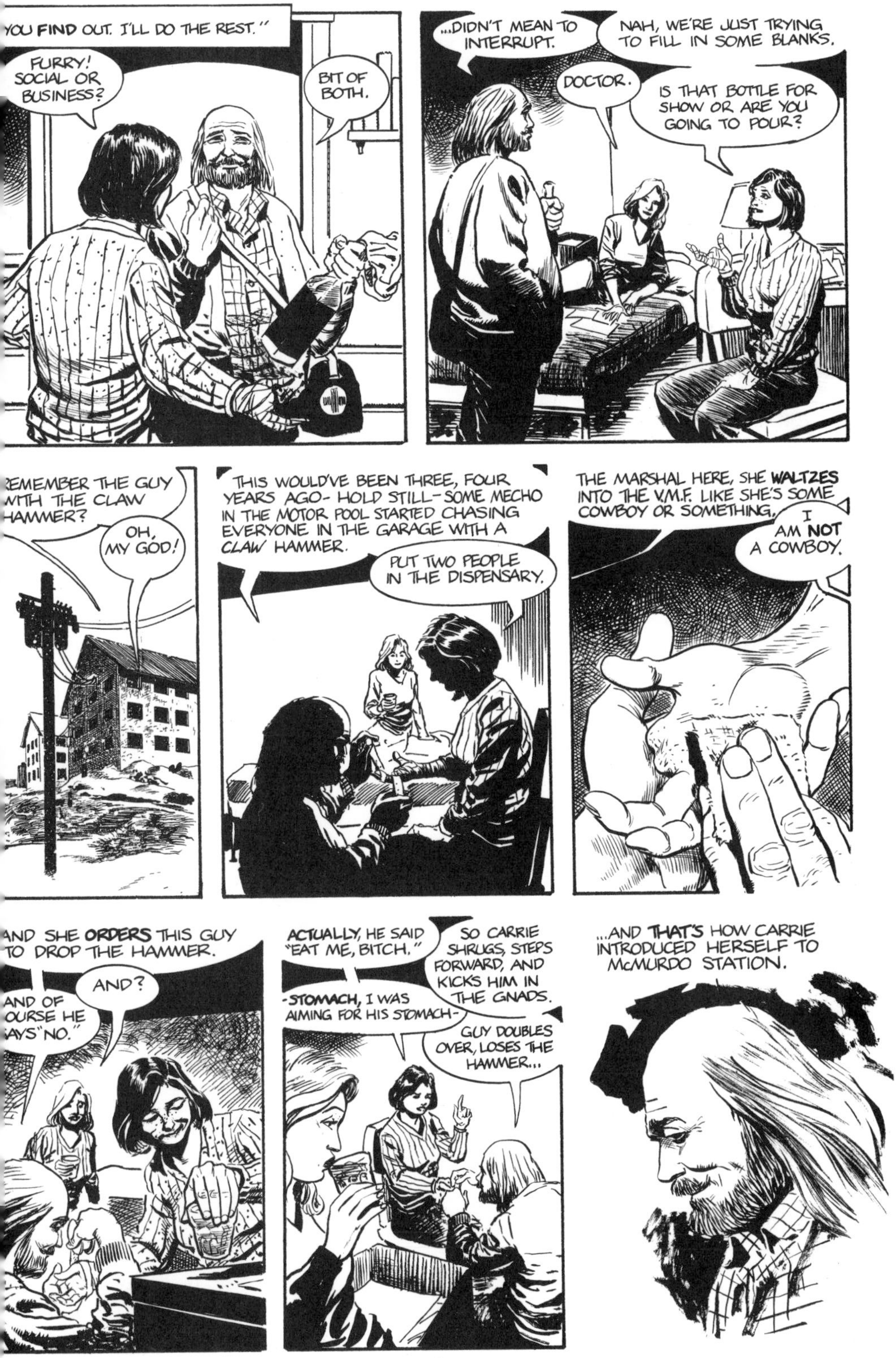
YOU FIND OUT. I'LL DO THE REST."
FURRY! SOCIAL OR BUSINESS?
BIT OF BOTH.
...DIDN'T MEAN TO INTERRUPT.
NAH, WE'RE JUST TRYING TO FILL IN SOME BLANKS.
DOCTOR.
IS THAT BOTTLE FOR SHOW OR ARE YOU GOING TO POUR?
REMEMBER THE GUY WITH THE CLAW HAMMER?
OH, MY GOD!
THIS WOULD'VE BEEN THREE, FOUR YEARS AGO- HOLD STILL- SOME MECHO IN THE MOTOR POOL STARTED CHASING EVERYONE IN THE GARAGE WITH A CLAW HAMMER.
PUT TWO PEOPLE IN THE DISPENSARY.
THE MARSHAL HERE, SHE WALTZES INTO THE V.M.F. LIKE SHE'S SOME COWBOY OR SOMETHING,
I AM NOT A COWBOY.
AND SHE ORDERS THIS GUY TO DROP THE HAMMER.
AND OF COURSE HE SAYS "NO."
AND?
ACTUALLY, HE SAID "EAT ME, BITCH."
SO CARRIE SHRUGS, STEPS FORWARD, AND KICKS HIM IN THE GNADS.
-STOMACH, I WAS AIMING FOR HIS STOMACH-
GUY DOUBLES OVER, LOSES THE HAMMER...
...AND THAT'S HOW CARRIE INTRODUCED HERSELF TO McMURDO STATION.

BRAVO!

THANK YOU. IT WAS NOTHING.

AFTER THAT, NO ONE DARED FUCK WITH THE MARSHAL.

I AM SERIOUSLY GOING TO MISS YOU WHEN YOU GO, FURRY.

I'M GOING TO MISS YOU, TOO.

YOU PACKED?

YOU'RE LEAVING?

TOMORROW. LAST FLIGHT OUT.

HIS TOUR'S UP. THEY THINK HIS OLD ANTARCTIC EXPLORER ASS HAS GOTTEN TOO OLD AND TOO COLD...

THEY'LL COME FOR **YOU** TOO SOMEDAY. DRAG YOU OFF THE ICE KICKING AND SCREAMING...

NO WAY. I'M **NEVER** GOING BACK. I'LL DIE HERE, AN O.A.E. WHOSE ASHES GET SCATTERED OVER THE POLE.

THEY WON'T GIVE YOU THE OPTION.

NOUGH OF HAT, HUH? SS ME THE BOTTLE.

YOU SHOULD HAVE GIVEN US MORE WARNING. I'D HAVE PLANNED A BIG BLOW OUT FOR YOU...

...AS IT IS, YOU CAUGHT US TRYING TO DO SOME WORK.

SO YOU SAID WHEN I ENTERED. WHAT SORT OF MUCK ARE YOU LOOKING FOR?

KELLER'S ACCOMPLICE. HE HAD TO HAVE HELP.

I'D THINK SO. SOME SUPPORT FROM OUTSIDE THE CAMP.

ERE THINKING IT'S A PILOT. HAT CAMP SURE AS HELL IDN'T **WALK** OFF THE PLATEAU.

ANY SUSPECTS?

POTENTIALLY.

IF YOU SEE HADEN, TELL HIM THAT I'D LIKE TO TALK TO HIM.

HADEN? OH... IF I SEE HIM, I'LL LET HIM KNOW.

WE'LL FIGURE IT OUT. JUST TAKES TIME.

HAVE YOU CHECKED THE INDEPENDENTS? ONE OF THE FIRMS OUT OF CHEECH OR CHILE?

I'LL CALL NZ TOMORROW...

YAWN> AFTER I GET OME SLEEP. WHAT TIME IS IT?

PAST THREE.

I'LL COME BY YOUR OFFICE IN THE MORNING, ALL RIGHT, CARRIE?

HAVE A GOOD REST.

YOU AS WELL. GOODNIGHT, DOCTOR.

GOOD NIGHT.

SLEEP WELL, FURRY. STAY WARM.

YOU, TOO, CARRIE.

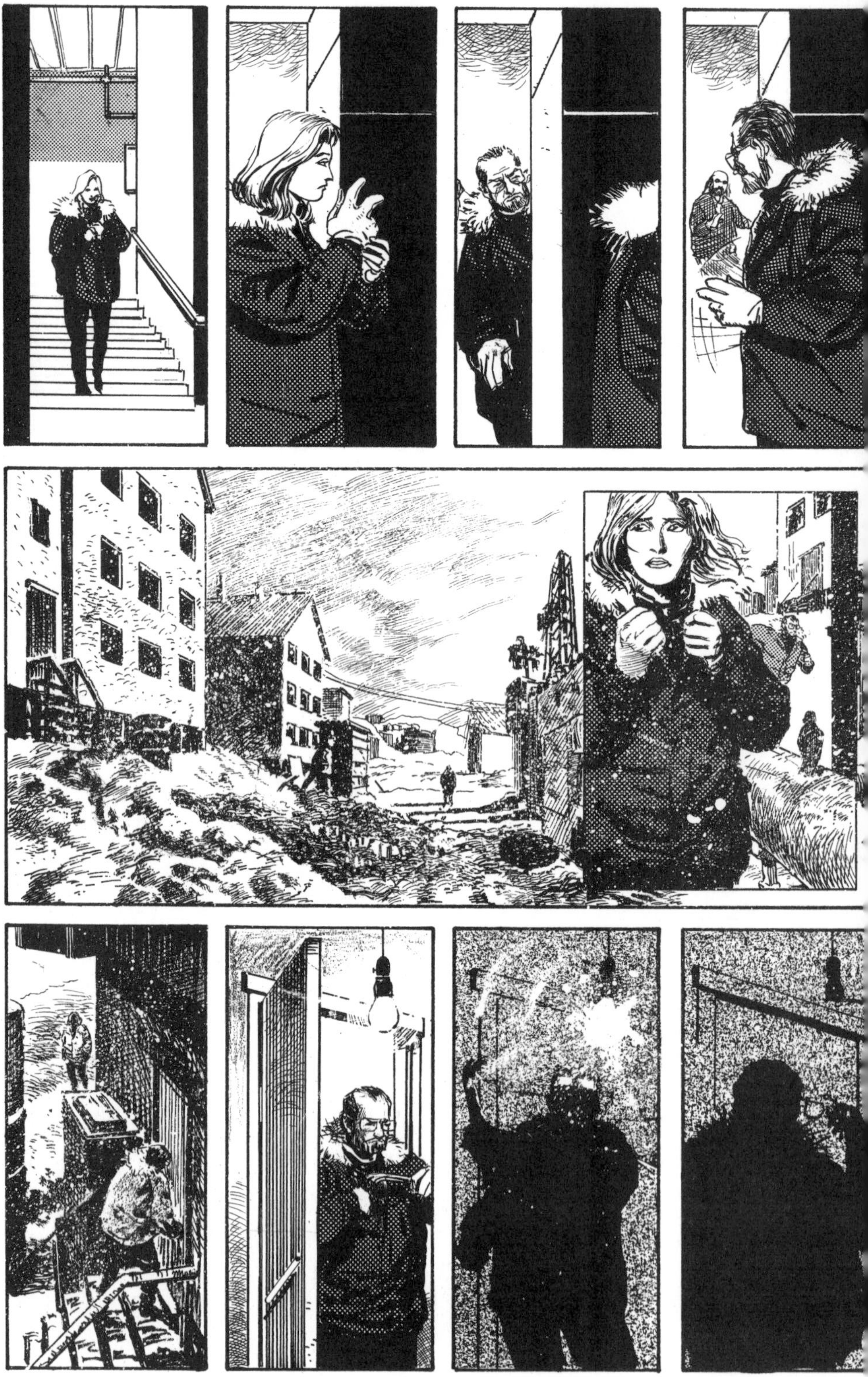

oh, bloody
motherfucking
he—

As it me...

...or am I having a rotten
run of luck lately?...

CHAPTER FOUR

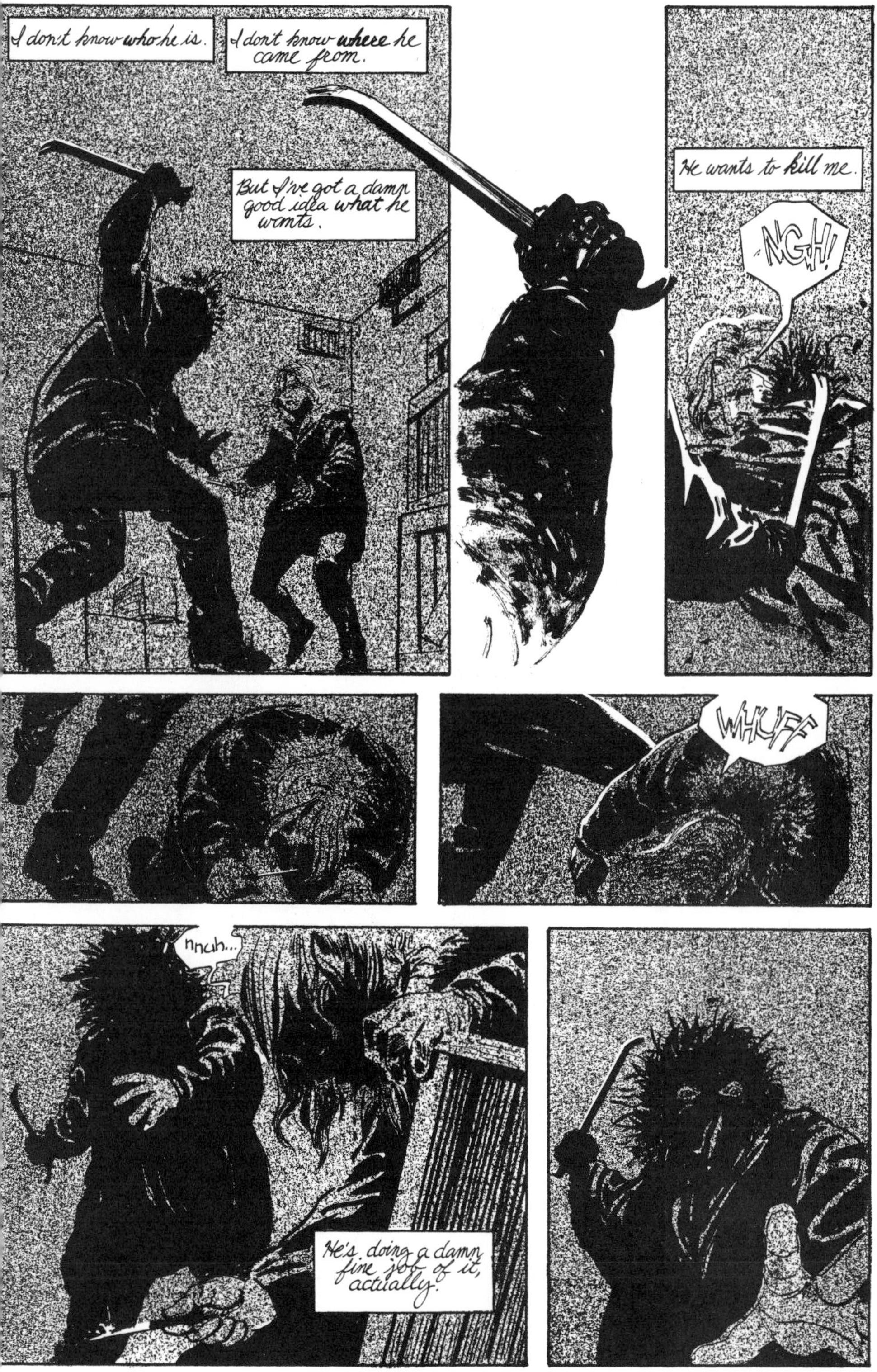
I don't know who he is.
I don't know where he came from.
But I've got a damn good idea what he wants.
He wants to kill me.
-NGH!
WHUFF
nnuh...
He's doing a damn fine job of it, actually.

The knife's made by Earl Emerson...

...gift from an S.A.S. bloke I went with once.

David, his name was.

David's dead now...

...*knife* still works.

DAMN BITCH!

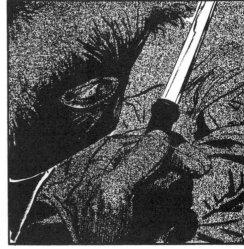

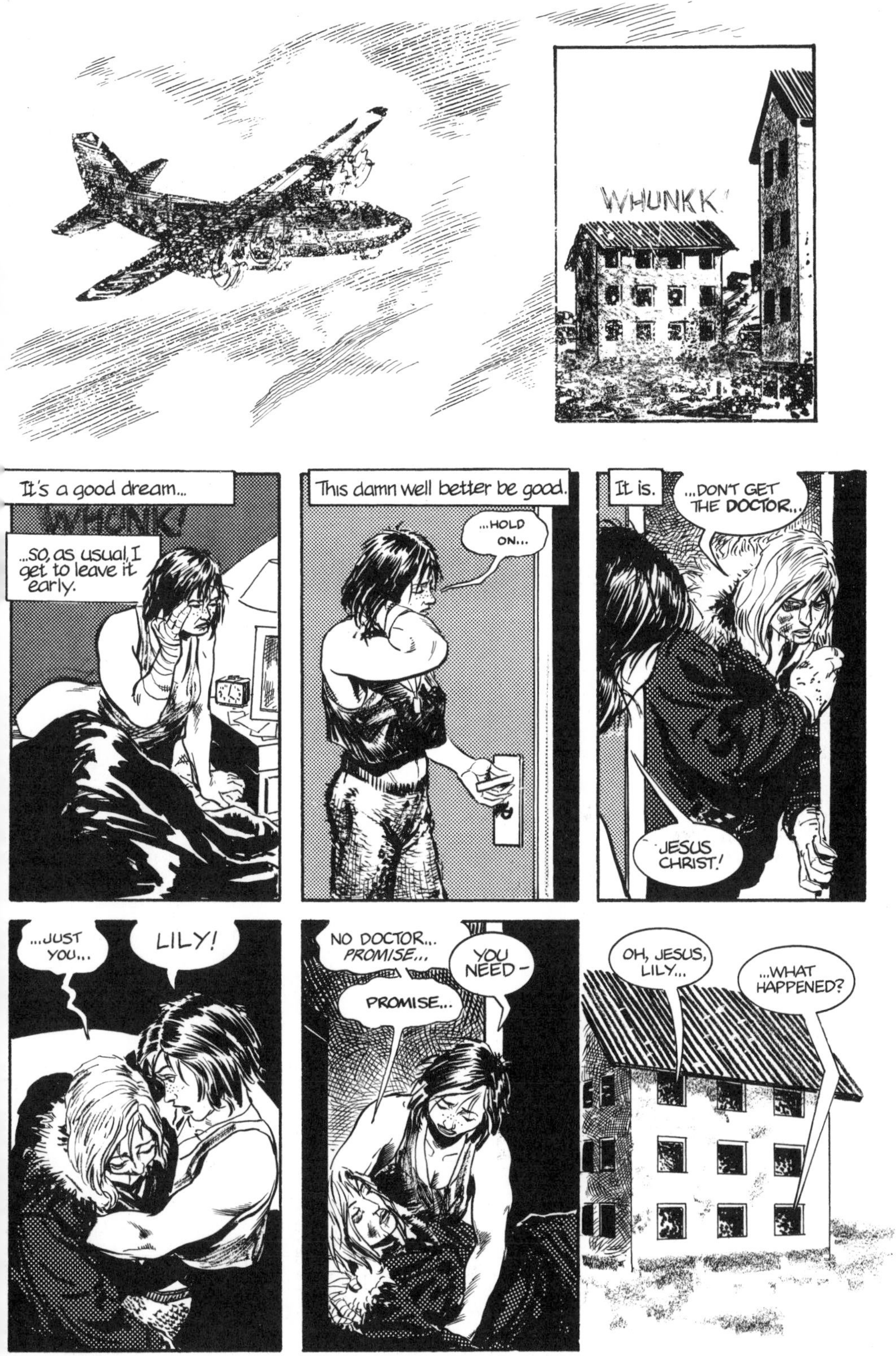
WHUNKK!
It's a good dream...
WHUNK!
...so, as usual, I get to leave it early.
This damn well better be good.
...HOLD ON...
It is.
...DON'T GET THE DOCTOR...
JESUS CHRIST!
...JUST YOU...
LILY!
NO DOCTOR... PROMISE...
YOU NEED -
PROMISE...
OH, JESUS, LILY...
...WHAT HAPPENED?

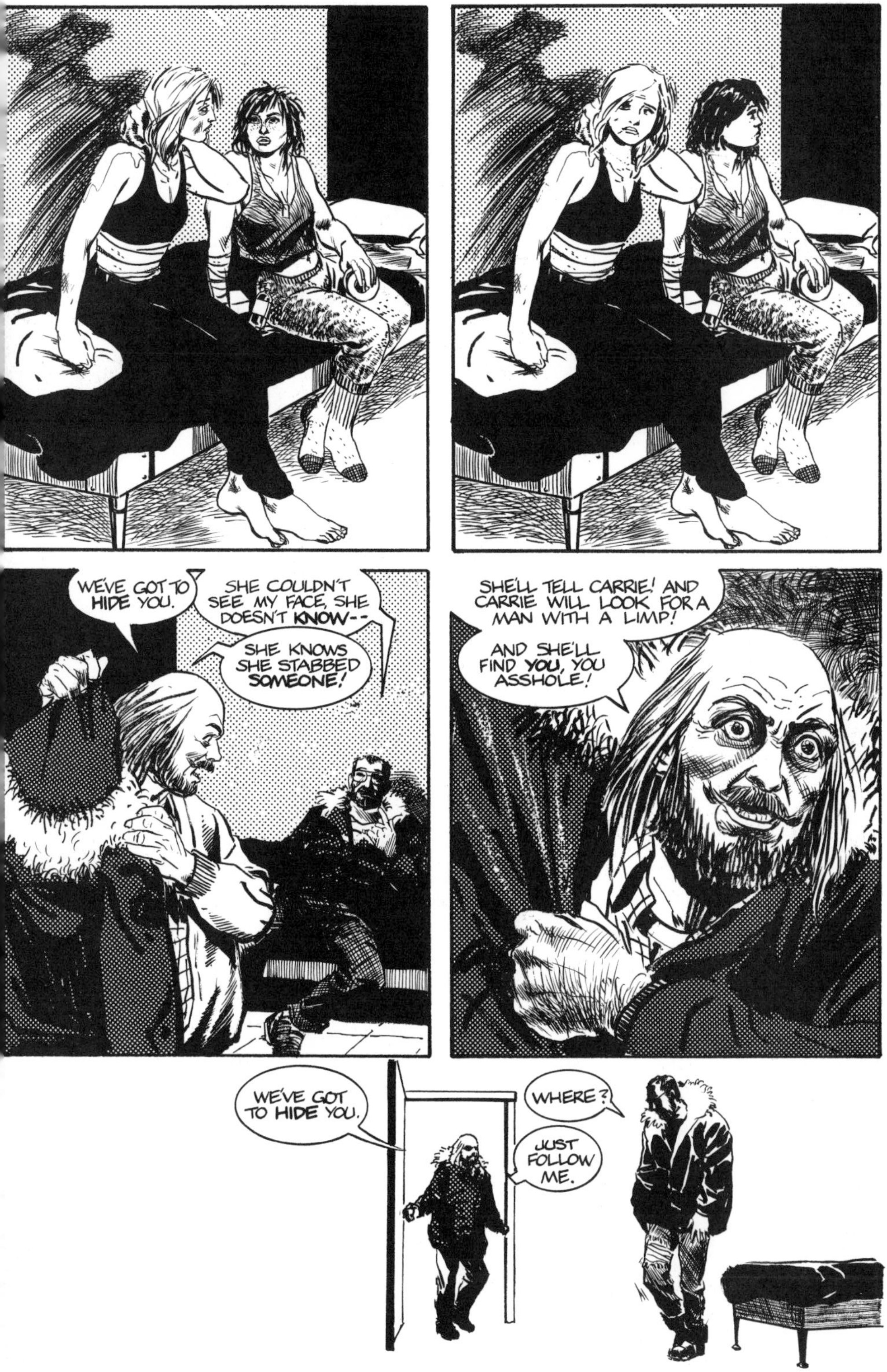

WE'VE GOT TO HIDE YOU.
SHE COULDN'T SEE MY FACE, SHE DOESN'T KNOW--
SHE KNOWS SHE STABBED SOMEONE!
SHE'LL TELL CARRIE! AND CARRIE WILL LOOK FOR A MAN WITH A LIMP!
AND SHE'LL FIND YOU, YOU ASSHOLE!
WE'VE GOT TO HIDE YOU.
WHERE?
JUST FOLLOW ME.

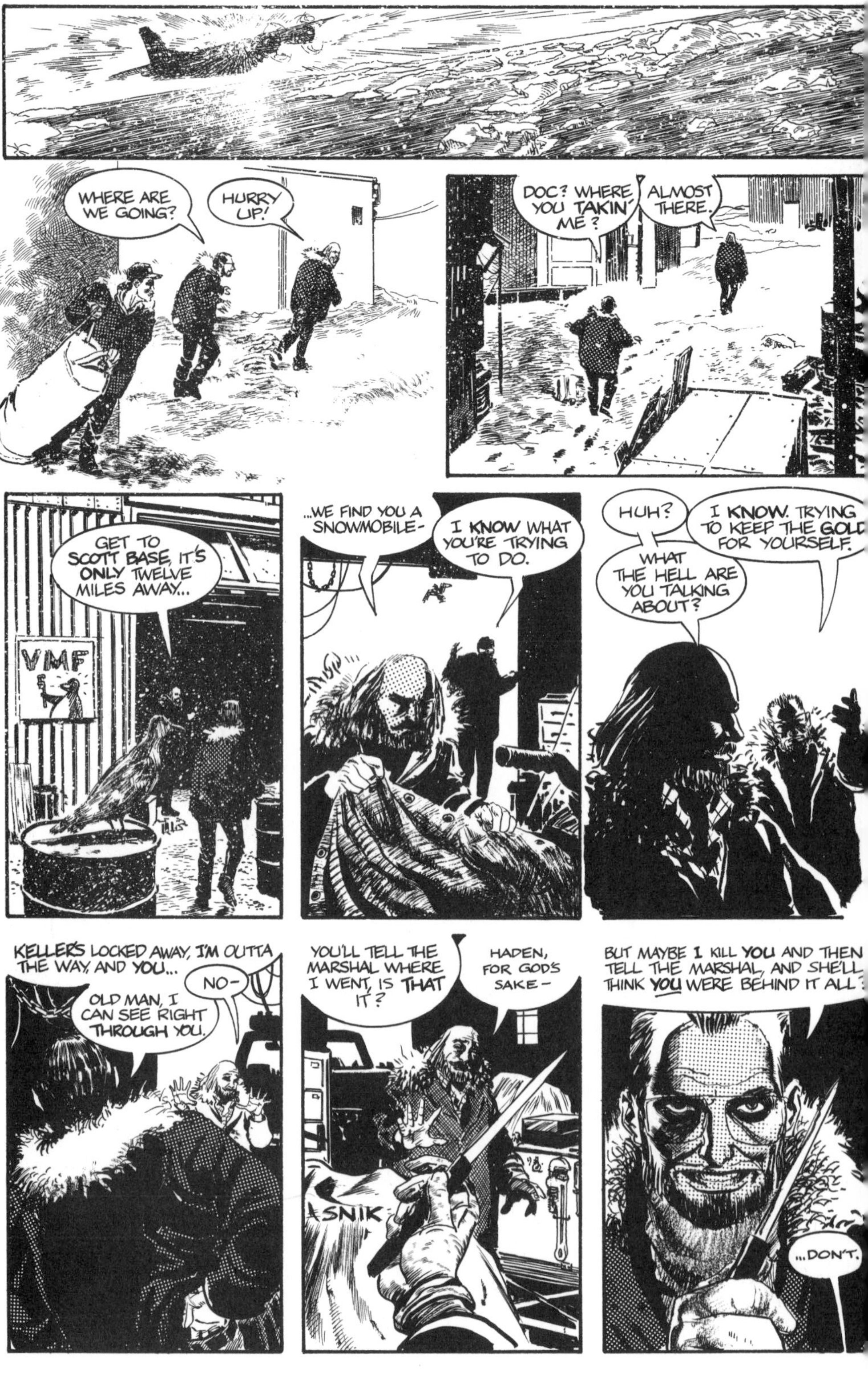

WHERE ARE WE GOING?
HURRY UP!
DOC? WHERE YOU TAKIN' ME?
ALMOST THERE.
GET TO SCOTT BASE, IT'S ONLY TWELVE MILES AWAY...
VMF
...WE FIND YOU A SNOWMOBILE-
I KNOW WHAT YOU'RE TRYING TO DO.
HUH?
WHAT THE HELL ARE YOU TALKING ABOUT?
I KNOW. TRYING TO KEEP THE GOLD FOR YOURSELF.
KELLER'S LOCKED AWAY, I'M OUTTA THE WAY, AND YOU...
OLD MAN, I CAN SEE RIGHT THROUGH YOU.
NO-
YOU'LL TELL THE MARSHAL WHERE I WENT, IS THAT IT?
HADEN, FOR GOD'S SAKE-
SNIK
BUT MAYBE I KILL YOU AND THEN TELL THE MARSHAL, AND SHE'LL THINK YOU WERE BEHIND IT ALL?
...DON'T.

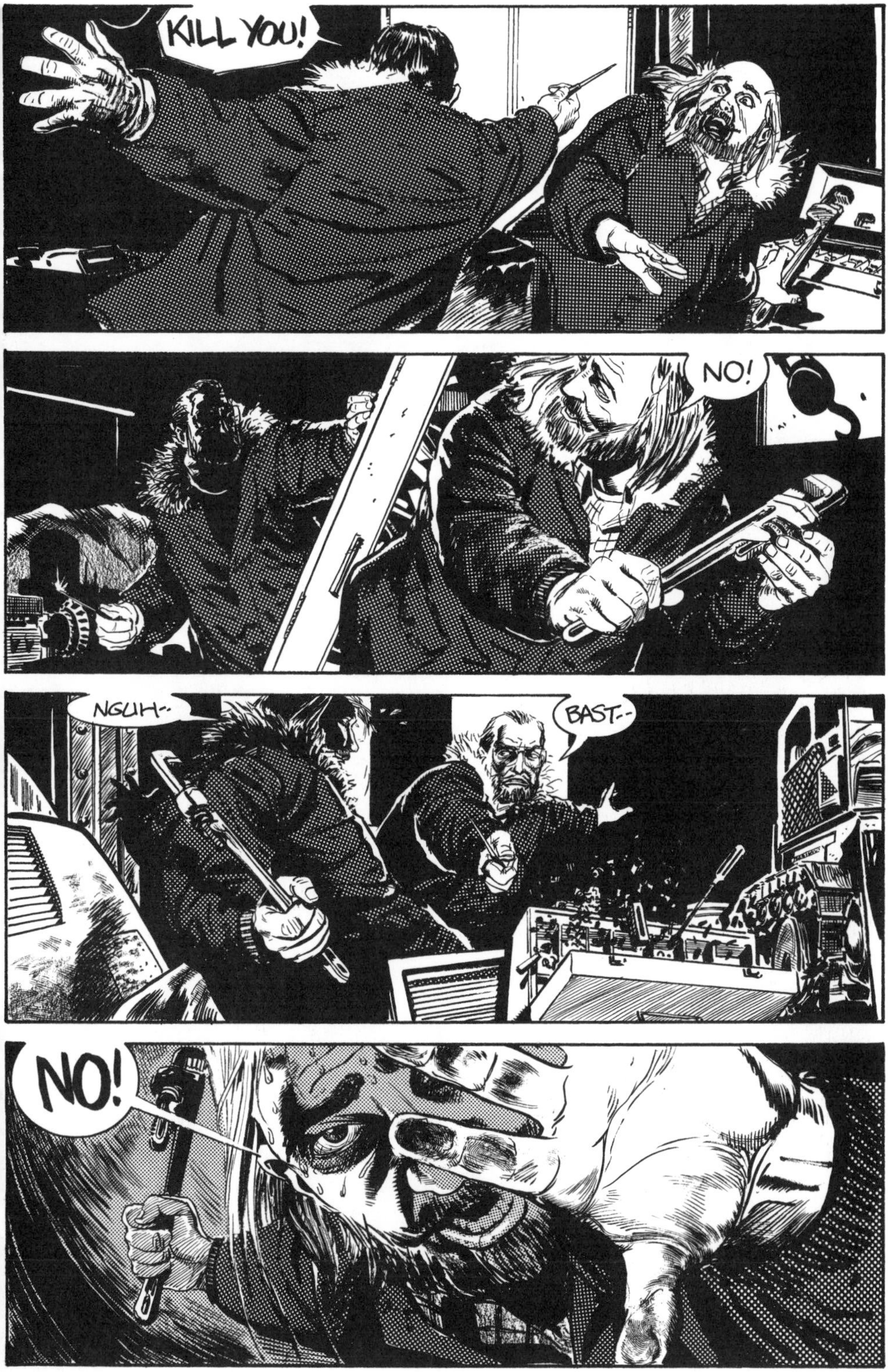
KILL YOU!
NO!
NGUH--
BAST--
NO!

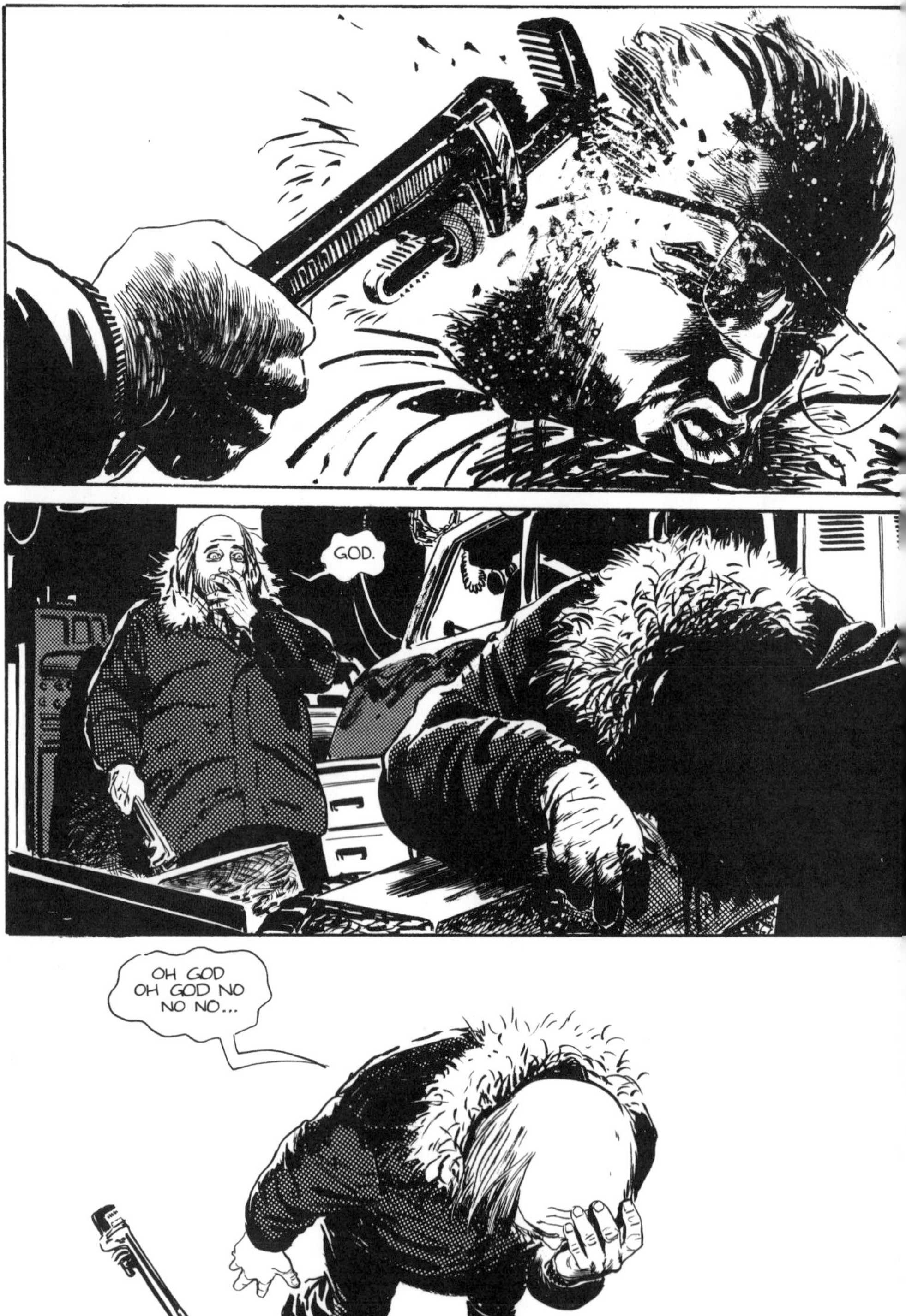
GOD.
OH GOD
OH GOD NO
NO NO...

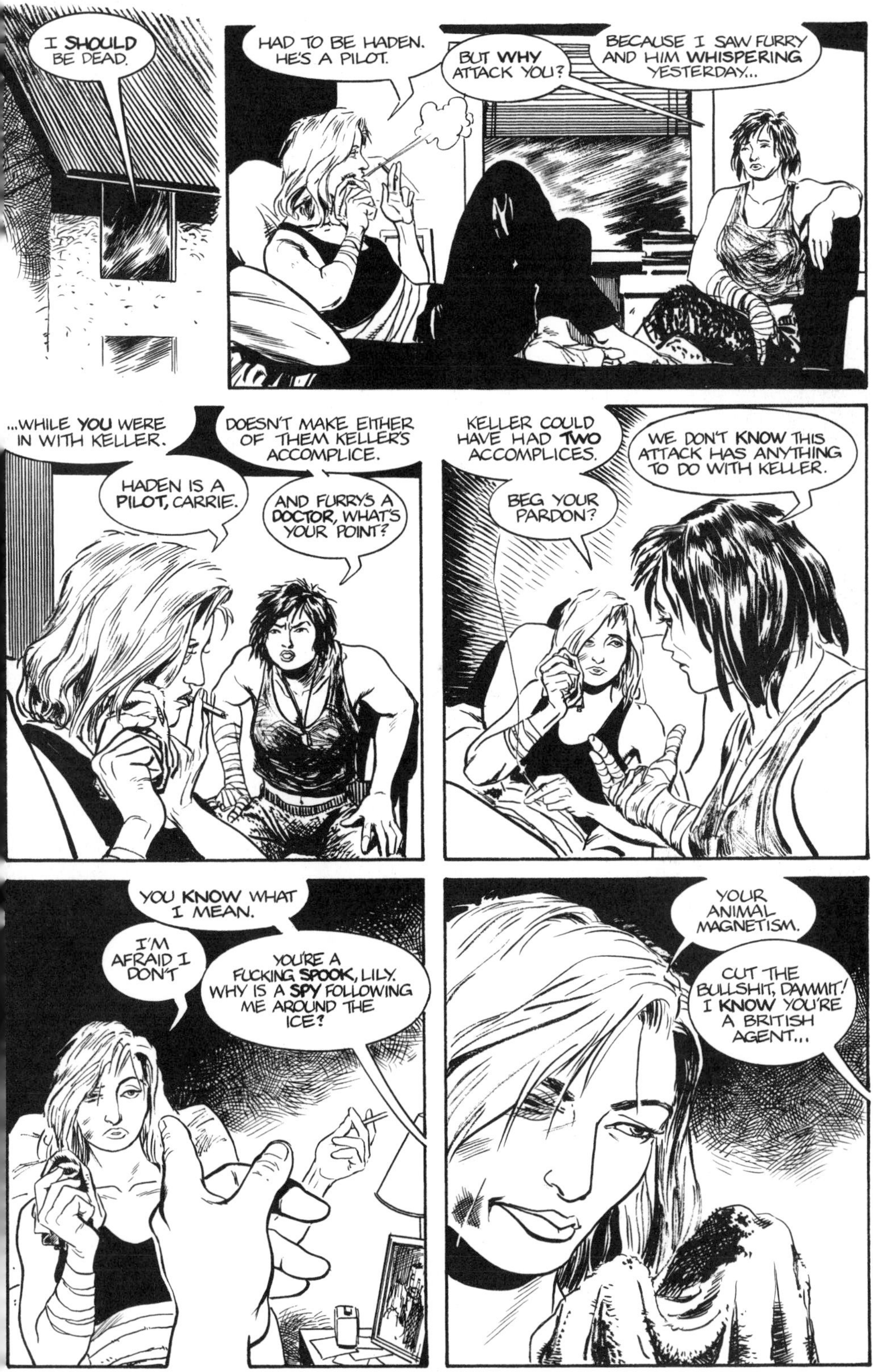
I SHOULD BE DEAD.
HAD TO BE HADEN. HE'S A PILOT.
BUT WHY ATTACK YOU?
BECAUSE I SAW FURRY AND HIM WHISPERING YESTERDAY...
...WHILE YOU WERE IN WITH KELLER.
DOESN'T MAKE EITHER OF THEM KELLER'S ACCOMPLICE.
HADEN IS A PILOT, CARRIE.
AND FURRY'S A DOCTOR, WHAT'S YOUR POINT?
KELLER COULD HAVE HAD TWO ACCOMPLICES.
WE DON'T KNOW THIS ATTACK HAS ANYTHING TO DO WITH KELLER.
BEG YOUR PARDON?
YOU KNOW WHAT I MEAN.
I'M AFRAID I DON'T
YOU'RE A FUCKING SPOOK, LILY. WHY IS A SPY FOLLOWING ME AROUND THE ICE?
YOUR ANIMAL MAGNETISM.
CUT THE BULLSHIT, DAMMIT! I KNOW YOU'RE A BRITISH AGENT...

WHY? IN CASE SOMEONE FINDS A VEIN OF COPPER AND THREATENS BRITAIN'S PLACE IN THE BRONZE INDUSTRY?

URAINIUM- OOF- IN CASE SOMEONE FINDS URANIUM...

...THEN MAKES A FISSION DEVICE WITH IT. D'YOU HAVE A SHIRT? THIS ONE'S **COVERED** IN BLOOD...

ALL THE NATIONS HERE CAN GET FISSIONABLE MATERIAL FRO—

NOT ALL AND **NOT** IN SECRET. ARGENTINA AND CHILE CANNOT, TO NAME TWO.

Cue the Hallelujah Chorus...

...as the Marshal finally gets a <u>clue</u>.

...WESSELHOEFT WAS ARGENTINE.

NOTHING?

EXACTLY. WHEN SIPLE AND MOONEY RETURNED TO VICTORIA, THEY DIDN'T DECLARE SAMPLES.

NOT A **PEBBLE.** I ASSUMED THEY WERE **HIDING** SOMETHING...

...THEN YOU ARRIVED, AND THEY SHOWED UP **DEAD**... **OBVIOUSLY** SOMETHING WAS GOING ON.

OBVIOUSLY.

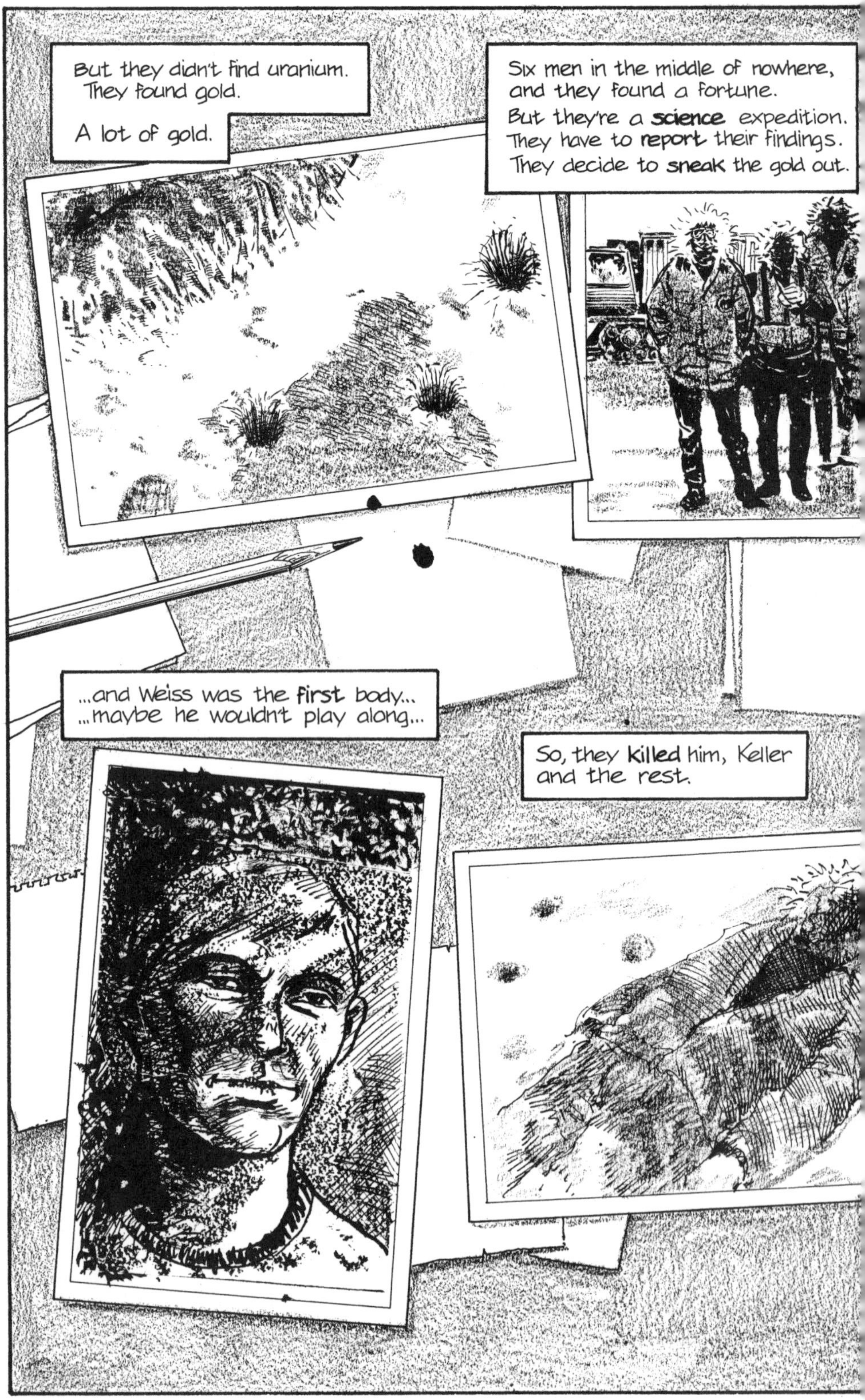
But they didn't find uranium. They found gold.
A lot of gold.
Six men in the middle of nowhere, and they found a fortune.
But they're a **science** expedition. They have to **report** their findings. They decide to **sneak** the gold out.
...and Weiss was the **first** body... ...maybe he wouldn't play along...
So, they **killed** him, Keller and the rest.

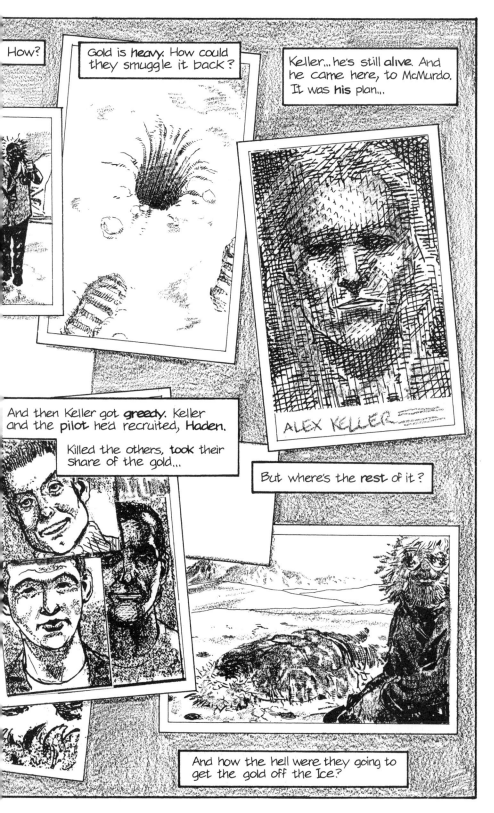

How?

Gold is **heavy**. How could they smuggle it back?

Keller... he's still **alive**. And he came here, to McMurdo. It was **his** plan...

ALEX KELLER

And then Keller got **greedy**. Keller and the **pilot** he'd recruited, **Haden**.

Killed the others, **took** their share of the gold...

But where's the **rest** of it?

And how the hell were they going to get the gold off the Ice?

THERE'S NO URANIUM.

I KNOW.

THIS IS ABOUT **GREED**. THIS IS ABOUT GETTING THE GOLD OFF THE ICE.

HADEN. HE'S A **PILOT**. FLIES FOR THE KIWIS.

KELLER WAS GOING TO THE U.S. HE WOULDN'T WANT HADEN HOLDING THE GOLD IN AUSTRALIA.

WE SHOULD GRAB HADEN THEN.

LET ME GET DRESSED...

...THIS IS A PAIN WHEN YOU ONLY HAVE ONE GOOD HAND.

I WOULD IMAGINE.

WHAT WAS HIS NAME?

MAL. MALCOLM. HE WAS AN ATTORNEY. A U.S. ATTORNEY...

HOW'D HE DIE?

IF YOU DON'T MIND MY ASKING, OF COURSE

...CANCER. RIGHT AFTER WE MARRIED...

THIS WAS AFTER I'D BEEN SUSPENDED FOR THE PRICE THING— **DAMMIT!—**

HERE.

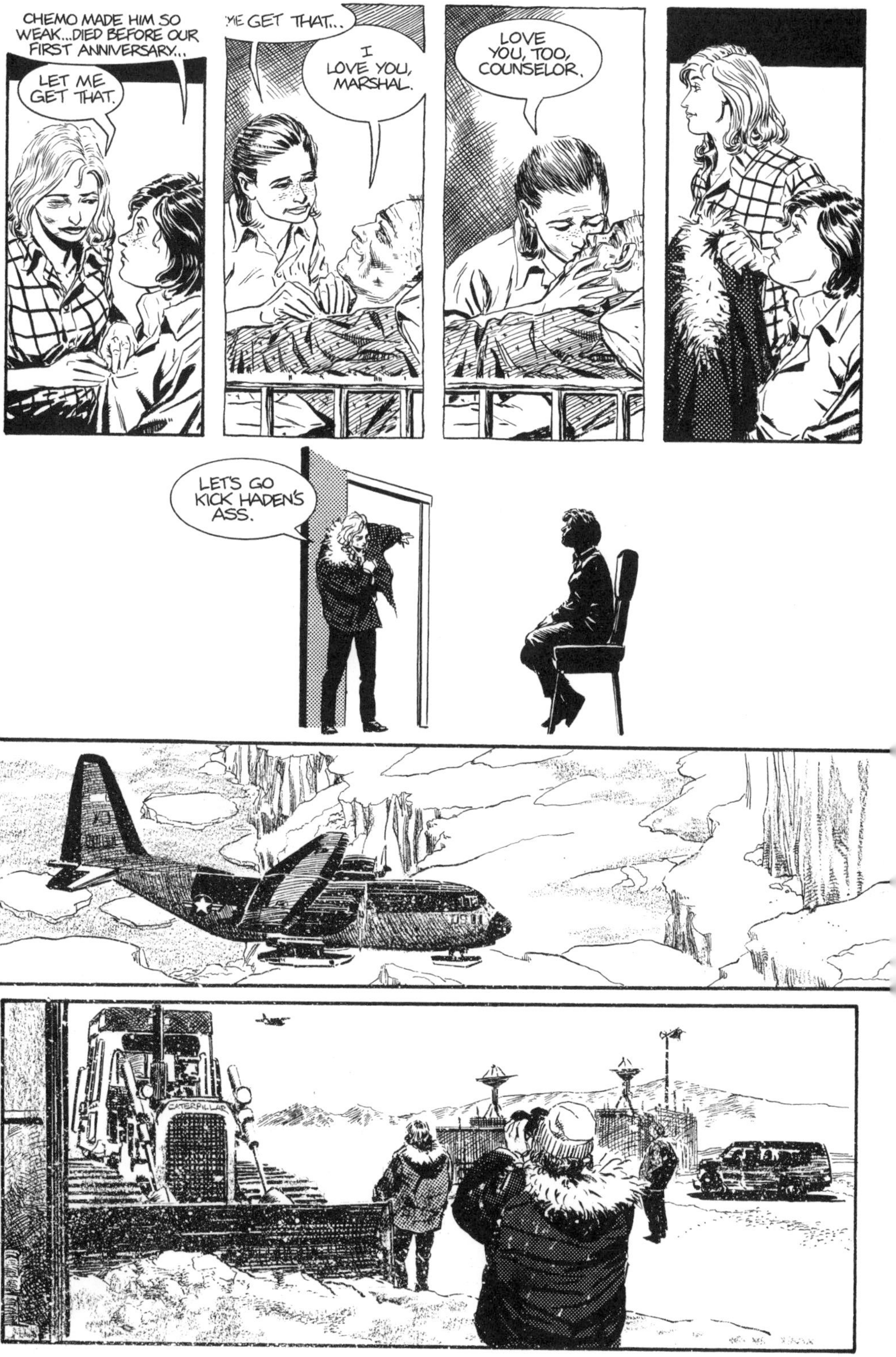
CHEMO MADE HIM SO WEAK...DIED BEFORE OUR FIRST ANNIVERSARY...
LET ME GET THAT.
ME GET THAT...
I LOVE YOU, MARSHAL.
LOVE YOU, TOO, COUNSELOR.
LET'S GO KICK HADEN'S ASS.
CATERPILLAR

The clock's ticking down, now.
McEwan or one of his cronies is on that flight...

...here to transport the prisoner back to the world.

The last flight out of town.

HOWDY, MARSHAL. HERE TO SAY **GOODBYE?**

That's **it**

YOU'RE ON THAT FLIGHT? BET YOUR CUTE ASS. WHAT HAP-

DON'T ASK, SEEN HADEN?

IF HADEN GRABBED A VEHICLE, HE'S HEADED FOR SCOTT--

YOU GO.

WHICH WAY? TOWARDS VMF, I THINK. WHY?

DURING BAG-DRAG THIS MORNING GOING SOMEWHERE WITH DOC.

FURRY? YEAH. LOOKED LIKE THEY WERE HURRYING. COURSE THAT MIGHTVE BEEN THE **COLD.**

TAKE THE LOO.

WHERE ARE YOU HEADED?

Let me be wrong.

Please let me be wrong.

  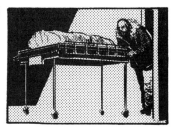

McEWAN. I'M LOOKING FOR **DEPUTY** STETKO.

CHECK THE GALLEY.

oving the gold around the **Ice,** hat's Haden's job...

...but getting it back to the **World**...that's **different**.

JAIL

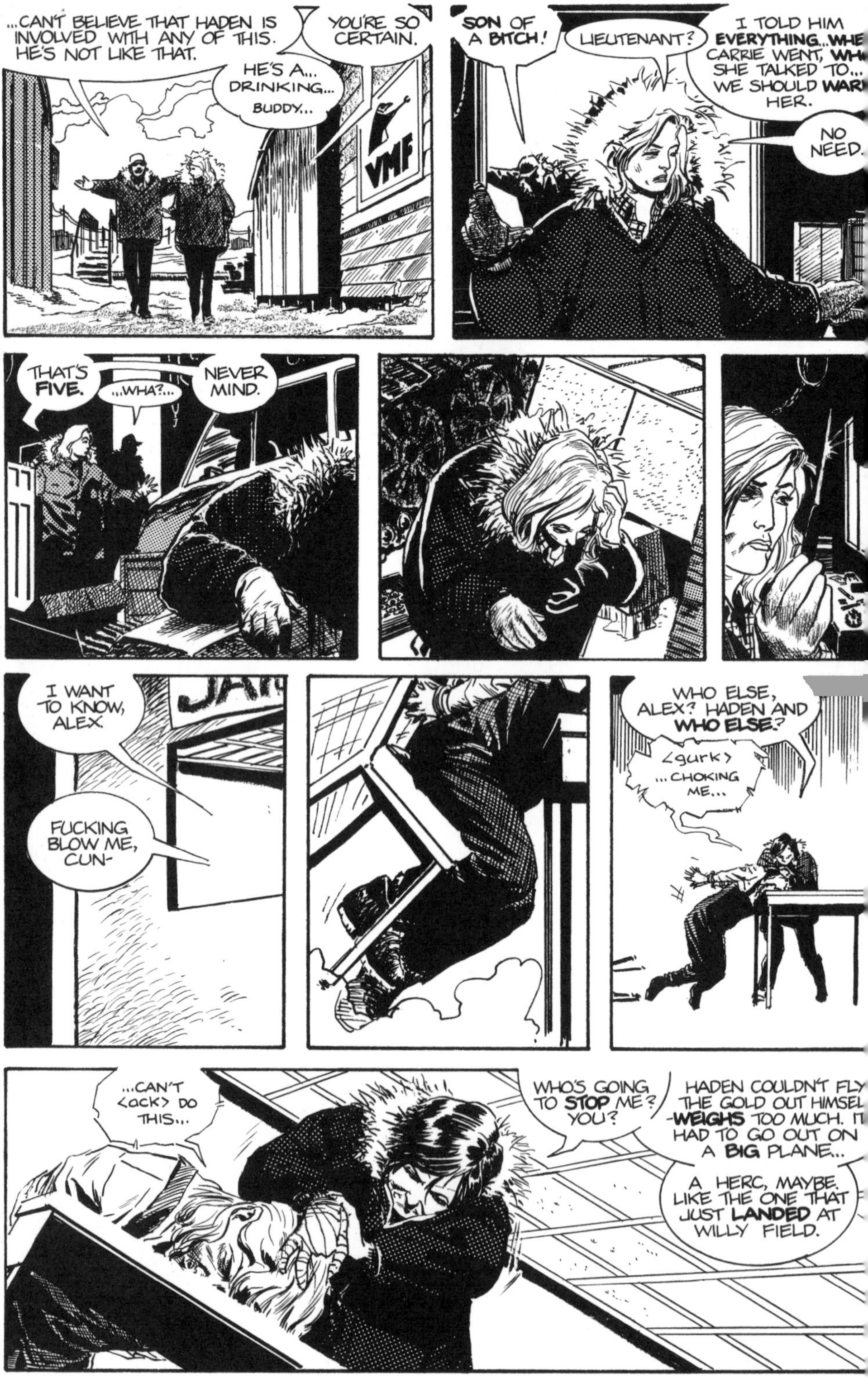
...CAN'T BELIEVE THAT HADEN IS INVOLVED WITH ANY OF THIS. HE'S NOT LIKE THAT.
YOU'RE SO CERTAIN.
HE'S A... DRINKING... BUDDY...
VMF
SON OF A BITCH!
LIEUTENANT?
I TOLD HIM EVERYTHING...WHE CARRIE WENT, WH SHE TALKED TO... WE SHOULD WAR HER.
NO NEED.
THAT'S FIVE.
...WHA?...
NEVER MIND.
I WANT TO KNOW, ALEX.
FUCKING BLOW ME, CUN-
WHO ELSE, ALEX? HADEN AND WHO ELSE?
<gurk> ...CHOKING ME...
...CAN'T <ack> DO THIS...
WHO'S GOING TO STOP ME? YOU?
HADEN COULDN'T FLY THE GOLD OUT HIMSEL -WEIGHS TOO MUCH. IT HAD TO GO OUT ON A BIG PLANE...
A HERC, MAYBE. LIKE THE ONE THAT JUST LANDED AT WILLY FIELD.

BUT HOW WERE YOU GOING TO GET IT ON BOARD?

...<AHK>...

HOW, ALEX?

I KNOW.

...CAN'T... BREATHE...

HOW, ALEX?

...TELL... YOU...

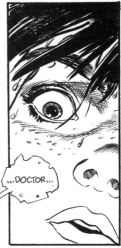

...DOCTOR...

FURRY...

FURRY... WHY?

DEPUTY! WHAT THE FU—

SIR, YOUR PRISONER IS READY FOR TRANSPORT.

AND WHERE THE HELL ARE YOU GOING?

...UNFINISHED BUSINESS.

DELFY WILL GIVE YOU A HAND.

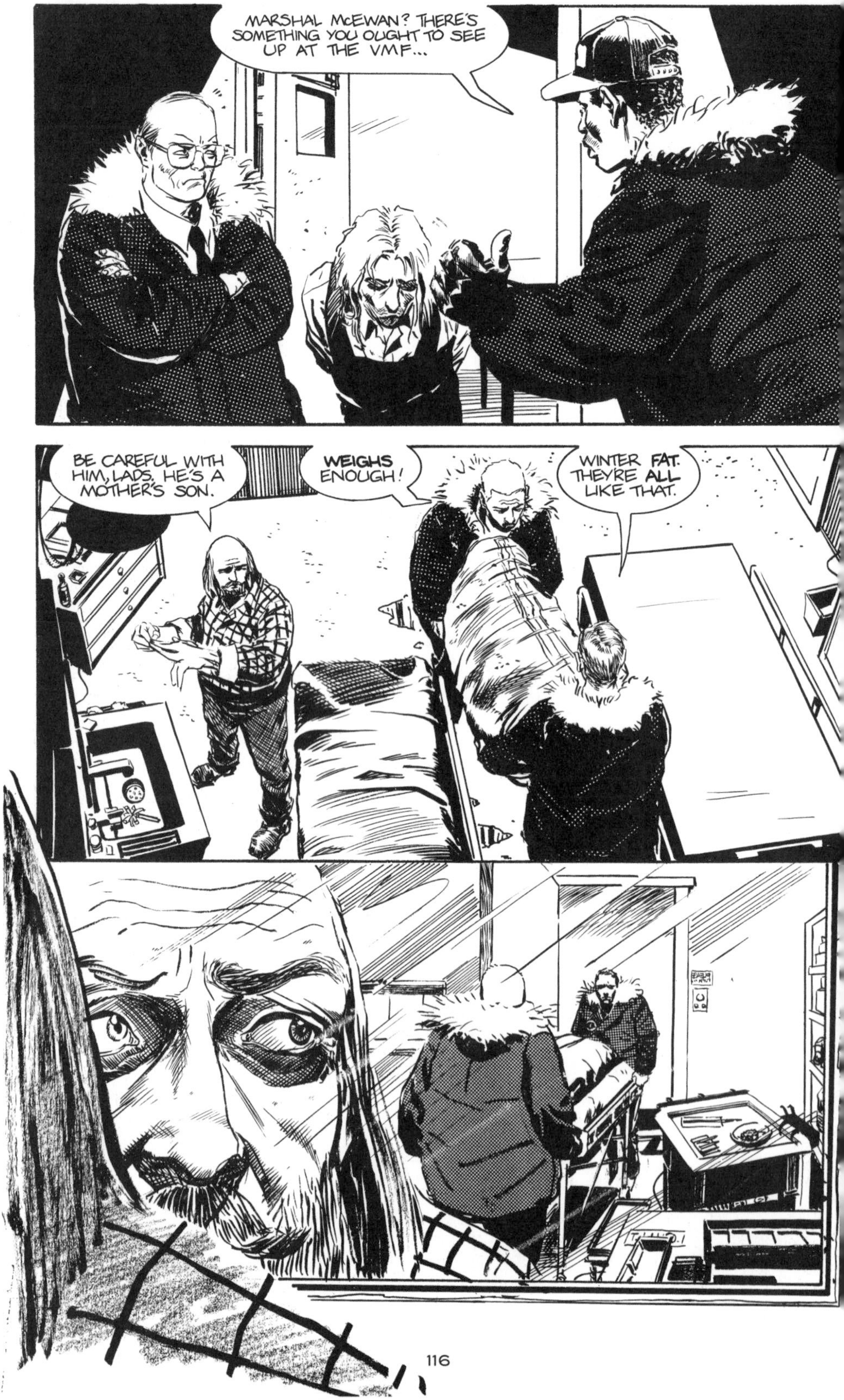
MARSHAL McEWAN? THERE'S SOMETHING YOU OUGHT TO SEE UP AT THE VMF...
BE CAREFUL WITH HIM, LADS. HE'S A MOTHER'S SON.
WEIGHS ENOUGH!
WINTER **FAT**. THEY'RE **ALL** LIKE THAT.

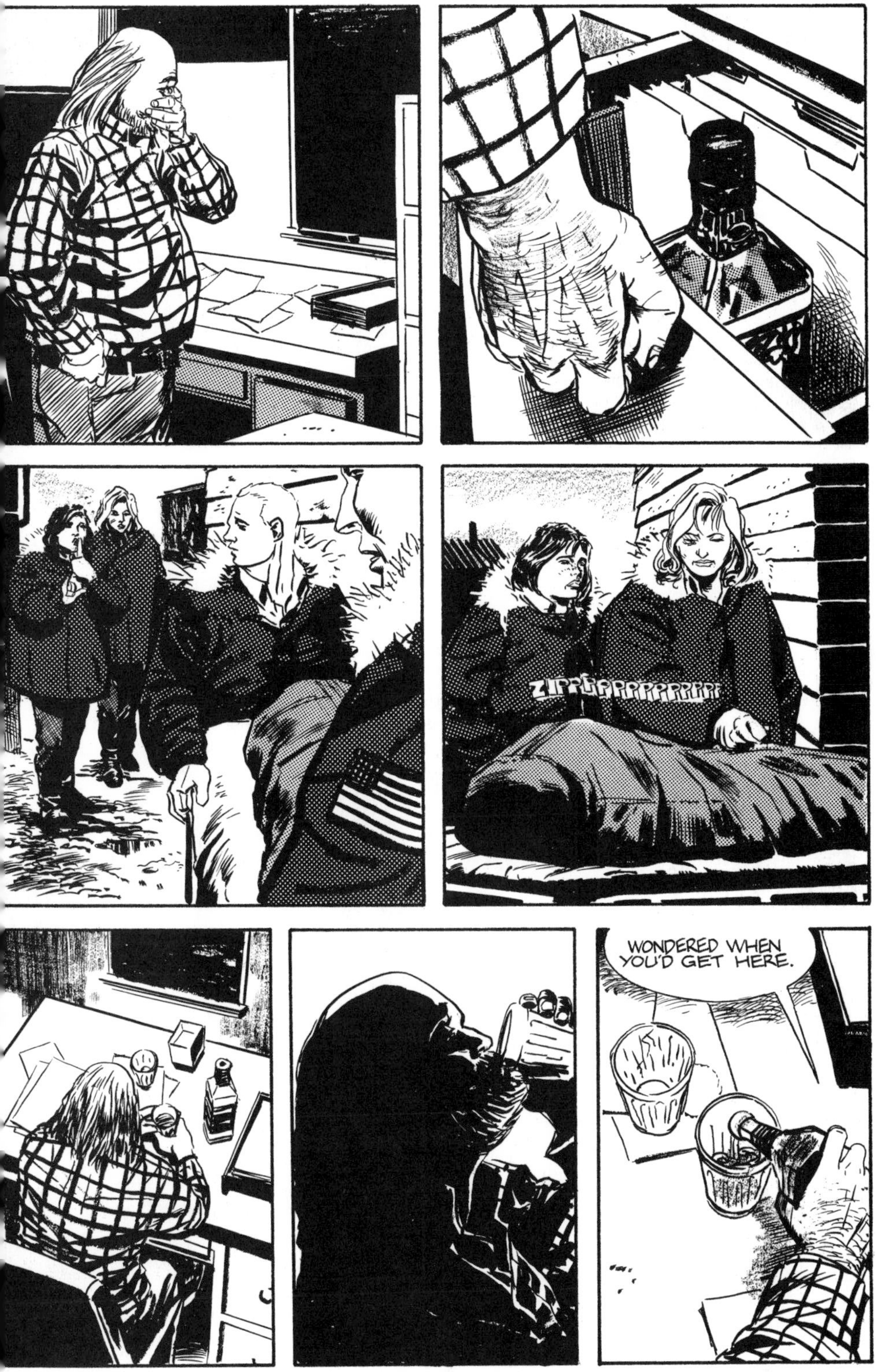
ZIPPPPPPPPPPPPPPP
WONDERED WHEN YOU'D GET HERE.

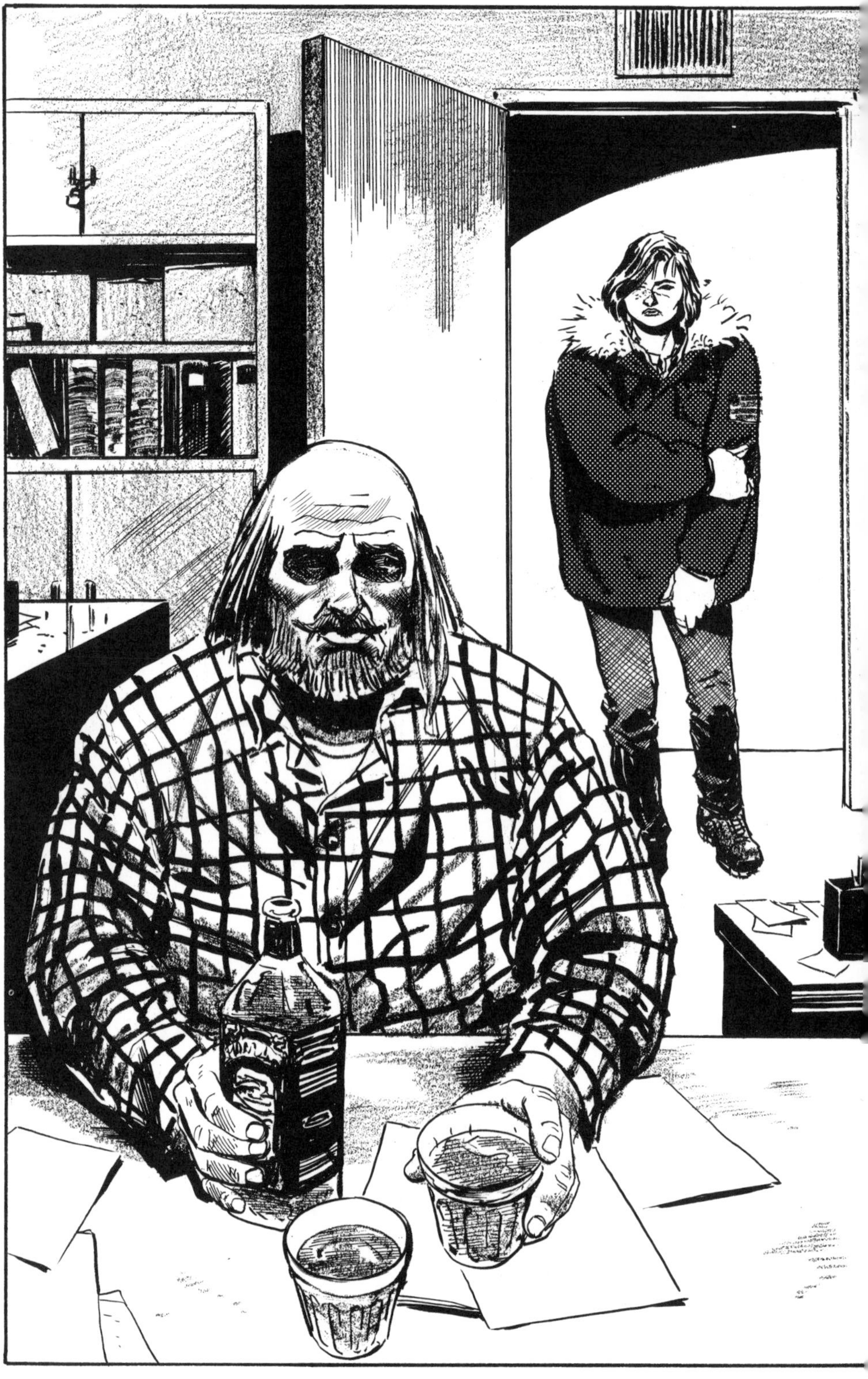

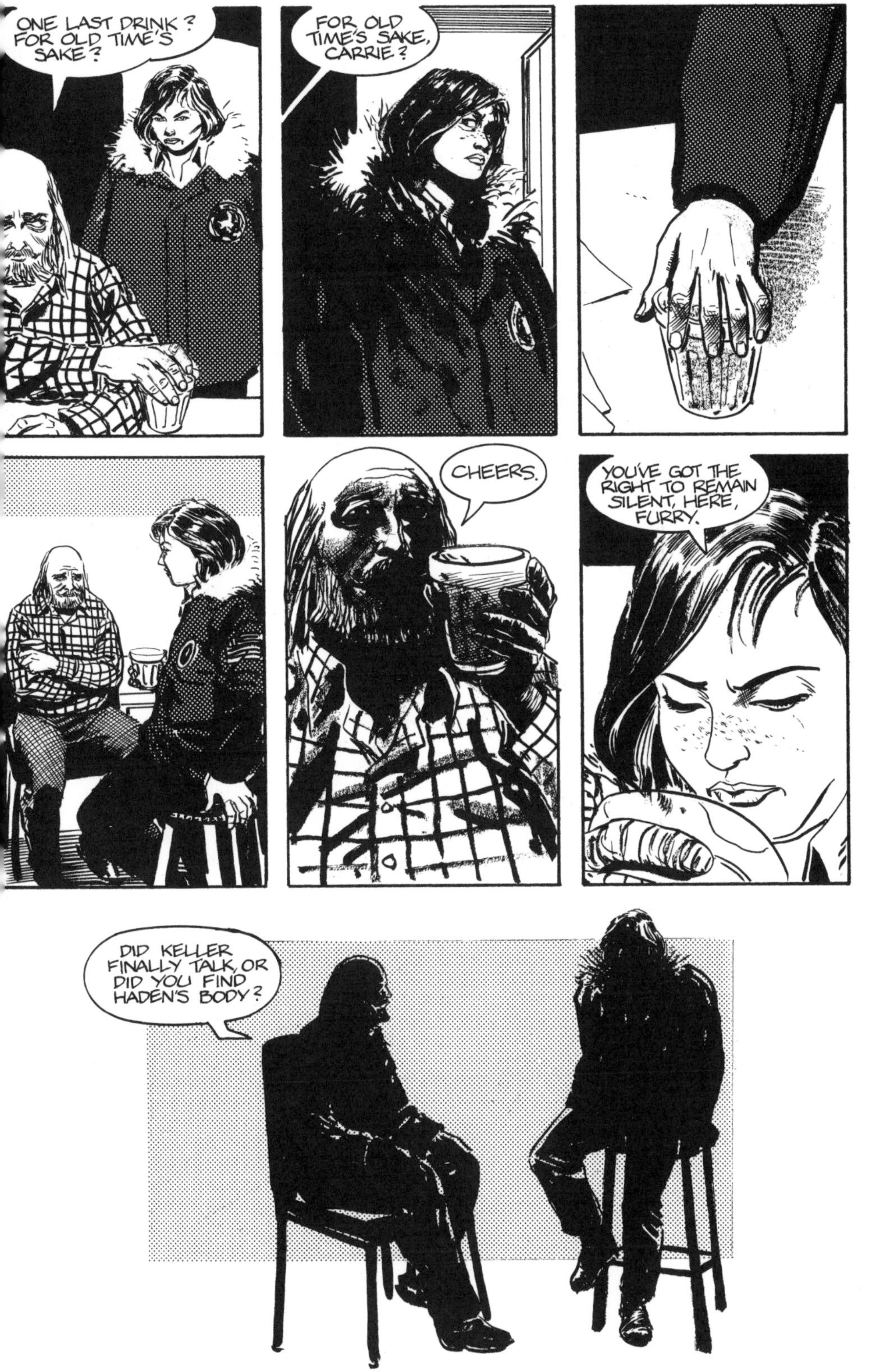
ONE LAST DRINK? FOR OLD TIME'S SAKE?
FOR OLD TIME'S SAKE, CARRIE?
CHEERS.
YOU'VE GOT THE RIGHT TO REMAIN SILENT, HERE, FURRY.
DID KELLER FINALLY TALK, OR DID YOU FIND HADEN'S BODY?

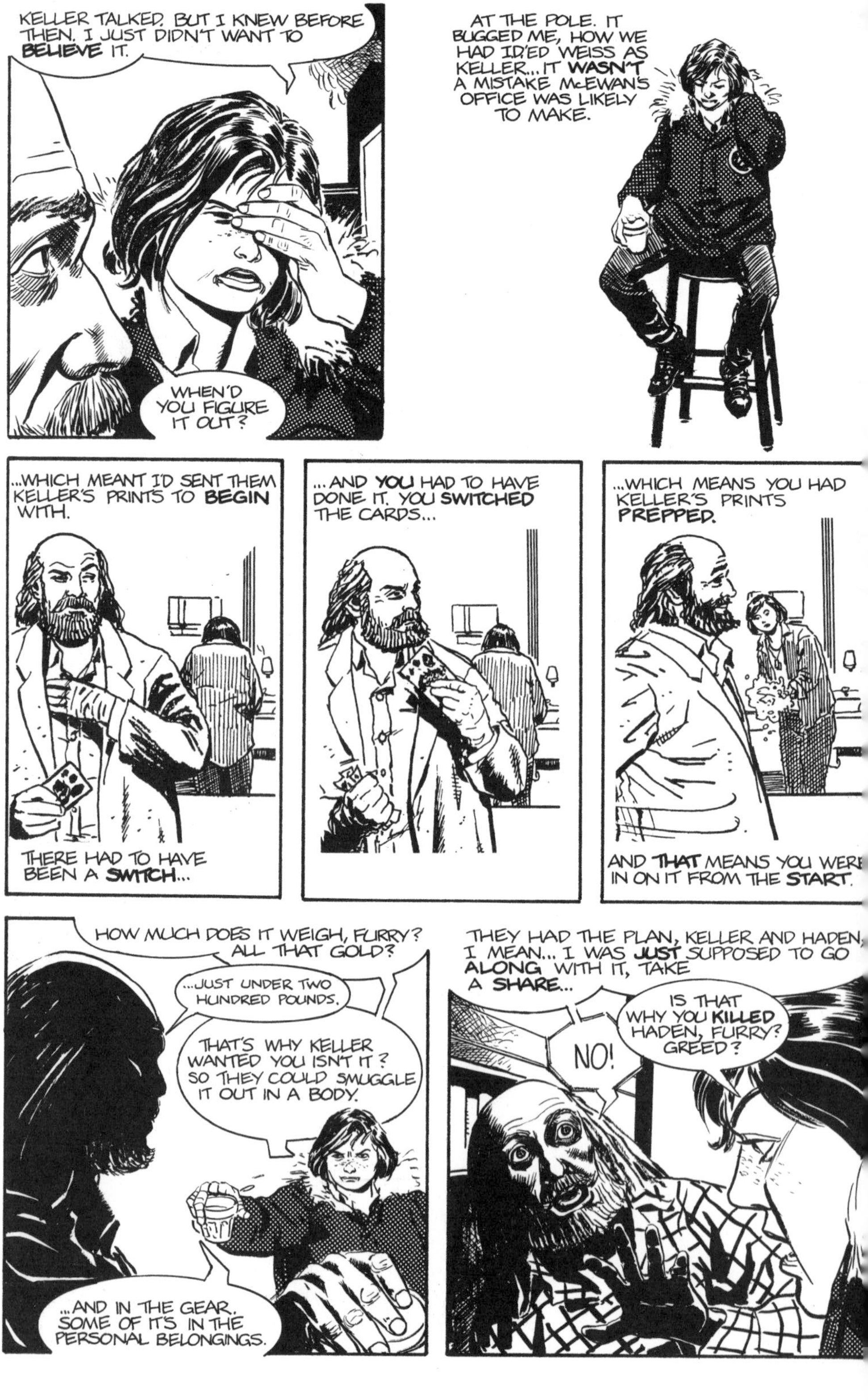

KELLER TALKED. BUT I KNEW BEFORE THEN. I JUST DIDN'T WANT TO BELIEVE IT.
WHEN'D YOU FIGURE IT OUT?
AT THE POLE. IT BUGGED ME, HOW WE HAD ID'ED WEISS AS KELLER... IT WASN'T A MISTAKE McEWAN'S OFFICE WAS LIKELY TO MAKE.
...WHICH MEANT I'D SENT THEM KELLER'S PRINTS TO BEGIN WITH.
THERE HAD TO HAVE BEEN A SWITCH...
...AND YOU HAD TO HAVE DONE IT. YOU SWITCHED THE CARDS...
...WHICH MEANS YOU HAD KELLER'S PRINTS PREPPED.
AND THAT MEANS YOU WERE IN ON IT FROM THE START.
HOW MUCH DOES IT WEIGH, FURRY? ALL THAT GOLD?
...JUST UNDER TWO HUNDRED POUNDS.
THAT'S WHY KELLER WANTED YOU ISN'T IT? SO THEY COULD SMUGGLE IT OUT IN A BODY.
...AND IN THE GEAR. SOME OF IT'S IN THE PERSONAL BELONGINGS.
THEY HAD THE PLAN, KELLER AND HADEN, I MEAN... I WAS JUST SUPPOSED TO GO ALONG WITH IT, TAKE A SHARE...
IS THAT WHY YOU KILLED HADEN, FURRY? GREED?
NO!

CARRIE, I'VE NEVER KILLED ANYONE BEFORE IN MY LIFE... ...I'M A DOCTOR.

I **KNEW** YOU'D LOOK FOR HADEN. I WANTED HIM TO HIDE UNTIL THINGS WERE CLEAR...

...HE ATTACKED **ME**... IT WAS SELF-DEFENSE...

GET UP.

CARRIE, **PLEASE!** THEY WERE SENDING ME **HOME**...

...MAKING ME **LEAVE**. I DON'T HAVE **ANYTHING** BACK IN THE WORLD.

THE ICE IS **OUR** WORLD. YOU **KNOW** THAT.

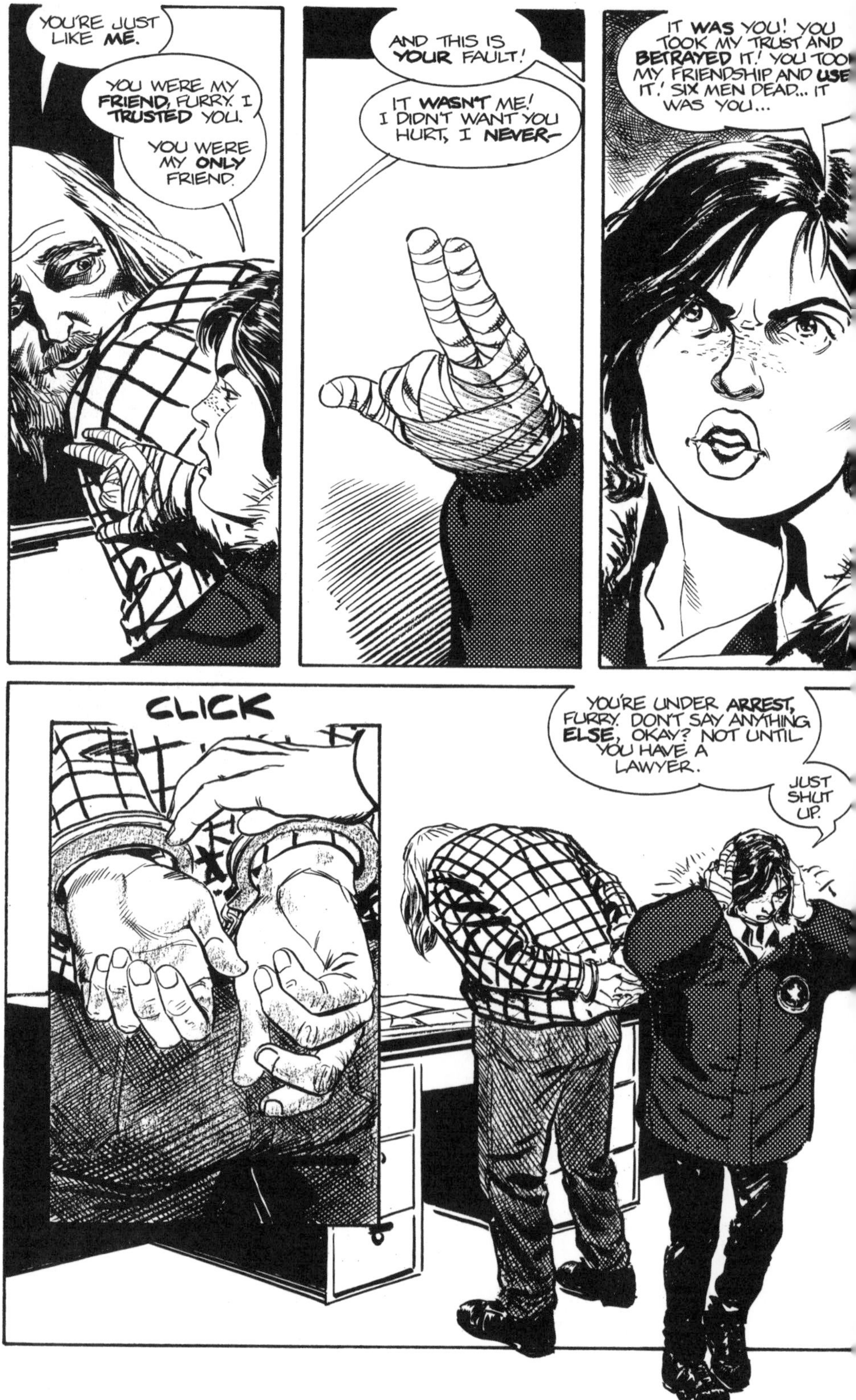

YOU'RE JUST LIKE ME.
YOU WERE MY FRIEND, FURRY. I TRUSTED YOU.
YOU WERE MY ONLY FRIEND.
AND THIS IS YOUR FAULT!
IT WASN'T ME! I DIDN'T WANT YOU HURT, I NEVER-
IT WAS YOU! YOU TOOK MY TRUST AND BETRAYED IT! YOU TOOK MY FRIENDSHIP AND USE IT! SIX MEN DEAD... IT WAS YOU...
CLICK
YOU'RE UNDER ARREST, FURRY. DON'T SAY ANYTHING ELSE, OKAY? NOT UNTIL YOU HAVE A LAWYER.
JUST SHUT UP.

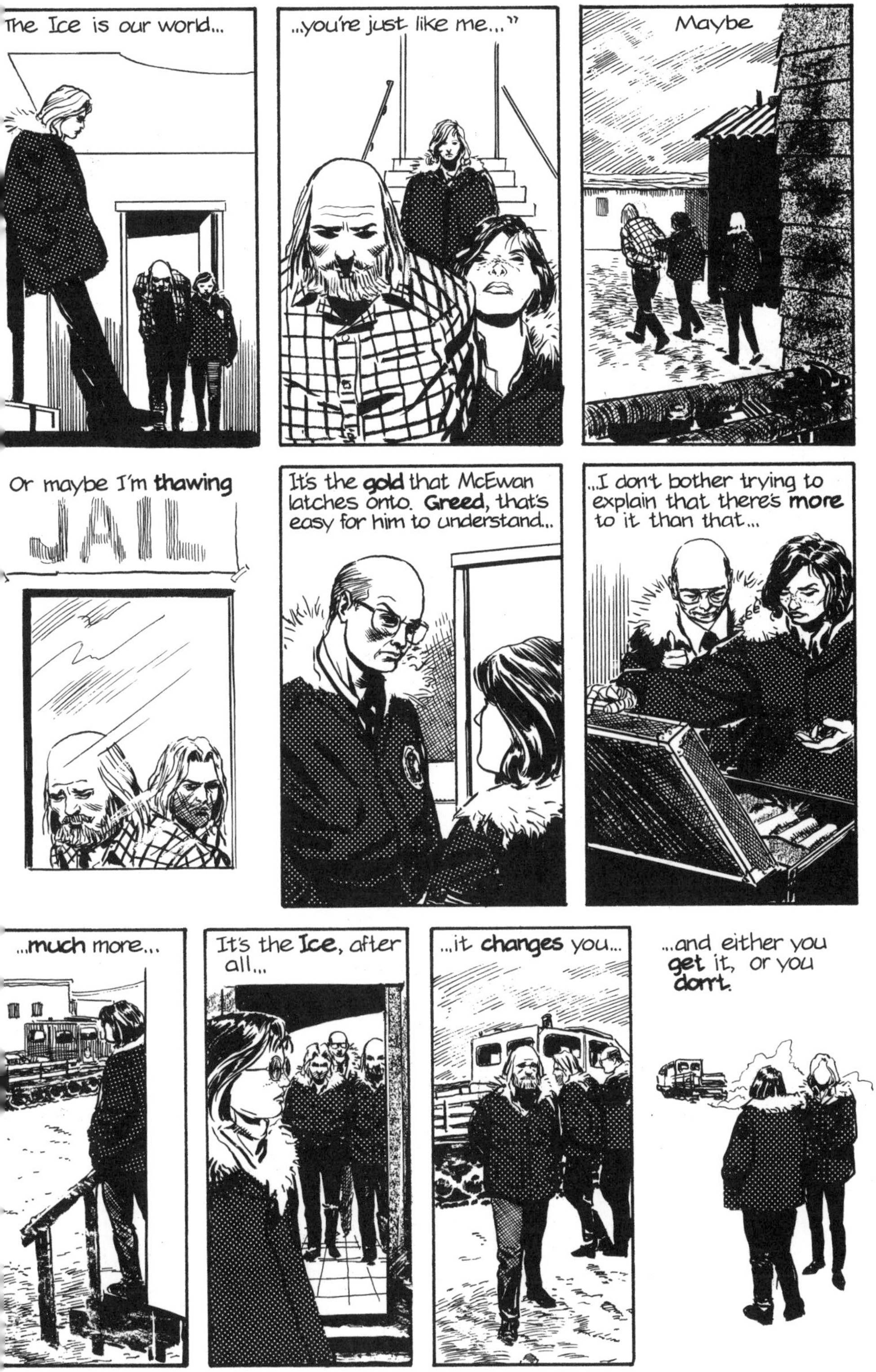

The Ice is our world...
...you're just like me..."
Maybe
Or maybe I'm **thawing**
JAIL
It's the **gold** that McEwan latches onto. **Greed**, that's easy for him to understand...
...I don't bother trying to explain that there's **more** to it than that...
...**much** more...
It's the **Ice**, after all...
...it **changes** you...
...and either you **get** it, or you **don't**.

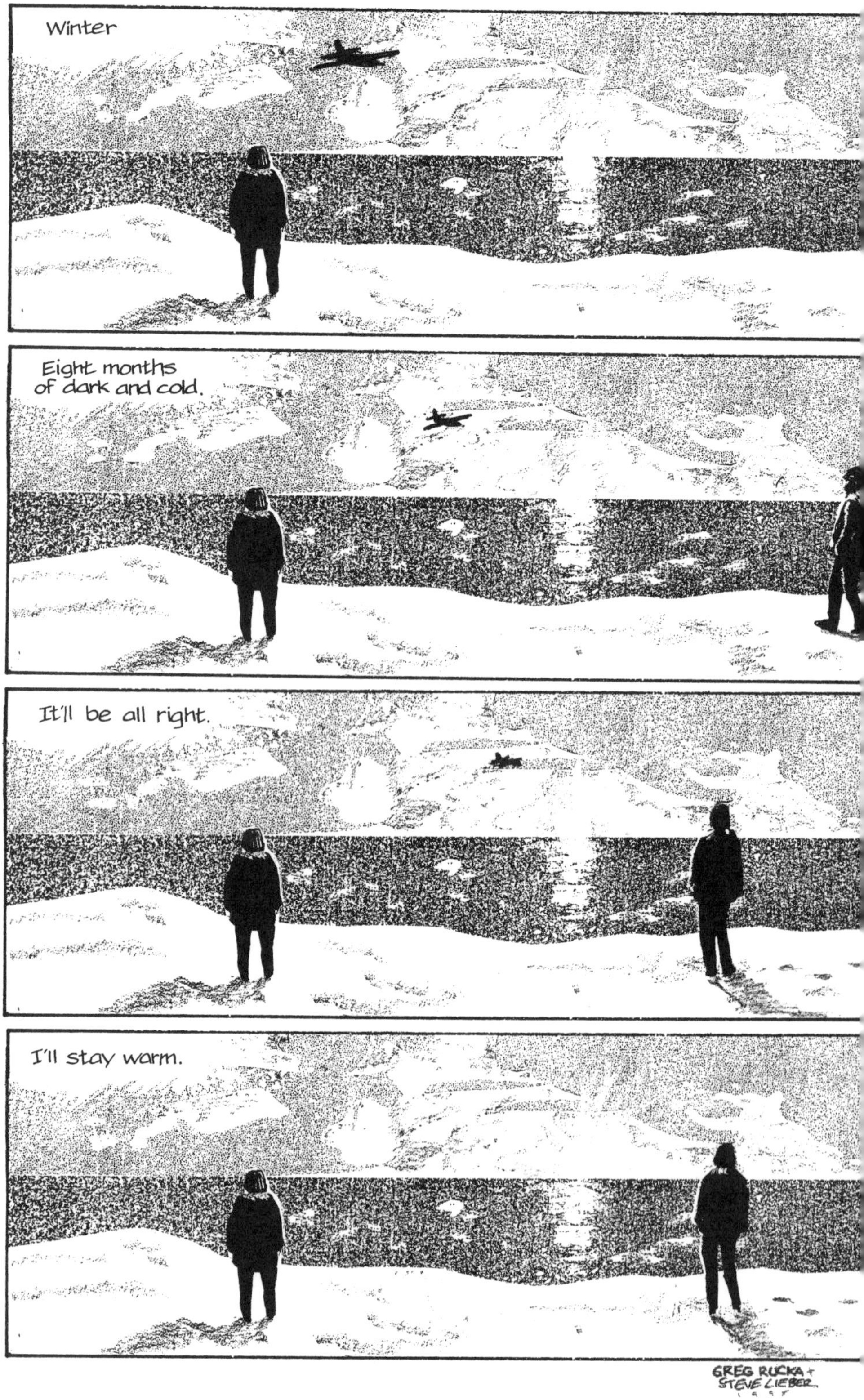
Winter
Eight months of dark and cold.
It'll be all right.
I'll stay warm.
GREG RUCKA + STEVE LIEBER

AFTERWORD

Ten years ago, when Bob Schreck first handed me a copy of Greg Rucka's first novel, *Keeper*, I was convinced I'd never make anything of myself in comics. I'd been working steadily for six years, but I couldn't look at anything I'd illustrated without vague feelings of regret. I knew I was capable of solid work, and I had a big pile of sketchbooks that supported that notion, but when I looked over my hundreds of pages of published stories, there just wasn't much to shout about. I hadn't figured out how to do good work on the industry's four color assembly lines, and that was the only place anyone could make a splash, right?

That's where Schreck comes in. Bob had given me my break at Dark Horse years ago, making him the first editor at a legitimate publisher to see any potential in my stuff. He'd just started a new company called Oni Press right here in Portland, where my wife and I had just moved. Bob said that he had a script that might be right for me, written by the same guy who wrote this novel.

I took the book home and devoured it in one sitting, and I felt like someone had built a writer just for me. Greg's novel was compelling, and compulsively readable, but more importantly, he worked the rhythms of storytelling the way I was desperate to do in comics[1]. I saw that we agreed on the ways the energy and emotional pitch of a scene should rise and fall. Our attitudes about violence and heroism were in sync, as were our sense of the rules that make for believable characters and action in fiction.

Long story short, Bob sent me the script for the first issue. I said yes, and oh boy was I eager to get started. If Greg had set out to write a script just for me, he couldn't have come up with something this perfect. Carrie and Antarctica were absolutely alive in my mind. I understood her frustration and her wonder at the place she'd wound up and her determination to find out what happened. All I had to do was tell the reader the story Greg told me and we'd have a great comic.

---

[1] It's best not to get me started on comics as a rhythmic—as opposed to a literary—medium. I tend to judge a page of comics by how the pictures sound, and I'm very aware of what a weird sentence that is. This isn't synesthesia. I just sort of hear panels and pages in my head as if I were reading a musical score. When the rhythm is off, the page doesn't work. When it's particularly good, the work comes to life in a way that's hard to communicate. Conversations with a number of other cartoonists lead me to believe this is a fairly common experience.

Greg's story was about a woman so frozen by anger and regret she'd found herself at home in the middle of millions of square kilometers of ice. How could I make that world as believable and compelling in pictures as it was in the script? Monochromatic could easily lead to monotony. Black and white comics, particularly crime stories, usually get their impact from the use of heavy areas of solid black. For obvious reasons, that wasn't going to work in this one. But those sketchbooks I mentioned earlier were full of black and white drawings where I'd played with all sorts of media and had been able to fully indulge my intertest in using texture as a both color and as a rhythmic element. I never worried about restricting myself to a slick comic book brushline in my sketches, I just worked to please myself. Suppose I treated the comic like it was my sketchbook, and just let myself whale away at every panel until it felt as cold, as dry, as windy, and as desolate as it needed to be. Sure, there was a danger that some panels might get overrendered, but certainly on *this* title I could feel okay about dealing with a bad drawing by just whiting it out.

That did it. I was free. For the first time in my career, I felt like I was producing drawings that looked like *I'd* drawn them. I used a dozen different brushes, any pen nib I could find, grease crayons, markers, ball points, white paint, toothbrushes, homemade zip-a-tones, xeroxes, charcoal, unerased pencil lines, sandpaper, razor blades, an electric eraser, even my own fingerprints—anything that could make or remove a mark on paper—I'd give it a try. I inhabited those panels and I think the struggle gave the pictures a lot of energy. Along the way, I tried to do what Greg had done when he wrote it – I buried myself in research, spending hours online or in the library researching Antarctica. And I'd call and fax him at all hours to discuss possible approaches to panel sequences. A twelve hour day at the board was slacking off. I drove my wife and friends insane. Greg, too, come to think of it.

Looking back, I'm grateful to everyone who was involved with this project: Greg, of course, his wife Jen Van Meter, for clarifying their concept of "hooskie" (which you, dear reader, can ask one of them about sometime); Bob Schreck, Joe Nozemack, Jamie Rich, and James Lucas Jones; graphic designers Sean Tejaratchi and Steven Birch; original cover artists Matt Wagner, Mike Mignola, Dave Gibbons, and Frank Miller; the guys at the now defunct website nextplanetover.com who gave away a metric ton of copies at the San Diego Comic-con; the readers of rec.arts.comics.misc, who were among the first to notice that something special was going on; Jeff Parker, who told me to quit being a puss when I was over-thinking; and most of all, my wife Sara Ryan, who supported me in my obsessiveness, inspired many of Stetko's expressions and gestures, and woke up with little bits of zip-a-tone in the blankets every morning for two years. From this day forward, it's all digital, hon, I swear.

STEVE LEIBER
MAY 2007

OTHER BOOKS FROM GREG RUCKA & ONI PRESS...

WHITEOUT

WHITEOUT, VOL. 2: MELT, THE DEFINITIVE EDITION™

By Greg Rucka
& Steve Leiber
128 pages
6x9 trade paperback
black & white interiors
$13.95
ISBN 978-1-932664-71-3

QUEEN & COUNTRY

QUEEN & COUNTRY, VOL 1: OPERATION: BROKEN GROUND™

By Greg Rucka
Steve Rolston
& Stan Sakai
128 pages
standard
black & white interiors
$11.95 US
ISBN 978-1-929998-21-0

QUEEN & COUNTRY

QUEEN & COUNTRY, VOL 2: OPERATION: MORNINGSTAR™

By Greg Rucka
Brian Hurtt
Christine Norrie
& Bryan Lee O'Malley
88 pages
standard
black & white interiors
$8.95 US
ISBN 978-1-929998-35-7

QUEEN & COUNTRY

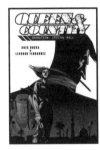

QUEEN & COUNTRY, VOL 3: OPERATION: CRYSTAL BALL™

By Greg Rucka
& Leandro Fernandez
160 pages
standard
black & white interiors
$14.95 US
ISBN 978-1-929998-49-4

QUEEN & COUNTRY

QUEEN & COUNTRY, VOL 4: OPERATION: BLACKWALL™

By Greg Rucka
& Jason Alexander
96 pages
standard
black & white interiors
$8.95 US
ISBN 978-1-929998-68-5

QUEEN & COUNTRY

QUEEN & COUNTRY, VOL 5: OPERATION: STORM FRONT™

By Greg Rucka
& Carla Speed McNeil
144 pages
standard
black & white interiors
$14.95 US
ISBN 978-1-929998-84-5

QUEEN & COUNTRY

QUEEN & COUNTRY, VOL 6: OPERATION: DANDELION™

By Greg Rucka
& Mike Hawthorne
120 pages
standard
black & white interiors
$11.95 US
ISBN 978-1-929998-97-5

QUEEN & COUNTRY

QUEEN & COUNTRY, VOL 7: OPERATION: SADDLEBAGS™

By Greg Rucka
Mike Norton
& Steve Rolston
144 pages
standard
black & white interiors
$14.95 US
ISBN 978-1-932664-14-0

AVAILABLE AT FINER COMICS SHOPS EVERYWHERE. FOR A COMICS STORE NEAR YOU, CALL 1-888-COMIC-BOOK OR VISIT WWW.THE-MASTER-LIST.COM.

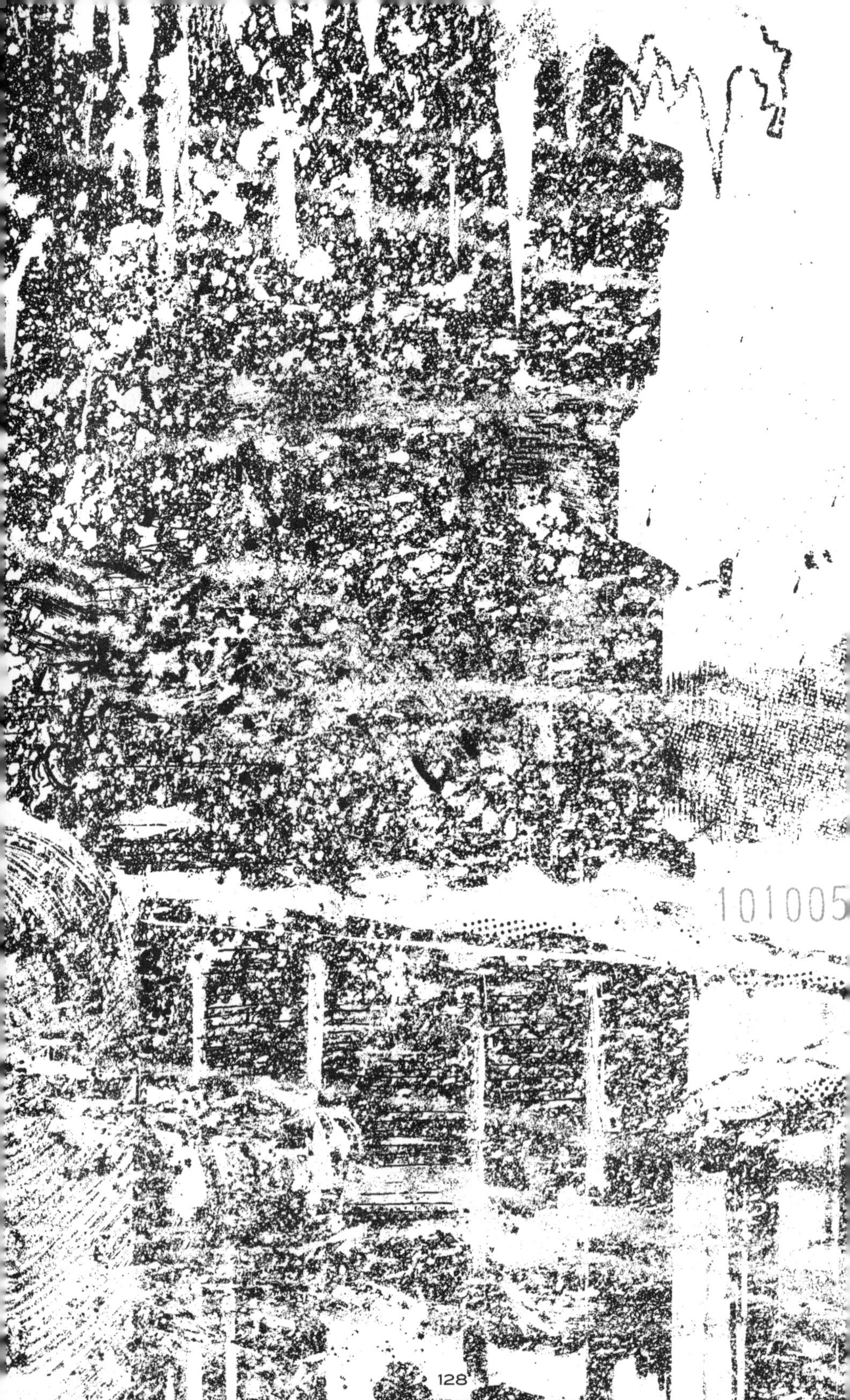